Medieval Mining and Power in Thirteenth-Century Europe

Jeannette Graulau

Medieval Mining and Power in Thirteenth-Century Europe

Bishop Wanga's Private Mine Drainage Works

palgrave
macmillan

Jeannette Graulau
Political Science
Lehman College
Bronx, NY, USA

ISBN 978-3-031-99238-4 ISBN 978-3-031-99239-1 (eBook)
https://doi.org/10.1007/978-3-031-99239-1

This Palgrave Macmillan imprint is published by the registered company Springer Nature Switzerland AG.
The registered company address is: Gewerbestrasse 11, 6330 Cham, Switzerland

To my father, who once endured the horrors of war, and insists that human courage and solidarity will in the end prevail.

Preface

This book tells the story of an imperial bishop and the dilemmas of political power he confronted when he sponsored private mine drainage works. It places the medieval silver mines of Monte Calisio in Trent in world history perspective. Why lords escalated political competition by plowing private capital in mines is a puzzling question. Marxist scholars have addressed the inquiry by emphasizing the role of 'politico-military' capabilities in the making of lordly power. Relying upon the force of monopolies of means of warfare that sustained land rights, lords extracted surpluses from agrarian labor and effectively resisted 'pressures from below.' Agrarian peasants cleared marshes and swamps, and expanded internal extractive frontiers, while lords exploited new sources of rents. Diseases, famines, plagues, wars, and climate change led to contradictions; generally, however, 'the system' remained fairly stable until the expansion of Iberian powers to the rest of the world.

The relation between political power and resources, however, was more complex. Ditches and water-retention ponds carved in mining mountains increased surpluses in a continental economy pierced everywhere by Afro-Eurasian divisions of labor and trade. Hydraulic works expanded mineral rent horizons while shifting power and profit relations in local societies. Caught up in antithetical forces of political change, a reactionary bishop by the name of Frederick Wanga mobilized entrepreneurs to carry out mine drainage works. In his fight against competing lords, the bishop exploited the mines of Monte Calisio. The city lived a short but enduring period of episcopal power and prosperity under the rule of Wanga. Situated on a plateau seemingly undisturbed by political violence, the mining mountain yielded mineral profits and rents. However, the subterranean wealth that increased hegemonic power favoring the bishop continually eroded the basis of political authority in mining lands. The book reconstructs the overlapping layers of political and economic conditions that led to this development.

Why mining carried on with its value-producing relations while refusing to yield to political power is a larger historical and theoretical problem. Marx approached the question from a Eurocentric perspective, taking for granted that the origins of capitalist mineral profits and rents were found in nineteenth-century England. After English lords committed the 'robbery of lands' in the form of enclosures, capitalist mining stood in its two legs for the first time in history. English coal basins became the 'theater of all controversies' between lords and capitalists over the gains of mines. It was there where capital first revealed the secret of *ground rents*—a secret that Adam Smith described a century earlier, according to Marx himself. 'It is one of the great merits of Adam Smith to have shown that the *ground rent* for capital invested in the production of such crops as flax, dye stuffs, independent cattle raising, etc., is determined by the ground rent obtained from capital invested in the production of the principal article of subsistence.' 'In fact,' Marx continued, 'no progress has been made in this since his time.' Marx added that it mattered little if it was wheat or minerals; the historical premises that explained the rise of agrarian rents applied to mineral rents as well. Marx concluded that landed property in its various historical forms, including feudal land rights, was the determinant condition of mineral rents.

The 'little pieces of evidence' available on Monte Calisio mining history show that capital plowed itself unto ore basins under conditions that antagonized the monopoly of landed property. It was not the monopoly of landed property *à la* Marx the fuel that moved the engine of mining. It was hegemonic competition the force that moved labor into a war against hydrogeological conditions of Monte Calisio. Binding together rivaling factions of the ruling class, hegemonic competition created favorable conditions for capital to extract value from mining labor. The result was a remarkable mine-drainage development in Monte Calisio. With systemic linkages to regional, continental, and global economic change, hegemonic competition was the invisible hand that moved mining labor and capital forward. As this book shows, monopolies of landed property and feudal rents afforded no unlimited hegemonic capability to lords, not even to imperial bishops. Capabilities to exert domination had to be continually renewed through wars, 'blood espionage,' alliances, loyalties, and marriages. Such renewals suddenly forced lords to drain mines, moving political change in particular directions. The picture that Monte Calisio presents is one where internecine economic warfare within the upper class, more than class struggle from below, unleashed economic change in this medieval society.

The arguments presented in this book are specific to Monte Calisio: a mining mountain that has witnessed mining booms, dreadful military campaigns, internecine aristocratic battles, and stood at the vortex of thirteenth-century Alpine agrarian change. They nonetheless suggest lineages for building a global history of rise and fall of resource hegemonies. The works of Bernard Léchelon on the mines of Languedoc and David Bourgeois on the mines of the Upper Rhine region offer rich evidence in the right direction. Ian Blanchard has studied capitalization of the mining industry in relation to Afro-Eurasian competition. Studies by Íñigo Mugueta Moreno on Pyrenees mines and the work done by Sima Ćirković on Balkan mines provide insights about mining money and local wars in crusading Europe. Emilio Gimeno and José Mateos Royo have also illustrated functional linkages between Iberian mines and the ascent of local Christian powers. Among many other works, this scholarship has stirred the grounds of political economy by showing that mining played a crucial role in the politics of economic change.

To this scholarship, this book provides a 'reliable outline' to argue that mining capital triumphed because hegemonic competition created possibilities for carving resource profits not available otherwise. This argument is consistent with some theoretical and historical assumptions. The first assumption is that mining played a role in the rise of capitalist rents, before and beyond nineteenth-century England. As such, mining exposed contradictions inherent to fiscal instruments rooted in historical forms of landed property. Contradictions emerged when drained mines became the space where feudalism confronted economic relations pushing for privatization of land. This assumption places my book in direct dialogue with Marxist political economy debates on economic change on a world scale. A belt of ore-yielding lands south of the Alps increased the mass of value of the world economy of the long thirteenth century. The same principle holds for mines situated in the Pyrenees, Islamic Andalusia, the gold hinterlands of Ghana and the Congo region, northern India, and all other mining lands as far as the coastal salt mines of China. All mines produced commodities bought and sold by international merchants, exerting influence upon the macro-economic conditions that affected mineral profits and rents in local European districts.

The second assumption of my argument is that hegemonies that strive to organize encompassing economic relations reach a point where they cannot hold the forces of economic change that sustain their grounds. Hegemonic powers progressively lose capabilities to organize and manage the 'temporal unevenness' from which they depend. This 'temporal unevenness' continues to move the wheels of accumulation forward. It is the most precious gift of capital to political power, and which capital yields when confronting value-producing labor everywhere. This assumption follows the work of the late Giovanni Arrighi, critical world system studies, and Marxist geography, on the role of inter-state competition in historical phases of expansion and contraction of capital accumulation. The third assumption of my argument is that metals played a role in the historical phase of accumulation that began in the twelfth century and lasted until A.D. 1349. Social historians have offered abundant evidence on the trade relations that linked Genoese, Venetian, German, Castilian, and all other European trading houses to a vibrant commercial world outside Europe. Drawing upon this vast body of work, my argument takes for granted that Europe *as a political system* had relative marginality in the world economy, as André Gunder Frank argued. However, European metals and minerals played pivotal roles in relations of commodity production, circulation, distribution, and capital valorizations. This assumption places my book in direct conversation with the work of economic and monetary historians such as Graeme D. Snooks and Dennis O. Flynn, which has provided an 'entirely different vantage point' and a 'birth of globalization' approach to the study of money and industry of the West.

This book sees the light in the midst of a new 'age of extremes,' borrowing the words of Eric Hobsbawm. Wars in Gaza, Sudan, and Ukraine, and political turmoil in every corner of the world, necessarily add other meanings to the questions on hegemony this book presents. I trust and hope readers see this work not in isolation from events shaping our times, but as an effort by its author to address the unsettled question of political power and resources that capital continues to revive with violence as if addicted to its effects.

Bronx, NY, USA Jeannette Graulau

Acknowledgments

Many friends and colleagues contributed in one way or another to the ideas contained in this book. Professors and colleagues Immanuel Ness and Corinna Mullin from Brooklyn College have taught me much about the dynamics of capital and labor relations from Marxist perspectives. Their groundwork on the history of Western imperialism has provided fertile grounds unto which I have stepped when in need for theoretical guidance. I thank them for their unremitting Marxist critique to my ideas and work. To our fortune, this has become the mark of enduring friendship.

I am deeply grateful to monetary historian Dennis O. Flynn, Alexander R. Heron Professor of Economics Emeritus at University of the Pacific, who enthusiastically welcomed and encouraged my inquiries about medieval silver and money. His extensive knowledge on 'silver monies' was invaluable and considerably enriched the arguments of my book. The work of mining archeologist Martin Straßburger was a pleasant discovery I made on a Summer afternoon a year ago while studying technical literature on mining. Since then, our Zoom conversations and lengthy email exchanges on mine geometry, drainage, ore smelting, and other technical aspects of mining have greatly enriched my research inquiries and imagination. I cannot thank him enough for sharing his time and fieldwork materials with me. The photos of Monte Calisio in this book come from his superb mining archeology archive.

Lehman College librarian Eugene 'Gene' Laper was instrumental in my acquiring many obscure titles listed in the bibliography. Gene never spared any effort to help me locating and finding sources in American libraries. Dean Pamela Mills and the Office of the Dean of Natural and Social

Sciences made possible the acquisition of copyrights for the publication of the historical images contained in the book. Her training in chemistry and the 'hard sciences' made her particularly adept to the mining story that the book narrates. I am deeply grateful to her for enthusiastically supporting my research endeavors.

I thank my siblings, Mayda, Jaime Antonio, and Orlando, and my parents, Irma and Jaime, for unconditionally encouraging all my pursuits. To Viviana, Diana, Noraida, and Caroline, thank you for bringing much joy and laughter to my life and work especially in these difficult times. To Peter, I thank you for cherishing my mining stories and more.

To all and the many more whose names I omitted for reasons of time and space, I could not have done this work without you by my side.

Competing Interests The author has no competing interests to declare that are relevant to the content of this manuscript.

Contents

List of Figures

on another shaft. Five miners work in the smelting factory,
while other miners transport crude ores from neighboring shafts
to the factory. This is how mining works at Pergine must have
looked like a few centuries after the death of Bishop Wanga.
ETH-Bibliothek Zürich, E-Rara 171

CHAPTER 1

An Imperial City Takes the Audacious Adige River as Its Guide

Trent occupies a *place majeure* in the annals of European land reclamation history. A city ruled by ecclesiastical lords until recent, Trent continuously challenged a landscape dominated by water, creating an early medieval economic boom that made it the jewel of the Adige Valley. Known to its German-speaking population as Etschtal, the valley stretches from Merano to Bolzano, and occupies the Alpine heartlands of the Italian autonomous province of Trentino Alto-Adige. Here, ongoing battles against water have forced political power to move between centralization and decentralization, responding to dynamic processes of agrarian change. To this day, the city surrenders its political fate to an ambitious and ongoing flood-prevention program that seeks to subdue the capricious hydrology of the Adige Valley. A tourist visiting the city for the first time cannot help but feel amazed at the modern hydraulic works built to control river waters. Dikes, embankments, drainage channels, and navigation canals extending from the Upper Adige below Bolzano to Verona in the Po Valley add a particular charm to the river. From the nineteenth century onward, these works transformed the Adige into a 'well-disciplined river.'[1] The Roman 'Ponte Pietra' bridge that crosses the river in Verona and the 'Ponte Scaligero' bridge are 'silent witnesses' *à la* Le Corbusier of an enduring love affair between the city and its river.

[1] Hatinguais, 'Catching the flood: river navigation from the Adige to the Po in Shakespeare's Italy.'

J. Graulau, *Medieval Mining and Power in Thirteenth-Century Europe*, https://doi.org/10.1007/978-3-031-99239-1_1

Inhabitants of this city have learned to live with seasonal floods. Alpine snow melting in the Spring creates a mild 'Spring flood' season. Historically, this flood was highly beneficial to navigation when unthreatened by what Italians call *Scirocco*, the warm wind from the southeast or heavy rains. A second flood season occurs every Fall. More violent and unpredictable, this flood season happens when prolonged, torrential rains descend upon the valley. Historically, it has created severe economic and environmental problems for the city. Hundreds of hectares of land between Casteller in Trent and San Giorgio in Valsugana currently undergo reforestation, after a 'Fall flood' three years ago swallowed the entire region.[2] Forestry experts have planted spruce, larch, beech, and pine trees since then, relying upon stocks of trees available in European nurseries. Increasing dependency upon a European farming industry impacted by climate change continues to worry local politicians, as yields of broad-leaf trees valuable for protecting forests from avalanches and landslides are not always available. The most catastrophic flood in recent history was the 1966 flood event. Then, the Adige River broke its northern banks at midnight when the city fell asleep. Its swollen waters engulfed industrial tanks containing sulfur and warehoused in the S.L.O.I. chemical plant, built during the fascist regime of Benito Mussolini, producing explosions that fueled fires everywhere.[3] Firefighters could not reach the dozens of fires that consumed valuable infrastructure, as waters continued to increase. It was a major disaster. Experts argued then that record-breaking high temperatures, snow melts, and heavy rains transformed the otherwise charming Adige River into the most destructive force of the valley.

Written evidence of floods goes back to the sixth century A.D., which indicates that this phenomenon has been an integral part of the history of the city.[4] This is an attribute that Trent shares with other societies that sprung from hydrological landscapes. Florence is as proud of its embankment battles against the Arno River as it is of its banking history. The *tempo del diluvio*, in the words of Giovanni Villani, left the buildings of the

[2] Micheletto, 'Ricostruire tre anni dopo la tempesta: dai vivai provinciali più di 350mila piante.'

[3] Editore, 'L'Adige rompe gli argini: 50 anni fa l'alluvione che sconvolse Trento.'

[4] Abballe and Cavalazzi, 'Flood risk and socio-ecological resilience in a late antique and medieval countryside: managing a post-Roman alluvial landscape in the Ravenna hinterland'; Brázdil, Glaser, Pfister et al., 'Flood events of selected European rivers in the sixteenth century'; Fontana, Ronchi, and Mozzi, 'The *diluvium aquarum*: geologic evidence and geoarchaeological constrains of extreme floods in northern Italy during early Middle Ages.'

city in ruins in A.D. 1333.[5] Inhabitants of Grosetto, in Maremma, to this day leave this charming city in the Summer, escaping the flood season. Medieval floods gave the prosperous city much cause for concern. Floods facilitated the spread of the malaria-carrying *Anopheles* mosquito, prompting city rulers to issue acts ordering inhabitants to 'leave the city during July and August every year' in the early fourteenth century.[6] The Dutch peoples, proud of their heroic struggles against waters, still write about the infamous 'St. Elizabeth's flood' that took place in A.D. 1421. Then, the Grote Waard of Holland County buried dozens of settlements in the grounds. Paris was perennially *au bord de l'eau* throughout the fourteenth and fifteenth centuries. The Siene River broke its embankments dozens of times, refusing to subordinate its hydrology to the whims of the urban quarter.[7] Canals, embankments, and river-dredging techniques eased the toil and trouble of living near rivers.

Trent, however, stands out for the role the battle against water played in the rise of ecclesiastic lordship-based hegemony in the twelfth and thirteenth centuries. The city stubbornly clings to the right side of the Adige River, which, running in a north-south direction, forces unto the settlement its characteristic semi-circle shape. The Adige has moved 'progressively to the right' in centuries-long pattern of slow motion pattern triggered by accumulation of sediments by the Talvera and Isarco rivers to its left side.[8] Not only the natural riverine barrier on the left side of the city has exposed it to continuous erosion, but dwellings have required solid, dry-stone foundations. The extravagant geological behavior of the Adige River placed a premium on the political control of the many improved lands organized around the *curtis* or lordships that proliferated in villages surrounding the urban quarter. The historic Verruca hill district stands at the center of the city. It attracts archeological research that continues to shed light on the history of human adaptation to this changing hydrological landscape. Archeologists Coltorti and Dal Ri state that human occupation of the valley has a millennia-long history. Such history took off in the colonizing waves that first occupied ridges in rock shelters during the Neolithic period. A second grand wave occupied the low-gradient slopes

[5] Villani, *Croniche di Giovanni, Matteo e Filippo Villani*, p. 510.

[6] Martini, Sarti, Pallechhi, 'Landscape influences on the development of the medieval-early Renaissance city-States of Pisa, Florence, and Siena, Italy,' p. 206.

[7] Roux, 'À Paris, au bord de l'eau.'

[8] Coltorti and Dal Ri, 'The human impact on the landscape: some examples from the Adige Valley,' p. 120.

during the late Bronze Age, before a third colonizing wave settled in the sides and floors of the valley during the Iron Age. These waves of colonizers created valley areas suitable for occupation, followed by Roman colonization of strategic hilltops, and an early colonization of valley floors in the Middle Ages[9] (Fig. 1.1).

Making habitation possible meant living with the extravagant geological habit of the river, which nonetheless places a premium on permanent agrarian occupation of the valley. Habitants have turned the impressive amounts of freshwater of the Adige valley into a Ricardian comparative advantage for agrarian specialization. The Adige River basin has 550 lakes, 'most of which have a surface of one hectare.'[10] Unlike southern Italy, where rainfall is concentrated in the mild winter and reduces plant growth for half a year, well-distributed rainfall allows here for 'continuous plant growth through most months of the year.'[11] Placing 'a systemic limitation *in sensu strictu* on the availability of open agrarian plains,' the hydrology of the valley created seasonal alternations of lowland pasture in winter, and highland pasture in the Summer.[12] It created, nonetheless, a magnificent mosaic of pasture grounds, meadow lands, and navigable waterways and marshes, stretching for more than 12,000 square km.[13]

To the west of Trent lies the extensive Giudicarie or *Iudicaria* region. It is a vast region of valleys bathed by the Chiese and Sarca rivers and dotted by medieval castles. A land of rock avalanches, mountain ridges, and hydrographic basins, the Giudicarie separated the urban quarter of Trent from Brescia and montane Lombardy. From castles such as Carmala and Romano and the group of castles built north of Garda Lake, lords attempted to regulate social life and commerce. As such, the region was part of the western trade corridor that connected Lombardy and Venice to northern Europe. The most famous castle was Castello di Arco on Riva del Garda, part of the patrimony of the lords of Arco. The castle was a potent structure built on a rock pinnacle from where lords avoided floodings

[9] Ibidem.

[10] Chiogna, Majone, Cano Paoli et al., 'A review of hydrological and chemical stressors in the Adige catchment,' p. 431.

[11] Postan (ed.), *The Cambridge Economic history of Europe*, p. 341.

[12] Stenico, 'Signorie rurali e risorse economiche,' p. 222.

[13] Franceschini, 'Le paludi dell'Adige diritti di sfruttanento,' p. 251. See also Brázdil, Glaser, Pfister et al., 'Flood events of selected European rivers in the sixteenth century,' pp. 265–266; Glaser, Riemann, Schönbein et al., 'The variability of European floods since AD 1500.'

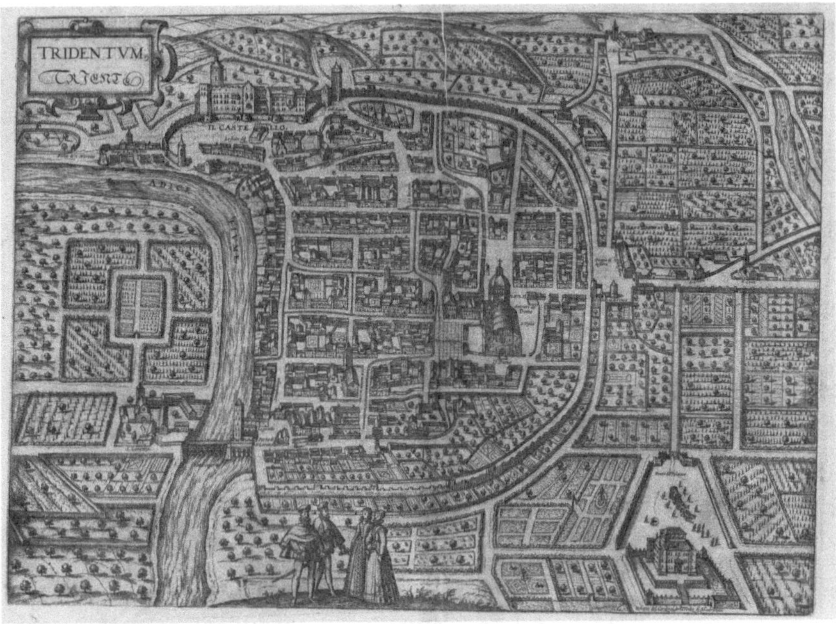

Fig. 1.1 Trent, by the renowned German mapmakers Frans Hogenberg and Georg Braun (A.D. 1581). Trent experienced a cultural revolution when the Italian Renaissance took hold of the city, forcing Germanic feudalism to hurry onward to its decay. The cultural influence of Prince-Bishops from the 'south' cannot be underestimated. With 27 years of age, Prince-Bishop Cristoforo Madruzzo brought pomposity to religious and civil rituals of the city in the sixteenth century. Balls, tournaments, sumptuous noble weddings, celebrations honoring local saints, and musical recitals were a legacy his nephew, Ludovico, carried on when he succeeded his uncle. The map intentionally portrays this Renaissance view of the city. Its neatly drawn land enclosures suggest that rivers surrendered to the city, for the nobility to take on 'recreational hydrology' at last. David Rumsey Historical Map Collection. www.davidrumsey.com

when the Sarca River emptied swollen waters into Lake Garda. Situated on the port city of Riva, it offered unobstructed views of Lombard ports on the other side of Garda Lake. It also gave the Arco lords open views of the road connecting Garda to Chiese Valley through Tenno, Bleggio, and Banale. Albrecht Dürer (A.D. 1471–1528) succumbed to the strange beauty of the castle, immortalizing its pinnacle in his painting titled *Adoration of the Magi* (A.D. 1504).[14]

[14] Zulberti, 'Il Castello di Arco nell'iconografia del Dürer.'

Rendena, the main valley of the Giudicarie, lies nested by two short mountain ranges. It offered strategic routes to merchants and pilgrims coming from Bavaria and western Lombardy into Trent.[15] Nature created in this region the startling 'splintered rock pinnacles' of the Brenta Dolomites, which divide the Sarca and the Adige valleys between Mezzolombardo and Trent.[16] Here, the Noce River, with its crystal clear waters, falls from the Tonale Pass into Trent. 'For centuries up to the present day, this little-known pass has marked the border between Italian Lombardy and German-speaking Trentino.'[17] The pass was a most frequented road that allowed Giudicarie villages to move agrarian surpluses into the urban quarter of Trent and beyond. Charlemagne crossed it once when he sought to avoid the dukes of Bavaria on his way to Lombardy.[18]

Trade took off very early, assisted by a river that dominates the entire orography and geography of the Adige valley.[19] The river runs deeply embedded in the floor of the valley for only few kilometers before it widens into the surrounding relief reaching between 2000 and 3000 meters.[20] The spruce forested mountains of South Tyrol are its birthplace, from where it grows in spring waters near Lake Resia at an elevation of 1586 meters. The river flows westward to Bolzano before turning southward to Trent on its way to Verona. It continues its run north of the Po River until it reaches the Gulf of Venice through Porto Fossone in Rossolina Mare.[21] The Adriatic Sea is its final destiny. The river is 340 km long, which makes it the second largest river of Italy after the Po River, and part of one of the largest watersheds of continental Europe.[22] This long fluvial corridor

[15] Cagol, 'Le Giudicarie e la val Vestino: i Lodron e i da Campo,' pp. 114–115.

[16] Coolidge, *The Alps in nature and history*, p. 354.

[17] Guckelsberger, 'Two great maps of Italy—a comparison,' p. 68.

[18] Stenico, 'Dazio al passo del Tonale,' p. 15.

[19] Mouthon, 'Les communautés alpines et l'État (milieu XIIIe–début XVIe siècle).'

[20] Coltorti and Dal Ri, 'The human impact on the landscape: some examples from the Adige Valley,' p. 106; Stenico, 'Signorie rurali e risorse economiche,' p. 222.

[21] Christie, *From Constantine to Charlemagne: an archeology of Italy*, p. 358; Perini, *Dizionario geografico, statistico del Trentino*, p. 175.

[22] Chiogna, Majone, Cano Paoli et al., 'A review of hydrological and chemical stressors in the Adige catchment,' p. 432. I also consulted the following works: Bassetti and Borsato, 'Evoluzione geomorfologica della Bassa Valle dell'Adige'; Bonoldi, 'La risorsa mutevole, l'Adige nell'economia della regione trentino-tirolese'; Bundi (ed.), *Alpine waters*; Campopiano, 'Rural communities, land clearance and water management in the Po Valley'; Corona, Guiot, Edouard et al., 'Millennium-long summer temperature variations in the European Alps'; Curtis and Campopiano, 'Medieval land reclamation and the creation of new societies'; Garçon, Chauvel, Chapron et al., 'Silver and lead in high-altitude lake sediments: proxies for climate changes and human activities'; Luetscher, 'Alpine permafrost thawing during the medieval warm period'; Taylor, 'Trent to the Reschen Pass, a cultural traverse of the Adige corridor.'

linked agrarian life of Trent to neighboring cities and above all, to the Queen of the Adriatic, Venice.

After the second half of the twelfth century, this *fiume rapidissimo* was a fluvial highway leading to the Brenner Pass. The competing Saint Bernard Pass absorbed the largest volume of traffic in the period, but the Brenner Pass was the nodal point for the expansionist policy of Emperor Frederick I or Frederick Barbarossa (A.D. 1122–1190; r. A.D. 1155–1190). This geopolitical condition substantially impacted the politics of riverine trade.[23] The Isarco River, a northern tributary of the Adige, still provides direct access to the Brenner Pass, rising gradually at an elevation of 1375 m above mean sea level.[24] A second commercial route leading to the northern Inn Valley of South Tyrol proved useful to merchants traveling from the newly founded town of Bolzano from the eleventh century onward.[25] Proximity to markets north of the Alps transformed Trent into the hub of 'easiest communication' lines connecting central Europe to Italy and the Venetian northern plains. A third but more challenging commercial pass was the Septimer, in the Canton of Grisons, the birthplace of Bishop Frederick Wanga (A.D. 1175–1218). Today a Winter tourist destination, the Septimer Pass was the highest of all passes (2310 m above mean sea level), with a difficult access ramp from Casaccia in Val Bregalia.[26]

Commercial traffic rapidly expanded after the late twelfth century.[27] Carriages, rafts, and Venetian *galeas* transported Levant pepper and other luxury commodities into the urban market of Trent.[28] From the north across the Alps, German, Flemish, and English merchants moved their goods through Bronzolo, south of Bolzano. From there, goods continued into Trent and Verona, loaded on timber rafts.[29] From 500 tons per year at the beginning of the thirteenth century, trade volumes increased to 3500 tons per year throughout the fourteenth century, reaching 5000

[23] Franceschini, 'Le paludi dell'Adige diritti di sfruttanento.'

[24] Freschi, 'L'axe du Brenner,' p. 47.

[25] Franceschini, 'Le paludi dell'Adige diritti di sfruttanento.'

[26] Frey and Rouger, 'Un axe transalpin méconnu et inutilisé: Le Septimer,' p. 289.

[27] Leonardi and Bonoldi, 'L'economia della montagna interna Italiana: un approccio storiografico.'

[28] Racine, 'Poteri medievali e percorsi fluviali nell'Italia Padana'; Stolz, 'Zur geschichte der organisation des transportwesens in Tirol im Mittelalter.'

[29] Corritore, 'Verona e Mantova nell'età comunale: *Mercatum* fori, granai privati'; Hatinguais, 'Catching the flood: river navigation from the Adige to the Po.'

tons in A.D. 1500; 8000 tons in A.D. 1570; and 10,000 tons in A.D. 1600.[30] Lords exploited the comparative advantage of fluvial trade by levying taxes for the use of bridges and river rafts. In time, rents paid for use of fluvial transport routes contributed to the development of roads, as in Valsugana and the Garda Lake region.[31] Attracting wool merchants, the Valsugana road linked Trent to Veneto. It brought 'Venice perceptibly nearer to Germany,' as a nineteenth-century observer noted.[32] The Garda lakeside road was busy in the Summer, afforded easy communication with Verona. In the long run, thus, waterways lowered the general level of rents by lowering the cost of land improvement. The classical Smithian effects of good fertile lands and proximity to trade corridors pulled labor in way that created erosion of onerous service obligations. The more this society accumulated capital, the more it lowered the cost of production and trade especially after the second half of the fourteenth century.

Trent exported agrarian surpluses produced by agrarian peasants, especially livestock, milk, timber wood, resins, saltpeter, and silver and lead ores.[33] In exchange for raw materials, Trent received wheat imported from Bergamo, Vicenza, and Brescia, and manufactured goods from Venice in the thirteenth century. The unequal exchange relations that sustained this trade pattern tied the ruling classes of Trent to foreign food imports. But it also tied the elite of Po Valley cities like Verona and Vicenza to foreign raw materials produced in Alpine hinterlands, especially cheese, timber, wine, and other agrarian commodities. Alpine hinterlands paid the highest environmental price of the imbalances of trade that linked them to the commercial orbits of rising communes of northern Italy. In A.D. 1488, the community of Tesino Castle purchased foreign grains and cereals from Venetian merchants. The community paid for imports by leasing the coniferous forest situated in Mount Agaro to Venetian merchants for 12 years. The community, however, reserved its rights of access to the grazing grounds of the mountain. Analogous to primary-commodity trade agreements today, the foreign grain suppliers paid the lease in kind and money.

[30] Racine, 'Poteri medievali e percorsi fluviali nell'Italia Padana,' pp. 223–224.

[31] Stenico, 'Signorie rurali e risorse economiche,' pp. 233–234. Unless otherwise noted, the rest of the paragraph comes from this work.

[32] McCrackan, *The spell of Tyrol*, p. 256.

[33] Denecke, 'Mining regions and metal trade in early modern Europe'; Orlando, 'Venezia, L'Adige e la viabilità nel Basso Medioevo,' pp. 104–105; Rossini, 'La Via dell'Adige e il commercio del legname nel Basso Medio Evo,' pp. 245–247; Stenico, 'Signorie rurali e risorse economiche,' p. 223.

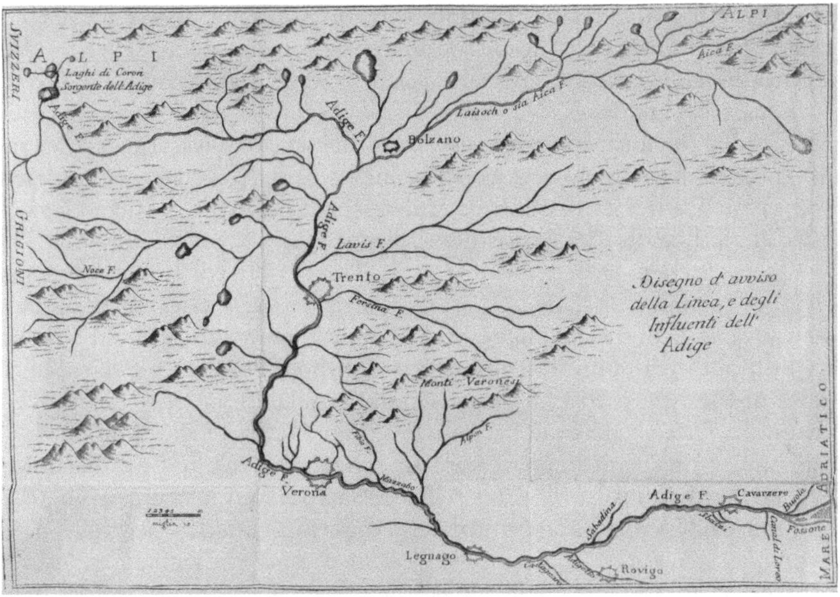

Fig. 1.2 The Adige River and its dozen tributaries, as depicted by Antonio Belloni in the eighteenth century. According to *I Dialoghi* by Gregorio Magno (A.D. 589), a swollen Adige descended upon Verona, destroying everything on its way on a sad day of October of the year A.D. 589. But when Zeno, Bishop of Verona, opened the doors of the Church, water refused to enter. The story of 'the miracle of Zeno' rapidly propagated in the high circles of Rome, for Zeno is today the patron saint of the city. Biblioteca Digitale Trentina

They supplied 421 bushels of wheat and approximately 170 bushels of rye and millet and paid the rest in cash in equal annual installments distributed over the 12 years of the contract (Fig. 1.2).

Abundance of water meant that hydraulic machines and techniques were at the core of economic development of the city. Farmers built ditches, intent upon expanding land available for cultivation. 'Drainage ditches led surface run-off into natural channels, curtailing erosion, and lowered the water table, facilitating root growth and soil workability: hence their laborious upkeep was worthwhile to cultivators.'[34] Ditches

[34] Magnusson and Squatriti, 'The technologies of water in medieval Italy,' pp. 224–225.

were structures that manipulated the direction of waterways but also controlled for sanitary conditions. Agrarian peasants adapted ditches to specific topographic circumstances, especially if water was meant to be driven back to rivers and lakes. Natural source and desired destination of water determined the form and construction of drainage ditches, argues Roberta Magnusson.[35] Archeological evidence indicates that ditches were unlined and opened, unlike the drainage and discharge systems that emerged in hydrological landscapes of northern Europe.[36]

Open ditches carried away wastes. They most likely had seasonal changes in water discharge, especially because they collected rainwater. The advantage of this hydraulic structure was that rainwater could be used to flush out the drains, in the direction of fishponds, pits, or rivers. Sluice gates of the type used in fishponds could regulate flow of water in open channels. There is no evidence of pipes built as part of the hydraulic system supporting land improvement in this period, suggesting that lords had no need to invest in water transport across long distances. There is also no evidence of distribution reservoirs built in this period. Those hydraulic structures were not needed in a land with abundant water sources, even though lead and earthenware pipes could be found in monastical houses and castles. Abundance of waters meant that ditches were built also to supply 'sub-potable river water' for various uses.

Efficient drainage ditches depended upon 'the gradient, the roughness of the channel walls, and the dimensions and shape of the cross section.' Builders assessed highest average gradient by calculating the difference in elevation between water source and terminus. Generally, they reduced gradients 'by following a sinuous course rather than a direct line.' Roberta Magnusson argues that crafters considered changes in gradient of single channels that affected depth and velocity of water current, 'running fast and shallow down steep slopes, deeper and more slowly when the slope was gentle.' Since floods could emerge if gradients in a single channel abruptly changed, crafters had to make difficult choices 'between channels with steep gradients and high velocities' which required frequent repairs, or 'channels with shallow gradients and low velocities.' The latter were by no means easier, given the problem of sedimentation. Agrarian lands most

[35] Magnusson, *Water technology in the Middle Ages: cities, monasteries, and waterworks after the Roman Empire*, p. 55.

[36] *Idem*, pp. 72–113. The paragraphs that follow borrow integrally from this work unless otherwise indicated.

likely looked like 'a grid of open drainage ditches,' forming a 'water-management system' that expanded agrarian possibilities of land, while escaping the monopoly power of lords.

Hydraulic machines allowed farmers to better control the 'three wild forces of soil, weeds, and climate,'[37] further expanding the agrarian frontier. The most important hydraulic machine was the watermill.[38] Wherever planted, it regulated the pace of agrarian production. Historian Lynn White stated decades ago that a feature of medieval Europe was that 'water mills were much more common than churches.'[39] Waterwheels and hydraulic techniques applied to farming lands rapidly spread in the Adige Valley, as they did across continental Europe from the eleventh century onward.[40] 'Watermills were much more common than churches.'[41] Mills were part of the engineering patrimony of rural lordships, alongside water-powered ore crushers and forges. Machines arrived at the region from Southern Germany, where mills appeared at *Schmidmühlen* before A.D. 1028. White summarized this development as the result of the 'passion for mechanization of industry' of the noble class.[42] Lords built mills, promoting increase in agrarian surpluses, as the Mezzo family did in the village of Rotaliana. Peasants had the obligation of using the mills built by lords, as well as other capital stocks provided by lords.[43]

North of Trent, floods were frequent on the Rotaliana plain, where the Adige River borders the eastern side of Atesina valley.[44] Despite the smooth topography of the plain, merchants avoided journeying through this land

[37] Georges Duby in Cipolla (ed.), *The Fontana economic history of Europe*, pp. 175–176.

[38] In addition to cited sources, I consulted the following works: Andersen, Jensen, and Volmar Skovsgaard, 'The heavy plow and the agricultural evolution in medieval Europe'; Arnold, *Negotiating the landscape: environment and monastic identity*; Campopiano, 'Rural communities, land clearance and water management in the Po Valley'; Cascio and Malanima, 'Mechanical energy and water power in Europe'; Classen, *Water in medieval literature*; Cortese, *L'acqua, il grano, il ferro*; Lanconelli, *Terra, acque e lavoro nella Viterbo medievale*; Lopez, *The commercial revolution of the Middle Ages*.

[39] Lynn White in Cipolla (ed.), *The Fontana economic history of Europe*, pp. 156–157.

[40] Cavaciocchi (cur.), *Le interazioni fra economia e ambiente biologico*; Centofanti, Brusaporci, Lucchese, 'Historical watermills, architectural, mechanical, and hydraulic heritage.'

[41] Georges Duby in Cipolla (ed.), *The Fontana economic history of Europe*, p. 155.

[42] Georges Duby in Cipolla (ed.), *The Fontana economic history of Europe*, p. 155; Gille, *Les ingéniers de la Renaissance*, p. 19; Magnusson, *Water technology in the Middle Ages: cities, monasteries, and waterworks after the Roman Empire*, p. 81.

[43] Franceschini, 'Castelli e campagne in area trentina,' p. 200.

[44] Tomedi, 'Tra nord e sud. Le signorie rurali in valle dell'Adige,' p. 62.

when they anticipated bad weather conditions. Instead, they relied upon the Cembra Valley, in the southeast fringes of Rotaliana plain, and which afforded communication with Monte Calisio. A new nobility families extracted rents from agrarian villages that specialized in viticulture, wine production, and hydraulic works. Bordering southeastern side of the urban quarter, the Fersina River nested various floating mills or *rotam*. The floating mill was an adaptation of the medieval waterwheel. The machine solved the problem of insufficient water due to seasonal hydrological changes.[45] Further south, the hydrological landscape made rice cultivation possible—on a large scale. This was the case of Piedmonte plains.[46] Watermills swept through the plains from the second half of the fourteenth century onward, coinciding with expansion of maritime trade. Back in Trent, the lords of Thun, representing family lines including Bragher, Castelfondo, and Thun, had ten or more watermills during the fourteenth and fifteenth centuries. These machines made agriculture possible in Non and Sole valleys, demarcating boundaries between rich lords and the rest. Machines also flourished in Cortaccia in Bolzano and Vigolana plateau in southeast Trent. The Khuen-Belasi family, lords of Arsio in Fondo, owned perpetual rights for lands and forges near Lovernatico River, in Brenta. Enjoying a preeminent position in lands running from Trent to Feltre, the Castellalto lords in Telve also owned watermills, which they obtained through leases granted in perpetuity by various bishops[47] (Fig. 1.3).

Proliferation of hydraulic works and exploitation of labor were two sides of one single coin, namely, economic development of the city. It is no exaggeration to say that unequal exchanges allowed Trent to join what medievalist Peter Spufford once called 'the nadir of the European road system' in the twelfth century.[48] Fluvial transport and traffic of goods had much to do with this process. Bishops and the old aristocracy put obstacles for imperial power to organize itself as a 'policing power' around the course of waters.[49] They were locked up in continuous competition for grabbing a higher share of the profits stemming from riverine trade and traffic, forcing emperors to increasingly withdraw from the political sphere where river usufruct rights were in the making. This vacuum strengthened

[45] Dai Prà and Allegri, 'Il fiume tra scienza e percezione,' p. 57.

[46] Bellero, 'I cistercensi e il paesaggio rurale: L'abbazia di S. Maria di Lucedio'; Grandis, 'I mulini ad acqua del Padovano.'

[47] Curzel, *Il capitolo della cattedrale di Trento dal XII secolo al 1348*, p. 499.

[48] Spufford, *Power and profit: the merchant in medieval Europe*, p. 174.

[49] Racine, 'Poteri medievali e percorsi fluviali nell'Italia Padana,' pp. 14–15; Varanini, 'Itinerari commerciali secondari nel Trentino bassomedioevale,' pp. 101–105.

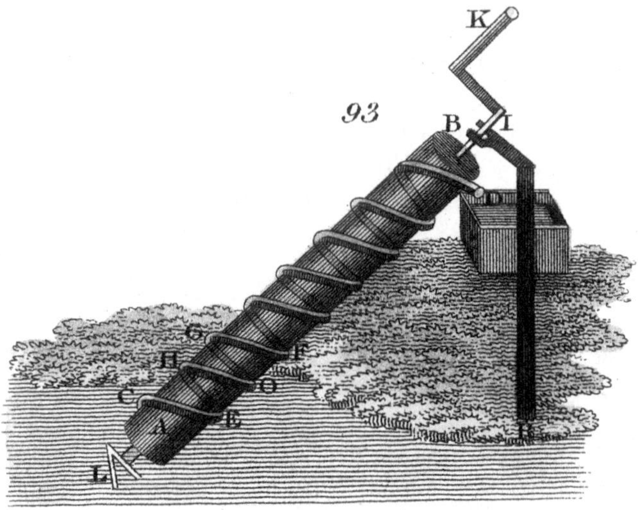

Fig. 1.3 Archimedean screw for raising water from one level to another. A modern design of the ancient *cochlea Archimedis* or 'water-snail' by Archimedes. The screw was employed in ancient mines for draining shafts. Driven by gearing from a vertical shaft, the machine had lugs turned as a treadmill. A man turned the treadmill while holding on to a fixed bar. Engineers have successfully adapted the machine for energy generation in Trent and other European cities. Ann Ronan Picture Library, London, Great Britain/Art Resource, N.Y.

local lordships and riverine communities, which joined bishops, monasteries, and the old aristocracy in the legal battles and alliances for water usufruct rights.

Lords continually attempted to monopolize river transport routes, triggering the rise of water transport rights. In the times of Wanga, *barcaioli* or shipowners from the village of Mori held riverine trade rights for the Ravazzone-Bolzano route.[50] They were protagonists of a rebellion against Bishop Wanga, and which the bishop repressed with the aid of *milites*, as discussed later. The strategic fluvial route they controlled had to be protected at all costs. More so given that fluvial commerce along Adige waterways reinforced the spatial agglomeration of extractive economies. Over

[50] Curzel and Varanini, *La documentazione dei vescovi di Trento*, pp. 388–389.

the long run, this geographic condition reduced the costs of agriculture and mining, in a process that distributed the gains of land improvement in uneven ways. However, it imposed upon labor the toil and trouble of controlling for floods. The 'early market-oriented agrarian development' was the outcome of land reclamation.[51] Pastoralists and farmers reclaimed lands between the northern Alpine tundra and Lake Garda south of Trent. Agrarian surface land expanded. Stocks plowed into lands by lords, shepherds, and farmers increased 'taxable wealth' of society. Farmers created a mosaic of improved lands surrounding the city. Stonewalls built on steep slopes were useful in the prevention of landslides. A tourist traveling through the vineyards of Cembra Valley can see the legacies of this technique in the mosaic of farming terraces encircled by stone walls. This technique organically resists mechanization of viticulture, given that terraces and stone walls alike require incessant care and maintenance against rains, snow, and Alpine frost.[52]

Bishops sponsored built public works, too. The most iconic structure built by Bishop Wanga was the *Torre Vanga*, a military tower which stands today near the old city gate of San Lorenzo. With its distinctive Romanesque architecture, the tower looks austere and melancholic, reminding visitors of the medieval heights of this ecclesiastical principality. Secular lords built castles everywhere, sharing with bishops the desire to extend and widen the jurisdiction of rent claims and privileges. Castles populated hilltops of difficult access, 'prefiguring the urban model' of the town that dominated the Alpine and all other European landscapes.[53] Here, economic development deepened ruralization of social life. Contrary to Adam Smith's idea that development always led to the rise of cities, the opposite was true in Trent, where extractive activities demanded colonization of rural lands by castles, *villae*, and *mansus*.

It was in a predominantly rural montane landscape where hydraulic techniques allowed peasants to conquer the 'three wild forces' of the feudal economy, *à la* Georges Duby—'soil, weeds and climate.'[54] Water mills expanded agrarian lands and yields, challenging the juridical, political, and

[51] Wickham, 'How did the feudal economy work? The economic logic of medieval societies,' pp. 7–10.

[52] Marcone, 'I vigneti terrazzati della Valle di Cembra: paesaggio e identità di un territorio.'

[53] Lynn White in Cipolla (ed.), *The Fontana economic history of Europe*, p. 75, footnote 1; Landi, 'L'incastellamento di fronte al diritto feudale.'

[54] Georges Duby in Cipolla (ed.), *The Fontana economic history of Europe*, p. 176.

economic horizon of hegemonic power, as discussed in the next chapters. The 'silver-mining mania'[55] that swept through Trent in the last quarter of the twelfth century gave bishops no time to ponder on the contradictions of ongoing land improvement processes that demanded the rise of hegemonic power. Trent bishops responded to the urge of expanding the battle against waters into the underground world of mines and miners.

Unholy Waters Agitate the City from Below

Mining also contributed to land improvement. In the times of Wanga, a silver mining boom began when German miners discovered *argento in prima linea* in Monte Calisio plateau in northeast Trent during the last decades of the twelfth century. Monte Calisio stands in one of the most important 'galena basins' of medieval Europe.[56] The mining territory was specifically located north of Monte Calisio, in an area covering 100 square kilometers. Archeologists Casagrande, Päffgen, and Straßburger argue that this area coincides with 'Bolzano Porphyry Platform' sediments. The sedimentary rock sequence here begins with Gröden layers, which reached 20 to 30 meters of thickness, and developed gradually from decomposed quartz porphyry.[57] This layer is represented by 'whitish grey, red or yellowish quartz sandstones.' Increasing amounts of dolomite and lime give way to the Bellorophon layer, which reaches 60 to 70 meters in thickness in the plateau. This sedimentary rock layer 'leads over' the upper layers of mineralized-rich rocks of Monte Calisio. It is this upper zone what distinguishes the 'Dolomitic southern Alps' from rest of the eastern Alps. Known as Werfen Formation, it creates a rocky belt of mineral-rich limestone that stretches from the Tyrolese Alps into the Dinaric Alps. Only the lower sections of Werfen rock formation remains in Monte Calisio plateau.

[55] Spufford, *Money and its use in medieval Europe*, p. 118.

[56] As late as the nineteenth century, various mining companies tried but failed to revive Monte Calisio mining works. After the First and Second World Wars, various companies tried to sink shafts in Monte Calisio plateau with little success. Later in the 1980s, a Canadian company held mining permits for Monte Calisio, but disappointed with prospection results, it quickly abandoned the site. Casagrande, 'Paesaggi minerari del Trentino'; Casagrande, Päffgen, and Straßburger, 'Mining archeological research of medieval silver ore mining at Trent.'

[57] Martin Straßburger, 'About Monte Calisio' Zoom video-meeting and emails to Jeannette Graulau, September 9–10, 2024. Unless otherwise noted, the rest of the paragraph comes from this work.

'The upper part is missing,' says Martin Straßburger, stressing the predatory character of mining. Werfen formations contain 'ore dolomite with galena, sphalerite and pyrite.'

Unlike silver workings in Devon and Chemnitz, where miners dug valley floors searching for ore veins, miners here carved shafts into Monte Calisio itself, fashioning a 'mining mountain' like no other in thirteenth-century Europe.[58] Miners discovered ore veins in a mineralized belt that stretches between the villages of Civezzano and Fornace. Situated between Fersina and Aviso, the plateau of *mons arçenterie* or Monte Calisio reaches more than 1000 meters of elevation. The toponym *mons arçentarie* appeared for the first time in the compilation of legal documents commissioned by Bishop Wanga and known as *Codex Wangianus.*[59] It speaks of a history of German miners or *omni metallorii* who descended from the Inn and Drave valleys into Trent, and whose labor removed constraints to mine improvement. They settled in Bolzano, Fiemme, Balsega di Piné, Folgaria, Ala, and Terragnolo.[60] Miners found in the Adige Valley a society enduring change, where processes of land reclamation presented a horizon of opportunities. They joined the population of the valley, mixing genetic pools and transforming the old Ladin tongue into *un vernacolo autonomo* as Italian linguist Giovan Battista Pellegrini saw it.[61] To a large extent, they were a 'labor aristocracy,' as economic conditions of early feudalism endowed this people with a certain *mobilité inquiète* denied agrarian peasants.[62]

Miners ferociously dug the ore veins of Monte Calisio, leaving a mountain 'entirely perforated by subterranean adits.'[63] Slags or residues of

[58] Martin Straßburger, 'About Monte Calisio' Zoom video-meeting and emails to Jeannette Graulau, September 9–10, 2024.

[59] Italian medievalists Emanuele Curzel and Gian Maria Varanini have dealt extensively with the Codex Wangiangus. They have transcribed the *Codex Wangianus*, making it accessible in Latin and Italian languages. See Curzel, *Il Codice Vanga: un principe vescovo e il suo governo, Tomo II*; with Varanini, *La documentazione dei vescovi di Trento*; also *Codex Wangianus, i cartulari della Chiesa trentina (secoli XIII–XIV), Tomo I.*

[60] Bonoldi, 'L'Adige nell'economia della regione Trentino-tirolese'; Cantù, *Illustrazione del Tirolo italiano*, p. 73.

[61] Battista Pellegrini, *La genesi del retoromanzo.*

[62] Borchgrave, 'Histoire des colonies belges qui s'établirent en Allemagne pendant le XIIe et le XIIIe siècle,' p. 2.

[63] Different spellings appear in the mining documents contained in *Codex Wangianus*, such as *arceterie*, *arçentarie*, *argentaria*, *argenterie*, *arzentaria*, and *arzenterie.* Cantù, *Illustrazione del Tirolo italiano*, p. 73; Perini and Lurati, *Illustrazione del Tirolo italiano e*

medieval smelting works discovered by Italian archeologists at the old site of Doss Le Grave in Monte Calisio reveal that miners exploited veins of *piombo solforato* or lead sulfide, copper pyrites, and chalcocite.[64] The mountain was a *monte calvo*, completely denuded of vegetation by the thirteenth century.[65] Archeologists estimate that the site of the medieval mines contains underground galleries extending for hundreds of kilometers and numerous shaft relics.[66]

The mines belonged to the bishopric since the second half of the twelfth century.[67] It is under Bishop Wanga that the problem of *fondiane aquaticae* or shaft flooding first emerged in the written law of the ecclesiastic principality. Historians speculate that Bishop Adelpert (r. A.D. 1156–1172) encroached upon patrimonial lands of the Counts of Eppan, relying upon his connections to Emperor Frederick I.[68] The bishop followed Emperor Fredrick I in campaigns against rebellious northern Italian cities during A.D. 1160–1162. Struggles among emperor, the pope and an antipope, and Lombard cities were fiercer than ever. Along with the bishop of Feltre, Bishop Adelpert witnessed when Frederick Barbarossa punished a member of his own class, Bishop Otto of Belluno, by removing the privileges of ecclesiastical principality from the city. Emperor Frederick was furious because Bishop Otto sided with Pope Alexander III, betraying the geopolitical goals of the emperor.[69] Bishops Adelpert remained loyal to the emperor, and Frederick I rewarded him well. The bishop received the Monte Calisio mines as a permanent donation of rights by the Counts of

della Svizzera italiana, p. 73; for historical geography of the region, see Dai Prà, 'La cartografia storica come interfaccia dialettica tra discipline e competenze territoriali.'

[64] Corniani Degli Algarotti, *Dello stabilimento delle miniere*, p. 19; Ferretti, 'Storia e geologia della "miniera d'oro" di Val Gerlano,' p. 199; Santi, Antonelli, and Renzulli, 'Provenance of medieval *pietra ollare*,' pp. 253–263; Tizzoni, 'Le scorie della riduzione di minerale argentifero dal Monte Calisio,' p. 12.

[65] Dai Prà, 'La cartografia storica come interfaccia dialettica tra discipline e competenze territoriali.'

[66] Ambrosi, *Trent e il suo circondario*, p. 11; Baillie-Grohman, *The land in the mountains, being an account of Tyrol*, p. 259; Collatera and Primerano, *Un vescovo, la sua cattedrale, il suo tesoro*, p. 22; Ferretti, 'Storia e geologia della "miniera d'oro" di Val Gerlano,' p. 199; Tizzoni, 'Le scorie della riduzione di minerale argentifero dal Monte Calisio,' pp. 284–288.

[67] Curzel and Varanini, *La documentazione dei vescovi di Trento*, pp. 154–157, 172–174; Kink, *Fontes Rerum Austriacarum*, pp. 41–42, 438–439.

[68] Landi, 'Non solo vescovi e imperatori. Dinastie comitali e attività mineraria in area trentino altoatesina,' pp. 384–385.

[69] Reich, 'I diploma dell'istituzione del Principato Vescovile di Trento,' p. 104.

Eppan, who ceded their jurisdiction of rights and privileges for Monte Calisio in an uneasy alliance that had consequences for bishops and the region. The Counts of Eppan remained fierce loyalists. In the schism between the empire and the Papacy, Counts Frederick and Henry imprisoned the Papal emissaries sent by Pope Adrian IV to negotiate with the emperor.[70] They remained loyal to their aristocratic class interests, joining the government of Wanga in the House of Canons of the *Capitulum Tridentinum* or Chapter of the Church of Trent (Fig. 1.4).

Monte Calisio mines appeared in an imperial diploma dated February 15, 1189, whereby Emperor Frederick I confirmed that the controversial Bishop Conrad of Beseno (r. A.D. 1189–1205) held mining rights for all metallic mines located in the jurisdiction of the bishopric, *argentifodinas in ducato Tridentino episcopatuve*. The donation excluded mines found in allodial lands of the counts of Eppan and Tyrol near Merano.[71] Debt and dangerous alliances characterized the government of Bishop Conrad. He tried to please Trent burgesses, the Tyrolean aristocracy, and allied canons,

Fig. 1.4 Monte Calisio viewed from the Adige River in Trent. The plateau with the mines lies north and north east. Courtesy of Martin Straßburger, Mining Archaeology Consultancy

[70] Castagnetti, *Governo vescovile, feudalità, 'communitas' cittadina e qualifica capitaneale a Trento fra XII e XIII secolo*, pp. 94–95.

[71] Curzel and Varanini, *La documentazione dei vescovi di Trento*, pp. 184–187.

who represented powerful local rural interests. The bishop founded a church and *eremitorium* in San Martino in Primiero valley north of the city, and members of the Chapter of the Church protested, fearing the ascent of a competing ecclesiastical jurisdiction undermining rent claims of the Church of Santa Maria. The political climate surrounding his ascent to power was different than the climate Wanga encountered. After the death of Emperor Barbarossa, competing interests between the old and the new nobility, the aristocracy, created a period of turmoil in the city. Bishop Conrad took advantage and joined others in the competition for the spoils of the episcopate. Historian Emanuele Curzel suspects that the bishop did a business transaction with money lenders, in return for cash.[72] The city revolted against Bishop Conrad, who had to flee only to return to his seat aided by his military vassals. Revolts or *discordiae* against him forced him to resign and retire to St. Georgenberg monastery near Schwaz.[73] As he communicated to the Pope in the first months of A.D. 1205, his parishioners afflicted him with *iniuriae et molestiae* and *homicidia, periuria et incendia* on his advanced age.

The diploma was by no means the first time the emperor donated mining rights to his vassals. Two previous imperial diplomas donated to similar rights to Count Palatine Hildebrandt of Tuscia and Margrave Otto II of Meissen in A.D. 1160s, suggesting that mines played a geopolitical role on behalf of rising sub-hegemonic power on behalf of Carolingian Europe.[74] By then, Frederick I had demanded that all cities 'should recognize his imperial suzerainty' based on *iura regalia* that the Emperor confirmed in the Diet of Roncaglia in A.D. 1158.[75] Nothing further is mentioned about the mines, until Bishop Wanga came to power in A.D. 1207. That same year, Wanga confirmed his rights to the mines of Monte Calisio, mentioning that the mines were flooded. A flooded shaft was a problem no lord could afford to ignore in this Alpine hydrological landscape. During Autumn and Spring rainy seasons, water levels of the Adige River and its tributaries tended to rise, increasing the volume and speed of surface and underground water-accumulation. The tributary closer to the urban district is the Fersina River. It borders the left side of the Adige watershed, reaching 'down as the falls of Pontalto.' Its waters reach Trent

[72] Curzel, *Il capitolo della cattedrale di Trento*, pp. 65–66.

[73] *Idem*, pp. 64–68.

[74] Landi, 'Non solo vescovi e imperatori Dinastie comitali e attività mineraria in area trentino altoatesina,' p. 375.

[75] Parker, *Sovereign city: the city-State through history*, pp. 100–101.

in a locality Italians called *il Deserto*, a menacing watery frontier space separated from the heart of the district.[76]

Snowmelt increased groundwater storage in the watershed of the river, oftentimes creating floods in neighboring farming valleys, turning lands into swamps, and altering water table of mines.[77] Because the snow melts early in this highland, the rainy season carries away moisture, and turns the Adige into a furious torrent. The Alps, aptly known as the 'water tower of Europe,' added to the seasonal changes in surface and underground water-levels.[78] This scenario could dramatically increase the cost of labor, threatening rents and profits, and political power. The multiple springs of water that flow from this range added to the volumes of water penetrating slits of rocks.[79] Neighboring shafts and transportation tunnels could be lost to mine drainage.

Because it halted production, shaft flooding severely impacted land improvement and metal trade. Moreover, while draining agrarian lands 'could be organized locally by peasants,' mine-drainage works required very specific capital and labor relations. It could entail improvement works on a large scale.[80] In the case of ordinary underground mines, a shaft on the verge of flooding left little time for miners to escape. One can imagine that waters warned their coming with a thunder-like noise, dreadfully reverberating in the rock walls of a pit, giving miners no time to escape. When and if miners escaped from a rush of water flooding a pit, they bore the responsibility of returning to the flooded mine as soon as the flood subsided. An expert foreman assessed the damages done to infrastructure and mining works, while a scribe or learned officer, related to the local nobility or aristocracy, took notes about expenses lost to the mine. A supervisor performed the difficult and risky task of going back inside the 'dry' tunnels of the mine along with trusted miners. He made a rapid assessment of what went wrong with the thickness of the roof of the mine-work, types of rock and materials forming the roof, and the condition of mine-roof and walls when the mine flooded. The freezing of flooded shafts

[76] Ambrosi, *Trento e il suo circondario, descritti al viaggiatore*, p. 6.

[77] Giulio, 'Sull' insalubrità della Valle dell'Adige,' p. 116; Christoph H. von Hartungen in Museo delle Semirurali, *Semirurali e dintorni*, pp. 67–68.

[78] Bundi (ed.), *Alpine waters*, p. 50.

[79] Brázdil, Glaser, Pfister et al., 'Flood events of selected European rivers in the sixteenth century,' p. 266.

[80] Magnusson and Squatriti, 'The technologies of water in medieval Italy,' p. 224.

in winter could make matters worse. Since no one needed nor wanted the work of digging out ice from a flooded shaft, supervisors preferred to do rapid infrastructure improvements and take advantage of the 'unwatering period' of a mine (Fig. 1.5).

Mines, however, are not all the same. In the same way in which sheep farming and pig farming differed considerably in terms of inputs, throughputs, and outputs even though both are livestock economies, Monte Calisio mines significantly contrasted to other mines of medieval Europe. Most mines of the medieval world had underground shafts dug from the ground surface into the targeted ore body. Such was the case of Kutná Horá or Kuttenberg in the kingdom of Bohemia. In those mines, *rotam* or waterwheels and windlasses adapted to drainage purposes solved the

Fig. 1.5 A miner of antimony, in *Compendium Salernitanum*, by Matteo Platearius (c. A.D. 1161). Abundant in dolomite formations of Tyrol, antimony was a metal sought after by experts in medicine and alchemy. It was used in metallurgical factories to produce copper alloys, as well as the medieval glass industry. However, its highest demand came from medieval artists. Artists preferred the antimony smelters obtained after prolonged roasting of antimony-bearing lead ores. Miners dug for other metals such as lead and zinc which bear antimony as by-product of smelting operations. The Morgan Library and Museum, N.Y.

problem of shaft flooding. Expenses incurred in adapting, repairing, or rebuilding waterwheels, windlasses, and other machines increased the cost of drainage and mining works. Under the assumption of high fertility of mines, hydraulic machines generally tended to lower the levels of rent because they increased the cost of capital and labor. An expert foreman assessed the damages done to infrastructure and a *gastaldia* or tax officer estimated expenses lost to the mine. The foreman performed the risky and difficult task of going back inside the 'dry' tunnels of the mine, along with trusted and expert skilled miners. He made a rapid assessment of what went wrong with the mine roof and walls, before deciding where to build the drainage machine and organize labor accordingly. This expert had to rapidly estimate how much water was in the medium, as well as water movement in the medium, in order to calculate optimal pumping rate. Planning drainage works required an expert foreman, who received payment in ores or silver currency.

Works were labor intensive, and demanded a considerable number of miners to transporting water from the flooded shaft into an adit if miners opted for a method that included hoisting machines.[81] If the job was carelessly done, a miner could end up destroying neighboring shafts by blocking them with rocks and water.[82] In an extractive economy in which vandalism against feudal property was not uncommon, a foreman supervised that no miner let water run onto lower-level shafts for this was a serious problem triggering legal battles among miners involving jurisdiction of lordly courts. The lower-level shafts, when active, usually were the oldest mining claims of the mine. The foreman was aware that

[81] A Roman example of this tunnel can be seen today in Mazarrón, Murcia, Spain. Its dimensions are astonishing: 180 meters deep, 1800 meters long, 1.30 meters wide, and 2 meters high. The tunnel was connected to a series of wells built at intervals of eighty meters and with a diameter of six meters each. It facilitated extraction works in different shafts of the mines. Because of the location of ore-extraction shafts, the drainage tunnel ran in an east-west direction. Thirty meters below the drainage tunnel, there was an ore-extraction gallery, suggesting that drainage works were highly efficient and allowed miners to keep the mine under continuous operation. This type of drainage device was found in medieval mines, too. Hirt, *Imperial mines and quarries in the Roman world*, p. 78; Hoover and Hoover (transl.), *Georgius Agricola De re metallica*, p. 122.

[82] For a comprehensive description of measurement problems based upon archeological evidence of sixteenth-century mines, see Czaja, 'Mining and hydrological transformations in Upper Silesia.'

careful planning of drainage works was essential for avoiding problems in neighboring mining stakes. Miners working round-the-clock and hurrying away from a potential burst of water could aggravate the situation.

Bishop Wanga discovered that Monte Calisio required flood-resistant structures built in the mountain itself. Even if lords locally organized construction of this type of flood-resistant structure by imposing labor obligations to vassals, the entire mining operation was destined to run into the problem of diminishing returns. Western monastics had contributed centuries earlier to the exploitation of easily available ore outcrops. Besides clearing forests, draining swamps, and marshes, monks mined lead and iron deposits.[83] Benedictine and Cistercian monks adapted Mediterranean hydraulic techniques to diverse topographic and geological settings.[84] The twelfth-century contemporary biographer of St. Bernard described 'with pride the series of water-wheels in his Abbey of Clairvaux which operated several industrial processes.'[85] Monks contributed in this manner to an 'ecological rift' without which land reclamation was not possible. Early feudal Europe had already consumed the *Natura gratis*, borrowing the words of Marx. In the absence of fresh injections of capital, the bishop would sacrifice land improvement and the progress of rents (Figs. 1.6 and 1.7).

[83] Braunstein (ed.), *La sidérurgie alpine en Italie (XIIe-XVIIe siècle)*; Postan (ed.), *The Cambridge Economic History of Europe*, p. 76; Reynolds, *Stronger than a hundred men: a history of the vertical water wheel*, p. 112.

[84] For exploitation of metallic sites by monastical orders, see: Burton, *The Cistercians in the Middle Ages*, p. 74, 178, 181; Burton, *The Monastic order in Yorkshire, 1069–1215*; Crawley-Boevey, *The Cartulary and historical notes of the Cistercian Abbey of Flaxley*, p. 2, footnote 5; Górecki, *Parishes, tithes and society in early medieval Poland*, p. 28; Huesca, *Teatro histórico de las Iglesias del reyno de Aragón*, p. 208; Lucas, *Ecclesiastical lordship, seigneurial power and the commercialization of milling in medieval England*, p. 219; Monsalbatje y Fossas, *Monasterio de S. Martín de Canigó*, p. 21; Pallares, and Portela, 'El complejo minero-metalúrgico de la granja cisterciense de Constantín'; Rusu, 'On a possible abbatial crosier from Bizere Monastery (Frumuşeni), Arad County,' pp. 217–218; Simmons, *The Moors of England and Wales: an environmental history 8000 BC to 2000 AD*, p. 83; Stroll, *The medieval abbey of Farfa*.

[85] Georges Duby, in Cipolla (ed.), *The Fontana economic history of Europe*, p. 170.

Fig. 1.6 A miner of Armenian bole, in *Compendium Salernitanum*, by Matteo Platearius (c. A.D. 1161). Armenian bole is a red clay, popular in Mediterranean markets for its use in artistic pottery. Its chemical properties made it an excellent material as a ground for gilding. With 'repeated forceful strokes,' a medieval miner of Armenian bole cut the clay mass into transportable clay pieces ready for further processing. The bookbinding industry still employs the mineral as coloring material. The Morgan Library and Museum, N.Y

An Ecclesiastic Lord Anxious for Draining and Digging Land

Built upon the foundations of Merovingian and Lombardian institutions, the Carolingian Church of Trent nominally guaranteed continuation of the politics of the empire. But changing economic, military, and political goals of the empire opened the way for competing interests within the church itself. With expansion of land improvement, 'mutually beneficial' exchanges between canons and secular lords became normal, sometimes at the expense of the rent claims of bishops. Members of the episcopate mostly came from local noble families, although Wanga had one cannon from Cremona and two from German lands out of the forty canons who sat in the Cathedral during his tenure as bishop.[86] From the twelfth century onward, bishops consolidated their own curia by including vassals

[86] Curzel, *Il capitolo della cattedrale di Trento*, p. 75.

Fig. 1.7 A miner of alum, from *Compendium Salernitanum*, by Matteo Platearius (c. A.D. 1161). Alum mining absorbed considerable amounts of water. Miners separated the ore from unwanted materials by boiling the mined rock in large cauldrons filled with water, preparing the ore for enrichment. Mined in Sicily, Aegean Sea islands, and Tuscany, it enjoyed brisk demand in the fifteenth century. In the times of Wanga, Anatolian mines supplied alum to northern European markets, followed by the Tolfa mines in Rome. Alum was a good fixative of dyes used by medieval artists for adding colors to textiles. The Morgan Library and Museum, N.Y

from the nobility entrenched in their own local rural jurisdictions, representatives of the old aristocracy with rent interests in the urban quarter of Trent, and ministers of the new nobility who also enjoyed jurisdiction over strategic rural lands.[87]

Church politics reached explosive levels. Legal controversies, political clashes within the group of canons of the Church, rebellions against bishops, and even the assassination of one bishop took place in the Cathedral of Trent. The schism between the empire and the Papacy that destabilized episcopal government and changed the boundaries of the district had receded. The influence of Verona and the Lombardian League south of Garda Lake was relatively contained, but created certain instability in the eastern and southern frontiers of the ecclesiastical principality. *Milites* of

[87] Bettotti and Landi, 'Signorie rurali, coscienza nobiliare e autorappresentazione,' p. 298.

the Castelbarco and Arco lords, rooted in the upper Garda region and Lagarina Valley, made of this frontier a problem to the emperor.[88] These lords plotted various insurrections and conspiracies against bishops and Counts of Tyrol, and which culminated in the assassination of Bishop Adelpret.[89] They changed sides, too, as when the *milites* of Briano Castelbarco helped Bishop Conrad wage war against Trent decades later, in a series of events that led to the retirement of Conrad to the quiet monastery of St. Georgenberg. To Emperor Frederick II, having a bishop tied to the imperial family was a useful strategy for the recalibration of the administrative and ideological roles the Church played in the region. Frederick Wanga was ideal for the role.

Bishop Wanga came from a noble family of the Venosta Valley in South Tyrol.[90] Today colonized by Winter ski resorts, the valley was part of the trans-Alpine corridors of trade that linked northern Italy with German-speaking populations of Tyrol. More important was the fact that Wanga was a distant relative of Count Albert III of Tyrol (A.D. 1185–1253), the aristocrat who played a considerable role in the government apparatus of the bishop. His sister Agnes married the Count of Tyrol, making Wanga uncle of Count Albert III.[91] Wanga was also close to the imperial family, as he was a distant cousin of Emperor Frederick II.[92] He had been canon of Augsburg and dean of the Chapter of Brixen or Bressanone prior to his rise as Prince-Bishop of Trent. His native tongue was German, and his worldview was aligned with the geopolitical interests of the empire.[93] Like his predecessors, Wanga was the product of political institutions rooted in

[88] At the time of Wanga, Lagarina was a stretch of land that included the Scanupia and Folgaria mountains. Stenico, 'Signorie rurali e risorse economiche,' p. 227.

[89] Castagnetti, *Governo vescovile, feudalità, 'communitas' cittadina*, pp. 109–112.

[90] For the origins of the Wanga family, see Rasmo, *Cultura atesina/Kultur des Etschlandes*, p. 2.

[91] Curzel, *Il capitolo della Cattedrale di Trento*, pp. 72–73.

[92] Duke Frederick of Swabia (A.D. 1047–1105) had two children: Frederick II of Swabia or 'The One-Eyed' (A.D. 1090–1147), and Kunigunde of Swabia (A.D. 1100–1125). Frederick II was the son of Emperor Henry VI (A.D. 1165–1197) and grandson of Duke Frederick II 'The One-Eyed.' Kunigunde married Henry of Bavaria (A.D. 1098–1139) and had a Kunigunde (A.D. 1121–?), who married Count Berthold I of Tyrol (A.D. 1110–1180). Kunigunde and Berthold were the parents of Henry of Tyrol (A.D. 1145–1190) and Mathilde (A.D. 1150–?). Henry was the father of Count Albert III of Tyrol. Mathilde married Albero I *von Wangen* or Wanga (A.D. 1160–1193), the son of Adalbert of Eppan. She gave birth to Frederick Wanga. Curzel, *Il Codice Vanga*, p. 19.

[93] Cusin, *I primi due secoli del principato ecclesiastico di Trent*, pp. 7–8.

feudal jurisprudence that regulated lord-vassalage relations. He also shared with them the clear mandate to govern the city and serve the Church of Trent.

Wanga found a city politically different from the Germanic fiefdom his predecessors had governed centuries earlier. Previous bishops confronted the problems of political order created by the schism between the empire and the Papacy. 'Pope and emperor were natural allies,' comments historian David Abulafia, but cooperation had turned into conflict since Emperor Frederick I challenged the claims by Pope Hadrian IV to temporal suzerainty in imperial lands.[94] Even when the most bitter episodes of the schism were long gone by, two centuries of conflicts between the Papacy and the emperor had enduring consequences for the exercise of Sovereign power by bishops. Emperor Frederick I confirmed the authority of bishops to rule the city in A.D. 1182. The Sovereign government belonged to the bishops and their curia, who were called to rule the *cives* or citizens without resource to *consules* or elected councilors. Thus, Sovereign power meant what it did for all other cities of the Teutonic Kingdom, and *not* what was in ascent in Italian city-States, according to historian Castagnetti.[95] This was a public administration strategy by which the emperor sought to contain the spread of Lombardian League spirit into Trent. Veronese notaries had been employed by bishops in the mid-twelfth century, giving the Veronese aristocracy a certain influence in the internal and territorial affairs of the city. The emperor previously demonstrated his idea of Teutonic city government in a privilege granted in A.D. 1179 to the bishop of Bressanone. Similar to the privileges bishops had in all other ecclesiastical principalities, it meant that administration of civil and criminal justice, the agrarian census or *bannum*, mills, and market, coinage and minting rights were exercised by the bishop for common good of the city. Moreover, citizens were forbidden from building towers in the city or in villages without prior authorization of the bishop.

Governing the district demanded the exercise of privileges entailed in immunity rights and embedded in the title of 'Prince-Bishop.'[96] Granted

[94] Abulafia, *Frederick II: a medieval emperor*, pp. 63–64.

[95] Castagnetti, *Governo vescovile, feudalità, 'communitas' cittadina*, pp. 120–121.

[96] I consulted the following works: Abulafia (ed.), *The new Cambridge medieval history, vol. 5*; Alberti, *Annali del principato ecclesiastico di Trento*; Albertoni and Provero, *Il feudalismo in Italia*; Barthélemy and White, 'Debate, the feudal revolution'; Bellabarba, 'The feudal principalities: the east'; Bellabarba, Obermair, and Sato (eds.), *Communities and conflicts in the Alps*; Castagnetti, *Governo vescovile, feudalità, 'communitas' cittadina*; Cipolla, *Before the*

by Emperor Frederick Barbarossa, the title emphasized immunity rights or investitures held by imperial bishops.[97] Merovingian rulers had introduced 'immunity' to Italy centuries earlier. They also introduced Germanic political and administrative structures to consolidate Frankish domination and displacement of defeated Lombards.[98] The institution of immunity cemented 'the hard-won *iura regalia* of the empire,' endowing lords with the authority to claim jurisdictions of rent rights and privileges they considered to be legitimately theirs. It represented a centuries-long process of political change in one of the most strategic regions of Carolingian Europe. Other historical forces influenced the culture of authority and political order. Trent or *Tridentum* was born as a Roman city in the first century BC. Under the Roman Empire, its *municipium* extended northward, reaching the Noce and Avisio valleys up to Merano in Tyrol and the Isarco River into Chiusa.[99] The district also bore the weight of its Lombardian history. It had been an important Lombard duchy after the fall of the Roman Empire, partly because the city was spared from devastations created by Greco-Gothic wars. Trent joined the Carolingian politico-military world relatively early in A.D. 774, which thrusted upon its lands and peoples the institution of immunity. The city had once functioned as garrison strategically situated in the road connecting Germany to Rome. Its surrounding territory had gained the boundaries of *comitatus* included in the Verona Mark or military frontier of the Carolingian Empire.

The Carolingian notion of immunity evolved, so that by the thirteenth century, immunity rights implied absolute juridical and secular power or *potestas* over patrimonial lands granted to the Imperial Church.[100] While in earlier times, emperors granted immunity only to the Church and its feudal courts, including the *casae indominicatae*, bishops as well as secular lords received investitures of these rights in later times. The result was the

Industrial Revolution: European society and economy; Cusin, *I primi due secoli del principato ecclesiastico di Trento*; Drew, 'The immunity in Carolingian Italy'; Eck, *Les liens de vassalité et les immunities*; Landi, 'L'incastellamento di fronte al diritto feudale'; Rosenwein, *Negotiating space: power, restraint and privileges of immunity in early medieval lands*; Vallone, 'La costituzione medievale delle terre e le giurisdizioni di Federico II.'

97 Drew, 'The immunity in Carolingian Italy.'

98 Pivano, *Il contratti agrari in Italia nell'alto Medio-Evo*, pp. 9–14.

99 Curzel, *Il capitolo della cattedrale di Trento*, pp. 43–44. The rest of the paragraph comes from this work.

100 Albertoni, 'Law and the peasant: rural society and justice in Carolingian Italy'; Arnold, 'German bishops and their military retinues in the medieval empire'; Voltelini, *Immunität, grund- und leibherrliche Gerichtsbarkeit in Südtirol*, pp. 12–19.

rise of 'islands of lay immunity'[101] fragmenting the territoriality of power entailed in the jurisdiction of rent rights and privileges held by bishops. The specific juridical formula that immunity rights took is still a matter of controversy. What is certain is that the early formula included rights over the *comitatus districtus*. Immunity rights presupposed a jurisdiction of rent rights and privileges. As such, they took for granted a certain demarcation of the territory unto which immunity was meant to be exercised. Demarcating the territoriality of power was the core of immunity and the basis of political power. Feudal law contributed to the making of the territoriality of power by providing social mechanisms needed for expansion and transfer of surplus from agrarian labor to lords. The more dynamically it adapted and responded to changes in land improvement, the more feudal law supported the exercise of immunity rights (Fig. 1.8).

Wanga was anxious for exercising his jurisdiction of rent rights and privileges soon after he gained the seat of power. The chaos left by his predecessor Bishop Conrad of Beseno (r. A.D. 1189–1205), who barely escaped a plot against him led by a group of canons from the Chapter of the Church of Trent, demanded strong rule. Previous imperial diplomas defined the geographic boundaries of the district. Most likely, Manasse of Arles, first Carolingian bishop of Trent, governed a relatively smaller district after King Hugh of Provence and King of Italy (r. A.D. 926–947) granted district rights in A.D. 934.[102] While campaigning in Italy in the early years of the millennium, Emperor Henry II (r. A.D. 1014–1024) confirmed district rights to the bishop, which then included Venosta, Bolzano, and Trent. The first geographic definition of the territory appeared in an imperial diploma granted by Emperor Conrad II to Bishop Udalrich (A.D. 1022–1055) on May 31, 1027. Frederick I confirmed and possibly expanded the boundaries of the district in a diploma granted to Bishop Adelpret in A.D. 1161, before a third diploma in A.D. 1189 defined the jurisdiction of 'immunity lands' in Venosta, the Giudicarie, and Trent.[103]

The Venosta territory included patrimonial lands of the aristocracy of Tyrol to the north and east of Trent. The limits of Venosta were

[101] The Counts of Flavon originated in the dynastic families ruling over south Bavaria at the close of the Middle Ages when the lands belonged to the Bressanone Diocese. Mor and Schmidinger, *I poteri temporali dei vescovi in Italia*, p. 185.

[102] Curzel, *Il capitolo della cattedrale di Trento*, p. 44.

[103] Castagnetti, *Governo vescovile, feudalità, 'communitas' cittadina*, pp. 13–18; Curzel, *Il Codice Vanga*, pp. 102–104; Curzel and Varanini, *La documentazione dei vescovi di Trento*, p. 56, 64, pp. 104–106.

Fig. 1.8 Saint Vigil, patron saint of Trent. Bohemian goldwork embroidery, A.D. 1390–1391. Made of gold and silk threads, the panel is part of a four-series panels depicting the story of Saint Vigil according to *Passio Sancti Vigilii*. Saint Vigil was Bishop of Trent between the fourth and the fifth centuries. The panel was commissioned by Prince-Bishop Georg von Liechtenstein (r. a. d. 1390-1419). Museo Diocesano Tridentino

somewhere near Tel on the right bank of the Adige River, and the Gargazzone River on the left side, north of the Adige Valley where Trent stands.[104] The Church of Trent exercised ecclesiastical authority in Venosta, too, except in a small area in Ega Valley and Tires that belonged to rural lords who also belonged to the group of canons of the Church of Bressanone. Rural lords in this region relied upon warfare to assert their rent claims.[105]

The Giudicarie was an extensive region that included a large number of valleys separated by mountain ranges. From Non Valley, to Sole, Rendena, Rotaliana, and Banale valleys, a small number of old and new lordships, including the counts of Eppan and Flavon, and the Campo lords, held jurisdiction over a large number of villages and *curtis* in the region. As a general rule, to the north lay the castles and villages under the dominions of the aristocratic lords whose families played important roles in the opening of the territory for the Carolingian Empire. The old nobility provided military service to bishops and emperors. However, imposing unto vassals military obligation led to a class differentiation giving birth to a new rural nobility, such as the Campo and the Lodron lords. The latter were aggressively entrenched in their castles, surrounding the old patrimonial lands of the old nobility. The new rural nobility supplied *milites* to bishops, for which they were rewarded with land and rent rights.

The Giudicarie region also included lands north of Garda Lake, bordering the jurisdiction of the lords of Arco. The latter exerted uncontested political and economic power in the south of Trent, and because of their hold on to strategic lands connecting the Adige Valley to Lombardy and Verona, they were almost untouchable. The district of Bolzano (in modern-day South Tyrol) included Tinne, Isarco, and Bria rivers to the north, where the Tyrolean aristocracy enjoyed patrimonial rights. Bishops of Trent received a fixed share of the streams of tithes coming from the sentences dictated by the Tyrolean court, but the Counts of Tyrol held the coveted real estate of the region, including the famous Tyrol Castle. Lastly,

[104] For debates about the meaning of the diploma, see: Curzel and Varanini have a different interpretation. Curzel, *Il Codice Vanga*, pp. 102–104; Curzel and Varanini, *La documentazione dei vescovi di Trento*, p. 56, 64, pp. 104–106; Cusin, *I primi due secoli del Principato ecclesiastico di Trent*, pp. 119–121; Fumagalli, 'Il potere civile dei vescovi italiani al tempo di Ottone I'; Gazzoletti, *Della Zecca di Trent*, p. 27; Malfatti, 'I confini dei Principato de Trent,' p. 10, pp. 12–15; Mor and Schmidinger, *I poteri temporali dei vescovi in Italia*, pp. 178–179, 181–182; Voltelini, *Giurisdizione signorile*, pp. 13–16, p. 43.

[105] Bettotti and Landi, 'Signorie rurali, coscienza nobiliare e autorappresentazione,' p. 307.

the territory of Trent is generally referred to the old Langobard area of the Duchy of Trent. Its northern limit was 'Tell-Adige-Laives.' Its western border included Giudicarie, and Rendena and Sole valleys, where ongoing conflicts between local rural lords posed problems to the exercise of political power. The southern limits of the district included Ala, Avio, and Brentonico in the Garda Valley.

In all directions, the boundaries of immunity lands of Bishop Wanga overlapped, cut across, or dangerously intruded into jurisdictions claimed by other lords. This condition was intrinsic to the process of territorialization of ecclesiastical and secular powers. The strategic Garda Lake separated the dioceses of Brescia and Verona in the south, creating ongoing conflicts over trade and transport rights. To the east of Trent, the dioceses of Feltre, Padova, and Vicenza (this last one bordering the diocese of Verona) had certain ecclesiastical rights that occasionally triggered political conflicts. Ecclesiastical jurisdiction in the northern lands belonged to the dioceses of Belluno in the east, Bressanone and Coira in the west. The diocese of Como formed the western ecclesiastical frontier of Trent, flanked to the north by Coira and in the south by Brescia. In addition, the Chapter of the Church of Trent also held jurisdiction of rent rights.[106] It had obtained rent rights centuries earlier, when imperial monastic orders accumulated land by dispossessing small-scale rural land holders through military campaigns.[107] In the times of Wanga, canons of the Chapter of the Church were by no means colonizing monks of previous centuries. They were noble vassals. They belonged to the aristocracy of Tyrol as well as an old and new local rural nobility. Nominally, however, canons and their own vassals were all *vassi* of the bishop of Trent, as immunity confirmed that only bishops could exercise *publicae functiones* over lands and vassals of the Church of Trent.

No imperial diploma could firmly settle the boundaries of immunity lands in a district where land colonization forced the aristocracy, the nobility, and the Church to share the gains of extractive economies. Bishop Wanga soon discovered that his jurisdiction of rent rights and privileges remained a contested affair. What was certain to Bishop Wanga was that prosperity and political power possible of his district depended upon economic life in lands surrounding the Adige Valley. From the northwestern Non Valley to Fiemme and Fassa valleys in the northeast of the Adige, and

[106] Franceschini, 'Castelli e campagni in area trentina,' p. 199.

[107] Leicht, *Studi sulla propietà fondiaria nel medio evo*, pp. 78–79.

from Rotaliana in the southwest to Valsugana in the southeast of Trent, these lands held the key to the glory of Trent. The problem was that continuous shifts in the agrarian geography of these valleys made it difficult for feudal lords to live off labor without recourse to competition. Caught in these forces, Bishop Wanga turned his gaze to the prospects of profits entailed in Monte Calisio mines. The monetary rewards hidden in the 'wet ores' of Monte Calisio represented a new *agrarian* frontier for consolidating territorialization of his feudal power. More so given that the 'great drain of silver out of Europe' had begun to recede in A.D. 1160s.[108]

Metal mining on a continental scale accompanied the rhythm and tempo of land reclamation. Continuous flows of metal ores and bullion led to major economic and social change in Carolingian Europe and beyond. No ore-yielding land was exempted from the intensity of change created by mining activities. Surpluses hidden in the womb of Monte Calisio seemed a most stable source of rent, which could enhance the money-making capabilities of the bishopric. With no obligation to improve land *at meliorandum et colendum* as agrarian peasants did, foreign miners who brought to the city knowledge, techniques, and capital needed to drain the 'wet ores' of the mines. Facing dilemmas of hegemonic power, Bishop Wanga welcomed miners to his *mons Arçentarie*. Mining was about to take off, changing society and politics in 'the jewel of the Adige Valley.' The price paid by Bishop Wanga was, however, unforeseen by all.

[108] Spufford, *Money and its use in medieval Europe*, pp. 158–159.

CHAPTER 2

Land Improvement and the Progress of Rent

Pastoralism dictated the speed of land improvement. It required colonizing montane valleys conditioned by history to receiving 'an immense deposit of labor.'[1] Shepherds and flocks at first followed ancient Roman Alpine transhumance routes, settling in low-elevation valleys.[2] These valleys occupy one-fifth of all surface land of the district. Mountains reaching more than 1000 meters above mean sea level follow next, covering two-fifths of the landscape. They form the belt of Alpine forests that provided wood, limestone, and seasonal pastures. This vast warehouse of raw materials attracted more colonists in the early Middle Ages. Mountains of astonishing heights form the remaining northern fringe of the district, some exceeding 1500 meters above mean sea level. Here, heat, steep slopes, and sunlight turned unimproved grasses into good sources of high Summer pastures. Settlements surrounded the best available slopes, from the westernmost valleys of Sole and Non to the eastern valleys of Fiemme, Fassa, and Primiero. Each settlement had a unique shape and length, determined by the oppressive but generous hand of Alpine orography. All settlements shared the daring ambition of building a prosperous grazing and livestock economy.[3]

[1] I borrowed the phrase from Robertson, 'Agricultural regions of the North Italian Plain,' p. 575.

[2] Montanari, *L'alimentazione contadina nell'alto medioevo*; Tognon, Martellozzo, and Gretter, 'Collective properties of Trentino,' p. 7.

[3] Atilio Stella in Carrer and Gheler (eds.), *Invisible cultures: historical and archaeological perspectives*, p. 153.

J. Graulau, *Medieval Mining and Power in Thirteenth-Century Europe*, https://doi.org/10.1007/978-3-031-99239-1_2

In early Carolingian times, a rural nobility took the initiative to improve Alpine meadows. The legacies of Langobard economic institutions privileging individual owners of flocks gave it an upper hand. Inter-continental forces of economic change had imposed unto the Langobard society the need for communal labor.[4] Such conditions had paved the way for the rise of an autonomous class of shepherds which communally managed grazing and pasture lands. In high elevations, these shepherds built dispersed settlements devoted to animal husbandry. In time, they joined the feudal lower nobility, escaping the fate of shepherds in lower valleys who were soon swallowed by the tide of Germanic feudalism that descended unto the Alps from northern Frankish lands. Autonomous colonists disappeared, while feudal institutions thrusted their roots unto Alpine lands. Feudalism unleashed the forces that led to privatization of grasslands and flocks. It legitimized claims to property to livestock and pastures as *casae vaccariciae e bovulcariciae*.[5] From the eleventh century onward, the general pattern was the immiseration of the class of small-scale livestock owners. The course and rugged life of men, women, and children who depended upon grazing and livestock came to be the dynamic affirmation of the progress of land improvement. Losing autonomy, this class joined the ranks of subordinated vassals whose labor sustained the ascent of Alpine rural feudal lords.[6] Its labor nonetheless led to a revival of transhumance pastoralism by the late twelfth century.

Environmental historians argue that the 'medieval warm period' (A.D. 950–1250), characterized by warm hemispheric conditions, favored the spread of specific forms of transhumance and agriculture.[7] They argue that land development benefitted from the end of a long-term climate pattern of cold and humid weather, low temperatures, and increased precipitation that lasted until the eleventh century. Even when there is little consensus on the real impacts of climate factors in the rise of medieval extractive economies, what is certain is that transhumance and Alpine pastoralism took off in this period.[8] Geography reinforced these patterns of

[4] Carrer and Angelucci, 'Continuity and discontinuity in the history of upland pastoral landscapes.'

[5] Leicht, *Studi sulla proprietà fondiaria nel medio evo*, pp. 35–42.

[6] *Idem*, pp. 75–77.

[7] Paladin, Moghaddam, Stawinoga et al., 'Early medieval Italian Alps,' p. 15.

[8] Aberth, *An environmental history of the Middle Ages*; Bruce, *Ecologies and economies in medieval and early modern Europe*; Campbell, 'Panzootics, pandemics, and climatic anomalies in the fourteenth century'; Crowley and Lowery, 'How warm was the Medieval Warm Period?'; Hunt, 'The Medieval Warm Period, the Little Ice Age and simulated climatic variability'; Matthews and Briffa, 'The "Little Ice Age": re-evaluation of an evolving concept.'

specialization. Slope inclination and exposure to winds limited the amount of agrarian land available for crop cultivation, deepening specialization in livestock and pastoralism.[9] Above all, livestock created grazing grounds that led to the raising of more livestock, expanding the stock of capital available for pastoralism.[10]

Shepherds and pastoralists adapted breeding of livestock to differences in elevation of mountain pastures. Like pastoralist cultures have done in other soaring mountain chains, labor collectively responded to ecological constraints associated with 'altitudinal variability.'[11] Little is known about how shepherds responded to changes in weight gains and milk yields, or spread and seasonality of animal diseases.[12] What is certain is that flocks stayed in lower valleys during Winter season, shielded from harsh conditions and cold temperatures of high altitudes, where they fed upon uncultivated lands and hay available from previous Summer season.[13] In late Spring, shepherds moved their flocks to high pasture stations, taking advantage of fresh Alpine grass. They descended back to the lower valleys in early September. This general outline conceals a complex and ecologically rich reality governed by altitude rather than latitude. 'We can assume that in one of the two extremities of this spectrum there is transhumance.'[14] Transhumance entailed a wider range of spatial mobility and along with pastoralism made long-term, permanent habitation possible in the rising feudal district of Trent. Specialization in 'haymaking' or the cutting and storing of hay took off, followed by sheep shearing. The shearing of local sheep occurred only once a year, in May. Transhumant sheep, however, had to generously compensate the coffers of big lords. This sheep was shorn in Spring and again in early Fall, before returning to Lombardian plains where it spent Winter seasons. The practice of shearing twice a year guaranteed the fineness and whiteness of the thread, according to Varanini[15] (Fig. 2.1).

[9] Stenico, 'Signorie rurali e risorse economiche,' p. 222.

[10] Jones, 'Agricultural origins of industry,' p. 60.

[11] Carrer and Angelucci, 'Continuity and discontinuity in the history of upland pastoral landscapes,' p. 102.

[12] For a summary of the state of research, see Decker, 'Animal and zoonotic diseases in the ancient and late antique Mediterranean: three case studies'; Newfield, 'Human-bovine plagues in the early Middle Ages.'

[13] Archetti, '"Fecerunt malgas in casina" Alevamento transhumante e alpeggi nella Lombardia medieval,' p. 487.

[14] Carrer and Angelucci, 'Continuity and discontinuity in the history of upland pastoral landscapes,' p. 102.

[15] Varanini and Demo, 'Allevamento, transumanza, lanificio,' p. 279.

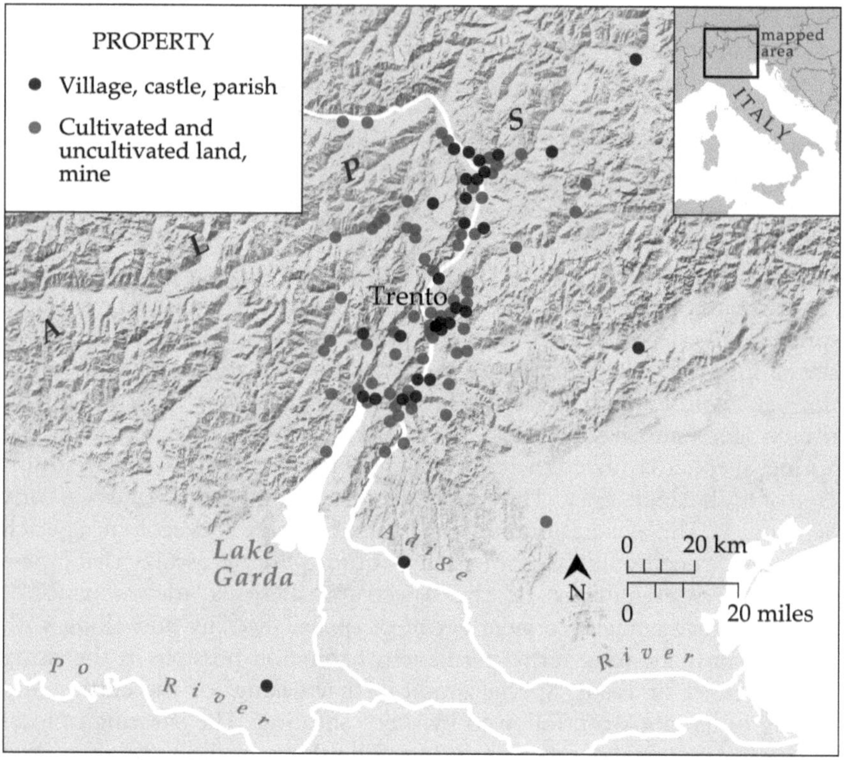

Fig. 2.1 Tax-paying property of Bishop Wanga, A.D. 1207–1218. Settlers of Trent were by no means intimated by the 'high hydrological activity' of the Alps. They stayed in the bottom of the Adige River valley, colonizing lands between the northern Alpine tundra and the southern mild-climate zone of Lake Garda. The result of long-term process of land improvement was the rise of 'taxable wealth,' borrowing a term coined by Roger Schofield, in the form of villages, castles, parishes, and agrarian and mining lands. The danger of floods, which increased as medieval settlers deforested riparian woodlands, was a modest price to pay for occupying coveted lands. Map based upon Codex Wangianus

In lower valleys, the ongoing and incessant action of livestock eating grasses turned marshes into improved land. Shepherds responded by patiently selecting the best grasses for grazing, and testing arable grasses for their own sustenance. Slowly, the 'war between men and nature'[16]

[16] Georges Duby in Cipolla (ed.), *The Fontana economic history of Europe*, pp. 175–176.

was giving way to larger areas of improved lands. Its corollary was a stronger presence of agrarian labor for an Alpine feudal peasant economy on ascent. Peasants continuously uprooted bushes from swamps and marshes to create *runcus* or newly cleared land. They added the plow, useful for clearing marshes and enlarge land available for habitation. Such was the way Bolognese Pietro Crescenzi (d. A.D. 1320) described it in *Opus ruralium commodorum*.[17] Crescenzi further described the use of a 'plough drawn by only one ox' and other 'different kinds drawn by two and four oxen' in neighboring Lombardy.[18] Peasants employed drives or wagons with 'a wooden axle and low wooden wheels; each wheel formed either of one piece or four pieces joined together.'[19] Above all, 'the asymmetric plough, an improved harness, the use of horses for ploughing and three-course rotation, all spread to the rhythm of urban growth.'[20]

Diffusion of agrarian tools, grasses, and livestock steadily eliminated the constraints that had acted against productive exploitation of land.[21] The urban grounds of the district benefitted by the incessant action of livestock feeding upon its surrounding *iscla*.[22] New lands available for grazing and agriculture soon encircled the Church of Saint Vigil and the Church of Santa Maria, before citizens encouraged the construction of a fortified wall around the urban quarter. The *pratum* or meadow required no capital expenditure besides livestock.[23] In settlements near the Adige Valley, one mowing per year was sufficient for sustaining improvement of this type of land. Two mowing per year were possible in some cases. The long-term result was forage management, an economy that was part of a 'vast agricultural enterprise,' 'where the breeding of cattle, the cheese industry, and an abundant production of dung permitted the permanent

[17] Curtis and Campopiano, 'Medieval land reclamation and the creation of new societies.'

[18] Loudon, *An encyclopedia of agriculture*, p. 33.

[19] Ibidem.

[20] Jacques Le Goff in Cipolla (ed.), *The Fontana economic history of Europe*, p. 81.

[21] Castagnetti, *Uomini e civiltà agraria in territorio veronese*; Carrer and Angelucci, 'Continuity and discontinuity in the history of upland pastoral landscapes'; Varanini and Demo, 'Allevamento, transumanza, lanificio.'

[22] Varanini and Demo, 'Allevamento, transumanza, lanificio.'

[23] Franceschini, 'Castelli e campagne in area trentina,' p. 200.

establishment of livestock, for which natural or artificial pastures, often irrigated, provided an essential supply of forage.'[24]

The *pratum* afforded high rents when not fragmented, as it increased livestock as well as related commodities. It was land that Bishop Wanga leased to herdsmen conditioned to the payment of the *fictum*. Understood as economic compensation owed to the lord for sharing the benefits of landed property, the *fictum* represented the price paid for leasing grazing grounds.[25] The *fictum* was a fixed rent, paid in money or kind. The produce of the improved *pratum* included hay, sheep, goats, lambs, rams, oxen, calves, cows, and related diary produce especially cheese.

Lords leased newly cleared lands or *runcus* with the expectation that peasants would provide dues, foods, and rents to their class. The legal formula *ad bonam et idoneam colturam* generally defined this reciprocal responsibility, which meant a strong dependence of peasants upon lords in some villages.[26] The *runcus* that proliferated around the urban quarter were property of the Church of Trent, its bishops, and the patrimonial families of the region. A *runcus* in *Borgonovo*, in the southern quarter of the city near the Church of Saint Vigil, was part of the real estate property of Wanga. *Borgonovo* took shape between the twelfth and the thirteenth centuries.[27] This type of land was prime real estate and taxable wealth; it was thus available for leasing. *Magister Ersignano* leased a *runcus* located near the gate of Sant'Apollinaire to Bishop Adelpret (A.D. 1156–1172) in A.D. 1193.[28] The price paid for the lease was two urns of wine. Two *runci* leased to *Palmerio* and *Capello* in Mesiano, both planted with vines when the lease was notarized on October 30, 1215, were priced as two urns of wine.[29] A lease dated March 4, 1178, for a *runcus* in Trent was priced at

[24] Montanari, *L'alimentazione contadina nell'alto medioevo*, p. 31, footnote 53; Sereni, *History of the Italian agricultural landscape*, pp. 133–134, p. 140.

[25] *Fictum* was the Italian name for that which was paid *ad fiscum*, 'according to a settled agreement,' in its original meaning. Franceschini, 'Le paludi dell'Adige, diritti di sfrutamento e tentativi di bonifica,' p. 257; Wiener, *Commentary to the Germanic Laws and medieval documents*, p. 183.

[26] The formula was still prevalent in the region after the second half of the fourteenth century. Curtis and Campopiano, 'Medieval land reclamation and the creation of new societies.'

[27] Curzel, *Il capitolo della cattedrale di Trento*, p. 429.

[28] Curzel and Varanini, *La documentazione dei vescovi di Trento*, p. 217.

[29] *Idem*, p. 526.

four urns of wine. It was Bishop Salomon who leased the *runcus* to *Aicardo*, son of *Teburgi* and citizen of Trent.

Individual farm-holding units proliferated as *tere arativa* and *tere ortalive.*[30] Each unit of *tere arativa* occupied limited surface space of elongated shape. It was designed to induce water runoff, avoiding formation of swamps. It added the 'convenience of not having to plow frequently,' which increased rent prospects.[31] For these reasons, it represented valuable land. Wanga leased *unam peciam tere ortalive* located in 'Broilo' for seven *soldi* or shillings and six *denarii* or pennies. The lease holder was *Fruzerinus*, son of the late *Gumpone*, who lived in the section of the urban quarter known as *Porta* or *Porta oriola* (also *porta auriola*).[32] The *ortus* was even more valuable land. As prime irrigated and cultivated land, it represented *la clausura per eccellenza*, in the words of Montanari.[33] It was the historical form that privatization of land took in an Alpine setting, and what Marx centuries later described as 'instrument of theft of people's land,' 'the form of robbery' against peasant farmers.[34] The *ortus* was a plot of drained land invariable surrounded by 'a ditch and a fence.'[35] As the space of viticulture, the *ortus* spread in lower-altitude valleys, below the belt of montane land dominated by pasture stations. Farmers cultivated vines using the terrace system, spreading vines that colonized the mountain slopes of the valley.[36] The grape variety cultivated in the region, the *Vitis vinifera L.*,

[30] In A.D. 1216, there is a conflict over rights for six plots of *terra arativa* in Tradorum, Pomarolo. *Idem*, p. 559.

[31] Castagnetti, *Uomini e civiltà agraria in territorio veronese*, p. 43. The rest of the paragraph comes from this work, unless otherwise noted.

[32] *Idem*, p. 463.

[33] Curzel, *Il capitolo della cattedrale di Trento*, p. 492; Magnusson and Squatriti, 'The technologies of water in medieval Italy,' pp. 233–234; Montanari, *L'alimentazione contadina nell'alto medioevo*, p. 23.

[34] Marx, *Capital, vol. 1, The process of capitalist production,* p. 796. For a history of enclosures, see Yelling, *Common field and enclosure in England 1450–1850.*

[35] Montanari, *L'alimentazione contadina nell'alto medioevo*, p. 23, footnote 19.

[36] I consulted the following works: Bertoldi, Roman, Larcher et al., 'Arsenic present in the soil-wine chain in vineyards situated in an old mining area in Trentino'; Laubenheimer and Notet, 'Les amphores produites à Gueugnon (S. et L.) et les débuts du vignoble bourguignon'; Martin, '"Vinum dulce, gloriosum ..." Le thème du vin dans la poésie latine médiévale'; Pereira de Souza, 'Les Barbares et le vin'; Higounet, 'Une carte agricole de l'Albigeois vers 1260'; Trabut-Cussac, 'Les costumes ou droits de douanes perçus à Bordeaux'; Carandi, 'L'economia italica fra tarda Reppublica e medio Imperio considerata dal punto di vista di una mercé: il vino'; Gandilhon, 'Henri IV et el vin'; Gras, 'Vin et société à Rome et dans le Latium à l'époque archaïque'; Panella and Tchernia, 'Produits agricoles

provided agrarian peasants with other commodities such as the *agresto*, a condiment made by adding salt to the juice of sour and fresh grapes.[37] The *Vitis vinifera L.* is not unique to the valley. The plant found suitable ecological conditions in lands located between 47 and 52 degrees latitude. This is the belt of land south of the northern European plains, where the *Vitis vinifera L.* found longer hours of solar day light and ideal solar radiation.[38] The *casamentus & ortus* was small farm-holding unit in an enclosed agrarian space.[39]

Enclosed lands were the result of advances in agriculture within the constraints of a rural Alpine economy. Farmers adapted agrarian techniques to the needs of the various species. They learned that 'in cool locations the leaves [of vines] surrounding the bunches were to be removed to let the grapes ripen in the sunshine; in warm places, [they] were to be shaded to avoid them drying out.'[40] 'Dry farming' and monotonous repetition of movements needed for turning the ground with a hoe were required for vines to flourish.[41] After plowing the ground, a farmer dug a hole and planted the vine. He plowed the land three times, pruning the grapes with care. Afterward, he propagated the plants by layering them and fertilizing the soil with residues of Fava beans and other plant remains.[42] Keeping the plant free from insects and pests required repetitive manual work, too. The toil of the farmer was completed when he fenced the cultivated land, something the he probably did before planting the vine, according to Montanari.[43]

Built to protect lands from thieves, travelers, and roaming animals, the *clausurae* became a symbol of boundaries of lordly property.[44] Wherever built, *clausurae* meant highly valuable land. It was not uncommon for villages specializing in viticulture to pay rents amounting to a one-half of total wine production. Land leases ranged from 5 to 20 years.

transportés en amphores'; Tchernia, *Le vin de l'Italie romaine: essai d'histoire économique d'après les amphores*; Boutoulle, 'La vigne et le négoce du vin en Bordelais et Bazadais.'

[37] Grasso, 'La viticoltura come indicatore paleo economico, paleo ambientale e paleo climatico,' p. 4.

[38] *Idem*, p. 6.

[39] Zadoks, *Crop protection in medieval agriculture*, p. 22.

[40] *Idem*, p. 45.

[41] *Idem*, p. 32.

[42] *Idem*, p. 45.

[43] Montanari, *L'alimentazione contadina nell'alto medioevo*, p. 28.

[44] Pini, *Vite e vino del medioevo*, p. 65; Rende, 'La vigna e la vite nella Valle del Tacina.'

Rents changed, as lords began to exploit stock-raising conditions pioneered by peasant cultivators. A lord in Segno increasingly incorporated the ecological demands of vineyard economy into lease agreements.[45] By A.D. 1311, this lord established the condition of land improvement *bene putare, rellevare, ligoniçare et remenare.* The legal formula meant making and planting stakes and trellis needed for raising vines 'in the Roman way,' which 'increased yields by exposing the grapes to the sun.'[46] Historian Marco Stenico discusses the manner in which this technique allowed agrarian peasants to diversify production and expand the stock yields of land. Other crops could be sown and planted in fields occupied by raised vines. Also, lords demanded the expansion of the surface area occupied by vines by using propagation techniques and spreading manure every five years. In exchange, the lord demanded annual rent payment equivalent to half of the total production of the vineyard for 50 years.

Cultivation of cereals and grains forcibly pushed land improvement forward. The right of *imblavare et disblavare* suddenly made their way into the feudal society. This right designated a plot of cleared land available for cereal cultivation.[47] The main cereals were foxtail millet (*Setaria italica*) and broomcorn millet (*Panicum miliaceum*), barley (*Hordeum vulgare*), and sorghum (*Sorghum bicolor*). One must take for granted that agrarian peasants took advantage of seasons when surface-water levels were low to fit land for crops that had 'a chance of success.'[48] Wheat, a competitive crop that flourishes in dry soils, reached the Central Po plains, stretching as far as southern Garda region. Even when geography of the Adige Valley was a formidable blockade to its advance, its presence south of Garda shows that lords 'hardly gave up on it.'[49] Less significant in shares of rents, lords still promoted its cultivation because it was a most profitable marketable cereal. A nobility obsessed with white bread on its table played a role in the spread of wheat in the region.[50]

Millet, an annual grass also cultivated in dry lands, was the insurance crop par excellence. The varieties that flourished in the region did not

[45] Stenico, 'Signorie rurali e risorse economiche.'

[46] Harding, *Oxford companion to wine*, p. 384.

[47] Kink, *Fontes Rerum Austrariacum*, p. 171, footnote 1; Franceschini, 'Le paludi dell'Adige, diritti di sfrutamento e tentativi di bonifica,' p. 265.

[48] Franceschini, 'Le paludi dell'Adige, diritti di sfrutamento e tentativi di bonifica,' p. 265.

[49] Curzel and Franceschini, 'L'agricoltura trentina nel tardo medioevo,' pp. 26–27.

[50] *Idem*, p. 27.

require that care and attention that wheat demanded. They were sown in deep and flat soils in mid-October.[51] A Spring-sown cereal, millet shared the agrarian space with other crops. It was used in soups, bread, and polenta, all part of the common food of herders, farmers, and miners.[52] Barley was a Winter or Spring annual grass; it slightly exceeded the one-meter height. Essential for bread-making, fodder, and brewing, barley was 'corn for the masses.'[53] It dominated all low-fertility soils. Sorghum reached all valleys, too, acquiring different names along the way, such as *melega*, *melica*, or *suricum*.[54] The cheapest grain in the market, sorghum was the basis of sustenance of the wretched of this Alpine feudal peasant economy. A team of forensic anthropologists, studying faunal and human bones collected in the Adige Valley, concludes that sorghum and millet dominated dietary options of peasants and shepherds in lower-altitude valleys.[55] The group of experts also noted sex-specific dietary differences in the region. Males of approximately 20 to 40 years of age had a diet richer in animal proteins than females.[56] The pattern suggests that household decisions about food allocation and consumption were determined by energy demands of individual work that members of the family unit confronted on a daily basis.

Blave, *frumenti*, *anone*, and *brayed* figured prominently in lordly rents, indicating that farmers succeeded in the planting and cultivation of cereals.[57] Villages in Mezzocorona north of Trent paid 20 *galetas* of cereals, 105 Veronese marks, and 9 *plastrum* of wine (each *plastrum* equivalent to 628 liters) to Bishop Wanga. A *galeta* was a unit of measurement of dry and liquid matter, usually grains, but also fruits and nuts in markets of the Garda Valley. It was equivalent to approximately 34 and 37 liters.[58] Rents

[51] Zadoks, *Crop protection in medieval agriculture*, p. 50.

[52] Curzel and Franceschini, 'L'agricoltura trentina nel tardo medioevo,' p. 29.

[53] Zadoks, *Crop protection in medieval agriculture*, p. 50.

[54] Castiglione and Rottoli, 'Il *sorgo* (sorghum bicolor) nel medioevo in Italia settentrionale,' p. 485.

[55] Paladin, Negahnaz, Stawinoga et al., 'Early medieval Italian Alps: reconstructing diet and mobility in the valleys.'

[56] *Idem*, p. 82.

[57] The word *anone* comes from *annōna*, or *annōnae*, and meant the yearly produce of a given land or fief, or the estimated price of the yearly produce, especially of grains and cereals. It generally referred to the 'grain tax paid to monasteries,' or 'grain dues.' Arnold, *Negotiating the landscape*, p. 79, 129.

[58] Curzel and Varanini, *La documentazione dei vescovi di Trento*, p. 285; Kink *Fontes Rerum Austrariacum*, p. 171, footnote 1; Schneller, *Quellen und forschungen zur geschichte*, p. 148.

paid by an individual leaseholder also from Mezzocorona included one *galeta* of cereals, one *galeta* of *siligo*, and four *galetas* of cereals. Further south, settlements in Arco, Cavedine, Drena, the small valley of Ledro, Nago, and Tenno paid 450 *galetas* of cereals in rents. In the second half of the thirteenth century, they paid 68 percent of tithes in millet, and 14.5 *galetas* of olive oil (of which 10 *galetas* came from Arco and the rest from Ledro). Ledro farmers also paid rents in wool, suggesting an early process of class differentiation rooted in resource specialization. A tithe record dated A.D. 1287 lists 490 *gallete* of cereals, equivalent to 59 percent of all tithes.[59]

Olive farming flourished south and east of Garda, where Lombardian geography favored the spread of *olivatum*.[60] The abbess of the Monastery of San Salvatore, in Brescia, obtained from *Andrea*, a cleric from Sirmione (in a small peninsula in the Garda Lake), numerous lots of lands: 10 *ioges* of land, each equivalent to 7900 square meters, and 63 olive trees in Caonno; 48 *tavole* of land and 6 olive trees by Castel Sirmione; 60 additional olive trees in Caonno; and 30 olive trees in Golegiano. Agrarian peasants built artificial terraces for the planting and cultivation of *olivatum* in the region.[61] The neighboring Monastery of Santa Giulia collected annually the astonishing amount of 2528 pounds of oil between the ninth and tenth centuries A.D. Its incomes included 1012 pounds from olive farms located at Iseo. The court of Cervinica added 580 olive trees, producing 1608 pounds of oil. The numbers are equally astonishing for the monastery of San Colombano of Bobbio: 2790 pounds of oil, of which 85 percent came from the court of Summolacu. Cervinica referred to Castelnuovo di Peschiera, a locality near Santa Giulia in Garda Valley.[62] The ecology of *Sylvestris Europea*, the variety planted in the region, favored the rent business of big ecclesiastical lords. This variety can live, if undisturbed, for approximately 1000 years. Sensitive to prolonged periods of freezing below 28 °C, its tree can reach a maximum height of 8 to 15

[59] Stenico, 'Signorie rurali e risorse economiche,' p. 226.

[60] Brugnoli and Varanini (cur.), *Olivi e olio nel medioevo italiano*, pp. 132–133, 137–140, 170–172.

[61] Brugnoli and Varanini (cur.), *Olivi e olio nel medioevo italiano*, p. 147.

[62] It was also known as Cervaneche, according to a document dated A.D. 1201; Cervaniga in a document dated A.D. 1202; Cervanige in A.D. 1203; Cervaniche in A.D. 1204. Summolacu referred to a locality to the north of Lake Garda. Brugnoli and Varanini (cur.), *Olivi e olio nel medioevo italiano*, pp. 132–133, 137–140, 170–172.

meters.[63] Its cultivation required care and labor: 'olives are hand-picked or harvested by hitting the branches with reeds and reaping the fallen fruit'[64] (Fig. 2.2).

Lords exploited the success of land improvement by organizing rural settlements around the *mansus*. The *mansus* represented a centralized unit of agrarian activity, and a powerful instrument for exercising lordly power.[65] Medievalist David Herlihy defined the *mansus* as 'somehow related to the land or farm of a single family'; 'certainly derives from *manere*—to remain.'[66] The institution appeared in Carolingian manorial surveys, indicating the spatial and economic unit dominated by serfs or *homine de masnada*.[67] Labor attached to the *mansus* formed the class of *macinatae* or vassals of lords.[68] These men, women, and children formed the bulk of agrarian labor of this Alpine feudal peasant economy. Although it occupied the lowest stratum of the social hierarchy, members of this class sometimes received pasture or rent rights.[69] Such circumstances created groups of *homini liberi* or free vassals who gained emancipation from lords.[70] The most important economic characteristic, however, was that feudal serfs had limited upward mobility. Vassalage relations kept this class attached to the *mansus*. Lords donated, bought, and sold men, women, and children *macinatae* as lords did with livestock, grains, agrarian tools, and capital. In A.D. 1191, *Guglielmo* of Velturno donated a woman named 'Ghenana' and ten children to two citizens of Tren. These serfs provided labor services to the court of Renon—*quos et quas dicebat esse suous de masnada*.[71] *Servus de macinata* and *femina de macinata* were mentioned in A.D. 1251.[72] Along *famulli* and *ancillae* that emerged in patrimonial lands, serfs belonged to the class of non-free vassals attached to the *mansus*.[73]

[63] Pfister, Luterbacher, Schwarz-Zanetti et al., 'Winter air temperature variations in western Europe during the early and high middle ages,' p. 549.

[64] Zadoks, *Crop protection in medieval agriculture*, p. 47.

[65] Franceschini, 'Castelli e campagne in area trentina.'

[66] Herlihy, 'The Carolingian *mansus*,' p. 79.

[67] *Idem*, pp. 79–81.

[68] Tomedi, 'Giuramenti di fedeltà e investiture nel comitatus Tridentinus (XII–XIII secolo).'

[69] Voltelini, *Giurisdizione signorile*, pp. 110–111.

[70] Pivano, *I contratti agrari in Italia nell'alto medio evo*, pp. 14–15.

[71] *Idem*, p. 108.

[72] This group was comparable to *familia*, a term denoting a group of non-free vassals that belonged to a single lord. Voltelini, *Giurisdizione signorile*, p. 109.

[73] *Idem*, pp. 110–111.

Fig. 2.2 Waterwheel at the forge of Fontenay Abbey, Marmagne, Cote-d'Or, France. The Cistercian Abbey, founded by Saint Bernard of Clairvaux in A.D. 1119, housed 300 monks who harnessed the power of water for iron mining and metallurgy. Its rents were heavily dependent upon productivity of waterwheels. Today a UNESCO World Heritage Site, the abbey forge is the oldest and best preserved metallurgical factory of Western Europe. Photo Credit: Manuel Cohen/Art Resource, N.Y.

In some villages, a *mansus* included a single-family house and a feudal court, and varied agrarian lands. In other cases, a *mansus* was an isolated settlement with a house and a plot of improved land, or a cultivated plot of land with a house situated in a neighboring vicinity. It could also appear as a plot of land demanding tillage.[74] As such, it was a productive space in route of developing a central farm holding unit. Its dimensions varied, too, tending to expand in proportion to settlement density, intensity of agrarian activity, and demarcation of boundaries.[75] Its economic relations were also dynamic, and created a distinction between public and private grazing grounds. Some pasture lands were small enough as to be managed by a single village. In time, groups of villages claimed pasture rights, creating a spatial demarcation between 'public' pasture rent rights held by the

[74] *Idem*, p. 102.
[75] Herlihy, 'The Carolingian *mansus*,' p. 82.

bishop of Trent and organized in the mansus and 'private' grazing rights monopolized by villages. In such cases, bishops exercised 'custody right' over newly privatized grazing lands. The right strictly referred to the power to appoint custodian officers.[76] Local *runcatores* gained functional linkages with the economic life of the *mansus*. Of Germanic origins, *runcatores* were 'rustic peasants' who cleared lands through deforestation to create open grazing grounds. They pragmatically targeted patches of lands that yielded high returns.[77] They were also found in southern lands as far as the Asiago Plateau and at lower altitudes near Verona, where they leased livestock farms and grazing lands. The latter attracted owners of large sheep flocks from Venetian and Lombardian communes, leading to high volumes of wool production and trade at a time of fierce competition among European wool producers for international markets.[78]

Rent gains of lords entirely depended upon the ongoing process of agrarian development. Rents paid in livestock-related products had higher prices than rents paid in grains. Their price increased in proportion to value created by economic activities sustaining livestock. These economies included salt mining, copper, tin, and lead mining, and all other productive activities yielding the raw materials needed for meat preservation and the making of tools and artifacts for slaughterhouses.[79] If certain types of livestock for both live animals and meat were earmarked for lords, its value increased in comparison to other types of livestock. Even when the 'enormous difference between the diet of the rich and the diet of the poor' allowed lords to tightly controlled circulation of expensive livestock and agrarian commodities, rents of livestock ultimately depended upon wider processes of land improvement. An *iscla* leased to a man by the name *Permannus* also paid *fictum* to Wanga—*duas urnas vinii*, etc.[80] Another lease of a vineyard located near the main urban settlement paid a more substantial *fictum*: a one-third of the total amount of wine produced annually by the leaseholder.[81]

In addition, Bishop Wanga leased grazing rights on Sadron Mountain (modern-day Malga di Sadron), located at an elevation of 1400 meters, to

[76] Leicht, *Studi sulla proprietà fondiaria nel medio evo*, p. 109.

[77] Ibidem.

[78] This was the thesis of John Murro, in 'The West European woollen industries and their struggles for international markets, c.1000–1500.'

[79] Lopez, *The commercial revolution of the Middle Ages*, p. 41.

[80] Curzel and Varanini, *La documentazione dei vescovi di Trento*, p. 485.

[81] *Idem*, p. 502.

representatives of Carbonara community (modern-day Croviana). The lease price was *X modios boni cassei*, or 10 *modios* of produce such as local cheese.[82] The *modium* was a unit of measurement for dry and liquid matter, equivalent to 170 liters or 8 *staria*.[83] Tithes paid by a family of Malé, in the frontier with Carbonara, included 63 *modium* of cheese, 36 *bestias* including cows, rams, and lambs, and 12 *urnii vini*.[84] The *urna* was a unit of measurement for wine equivalent to 62 to 78.5 liters. According to Schneller, it was common to pay three Veronese marks for three urns of wine (the mark being a unit of fineness and weight, as described below).[85] In Livo, the tithes owed to the bishop by one family included 83 *modios* of *siligo* (a wheat variety), 70 *modios* of cheese, 26 urns of wine, 28 animals (cows, rams, and lambs) and 5 *vaccas* & *porcos*. 'Teupus de Roveredo' paid Bishop Wanga one cart of hay for a specific meadow in 'Figniuncle,' part of a larger meadow located in Lagarina Valley (Vallagarina), which was divided among various leaseholders.[86] An inventory of agrarian produce available for the kitchen of Tyrol Castle offers an idea of the scale and magnitude of agrarian surpluses. The castle had 'at its disposal 1750 sheep, 800 chickens, 380 cattle, 40 pigs, no less than 8000 eggs, and at least 8000 cheeses each year' in the late thirteenth century.[87]

[82] Curzel and Varanini, *La documentazione dei vescovi di Trento*, pp. 562–564.

[83] Wheat and cereal rents in *Codex Wangianus* were reckoned in *modium*. When used for measuring dry goods, a *modium* was equivalent to approximately two and one-fourth pounds, although in some cases it was equivalent to 36, 45, 58, and even 72 pounds. Twenty-four *sextaria* or *staria* equaled one *modium*. There is another possibility, noted by Schneller, that *modium* meant *moçolus*, a grain weight, with three *moçoli* equivalent to one *modium*. The unit of surface land measurement was the *plodium*, equivalent to four *starium*, each *starium* equivalent in turn to 845.7 square meters. In Lombardy, *iugero* was the prevailing unit of measurement of land surface, equivalent to approximately 7900 square meters. A liter described the volume occupied by one kilogram of distilled water at 4 °C and at the standard atmospheric temperature of 760 millimeters. Curzel and Varanini, *La documentazione dei vescovi di Trento*, p. 286; Montanari, *L'alimentazione contadina nell'alto medioevo*, p. 33; Schneller, *Quellen und forschungen zur geschichte, litteratur und sprache Osterreichs und seiner Kronländer*, p. 151.

[84] It was also common to reckon one urn of wine as one pound reckoned in Verona marks. Curzel and Varanini, *La documentazione dei vescovi di Trento*, pp. 573–574; Schneller, *Quellen und forschungen zur geschichte, litteratur und sprache Osterreichs und seiner Kronländer*, p. 161.

[85] Malfatti, *Degli idiomi parlati anticamente nel Trentino*, p. 17, footnote 10; Schneller, *Quellen und forschungen zur geschichte*, p. 161.

[86] Curzel and Varanini, *La documentazione dei vescovi di Trento*, pp. 555–556.

[87] Flatscher, '(Self-) Supply in a medieval castle,' p. 118.

The numbers above confirm the 'astonishing speed at which animals were slaughtered or bought and sold in the region.'[88] Lords influenced the speed of agrarian change by granting leases for substantial periods of time. Land concessions represented in the *livello* contract, which were based upon the 29-year lease, changed in response to agrarian development. By the end of the thirteenth century, lords showed the inclination to grant contracts in perpetuity *in perpetualis* after the contract reached expiration date.[89] Such was the character of economic development and organization of a *rural* society driven by agrarian labor and capital. Trent was never meant to reach the socio-economic and political organization of its southern Veronese and Lombardian communes. The city remained loyal to its political destiny well into the sixteenth century. Its lords lived off rents paid in kind and money. Some commodities were more expensive than others, but all satisfied 'the necessaries and conveniences of life' either by direct consumption or by exchange. All commodities including silver coins were expressions of value produced by a society enduring rapid growth of monetized rents.

Rise of Monetized Rents

Production and circulation of agrarian surpluses sustained the triumph of the Carolingian money system. Based upon silver, the system was expressed in *libras* or pounds, *denarii* or deniers (pennies), and *soldi* (*solidi*) or shillings.[90] It originated with the system of account based upon the *denarius* introduced by Pepin or Pippin the Short.[91] Toward the end of the century,

[88] Archetti, '"Fecerunt malgas in casina" Alevamento transhumante e alpeggi nella Lombardia medieval,' p. 499.

[89] Castagnetti, *Le comunità rurali*; 'Enti ecclesiastici, Canossa, estensi famiglie signorili e vassallatiche a Verona e a Ferrara'; Ertl, 'Small landlords: land transactions in and around Bozen (south Tirol),' pp. 13–14; Fasoli, 'Città e feudalitá'; Keller, *Signori e vassalli nell'Italia (secoli IX-XII)*; Pivano, *I contratti agrari in Italia nell'alto medio evo*, p. 11; Reynolds, *Fiefs and vassals*, p. 186; Spicciani, *Benefici livelli feudi*; Tabacco, *The struggle for power in medieval Italy*; Violante, 'Un beneficio vassallatico instaurato con una carta di livello.'

[90] Feller, 'Measuring value in the Middle Ages'; Flynn, 'Six monetary functions over millennia'; Gorini, 'Aspetti della documentazione numismatica medievale nel Trentino-Alto Adige'; Kelleher, 'From the Commercial Revolution to the Black Death (c.1150–1350)'; Mueller and Lane, 'The first coins and moneys of accounts'; Naismith, 'The social significance of monetization in the early Middle Ages'; Wolff, 'Monnaie et développement économique dans l'Europe médiévale.'

[91] Naismith, 'The social significance of monetization in the early Middle Ages.'

Charlemagne created the *Carolingian denarius*, originally a pure silver coin weighing 1.7 grams, which became 'a fundamental unit for all European coinage.'[92] Also, the mark of Cologne set a new standard of weight for silver, equivalent to approximately 233 grams. The mint of Verona, one among the twelve imperial mints established by the Carolingians, minted coined the *denarii* and *soldi* that circulated in Trent. Decades later, a mint in Merano began operations under Florentine Masters, in the lands of the Counts of Tyrol.[93] Following Italian commercial conventions, Trent referred to money by emphasizing the origin of the mint that produced the coins available in its market. It identified money as *libras denariorum veronensium monete* or 'pounds of Veronese deniers'; *libras veronensium* or 'Veronese pounds'; *solidus veronensium* or 'shillings of the Veronese mint' or 'Veronese shillings.'[94]

The Veronese pound or *libra* originated in the Roman weight system. It was roughly equivalent to 327.45 grams, 'though the precise figure is uncertain.'[95] The *libra* functioned as local weight standard and money of account, divided into 20 *soldi* each of 12 *denarii* (equivalent to 240 *denarii*).[96] The *solidus* was 'originally the standard gold coin of the late Roman Empire,' weighing 24 carats (4.55 grams) of pure gold when first introduced in A.D. 309. The *solidus* was also a money of account, equivalent to four *taris* (2.78 grams of gold). In Western Europe, it was a multiple of 12 silver *denarii*. Merchants estimated the metallic value of the Veronese pound in coin or bullion. When estimated in coin, the metallic value was equivalent to the amount of fine silver contained in the 240 *denarii* of one pound. If estimated in bullion, the metallic value of the Veronese pound was equivalent to the number of pounds that made for one mark of silver bullion, which was in turn a money unit of account. For most of the period under study, 10 Veronese pounds 'of presumably pure silver' were equivalent to one mark of silver bullion.[97] Studying various

[92] Kinkade, 'Money in the Poema De Mio Cid: a reassessment,' pp. 109–110.

[93] Travaini, 'Mint organization in Italy between the twelfth and fourteenth century,' p. 19.

[94] Mueller and Lane, 'The first coins and moneys of account,' p. 108; also, Grierson and Travaini, *Medieval European coinage*, p. 466; Sperges, *Tyrolische bergwerksgeschichte*, pp. 263–264; Spufford, *Money and its use in medieval Europe*, pp. 225–239.

[95] Mueller and Lane, 'The first coins and moneys of account,' p. 108.

[96] Curzel and Varanini, *La documentazioni dei vescovi di Trento*, p. XXV.

[97] The talent or *talentum* was used as a weight unit or money of account. The *solidus*, or *solidi* in plural, was 'originally the standard gold coin of the late Roman Empire,' weighing 24 carats (4.55 grams) of pure gold when it was introduced in A.D. 309. The *solidus* was also

specimens of the *Henricus denarii* coin minted in Venice in the mid-twelfth century, Mueller and Lane argue that 10 Venetian pounds of such coins 'would contain 218.4 grams silver, slightly more than the marc [mark] in use at that time.'[98] This amount of silver corresponded to the metallic value of the Verona mark. Since coinage was an expensive operation, 'coined silver was generally worth more than silver bullion.' They suspect that the general equation of one mark equal to 10 Venetian pounds 'was not a current market price of silver bullion but a conventional way of reckoning' (Fig. 2.3).

The Carolingian money system was by no means universal. It was a small subsystem of an expanding world of production and trade where coined metals and a whole range of commodities played monetary functions side by side. The gold-based markets of Islam bordered the heartlands of Carolingian Europe. They formed a vast mosaic of markets including Andalusian Muslim kingdoms in the Iberian Peninsula, Sicily, southern Italy, northern Africa, and the Levant.[99] Gold-based money flourished in the Levant and Western Asia. A spectacular shift in the balance of power had favored Islam from the mid-twelfth century onward, despite a costly and futile Third Crusade in A.D. 1188–1192.[100] Afterward, Western Mediterranean currencies increasingly replaced the gold-based *nomisma* of Byzantium.[101] Carolingian Europe sustained commercial relations with these states. Occasionally, it minted gold coins, as the gold coin struck in Arles that was recently discovered during an archeological excavation, and which numismatist Garipzanov has discussed elsewhere.[102]

The high frequency at which *libras*, *denarii*, and *soldi* appear in rent documents of Trent bishops suggests that silver money facilitated the pricing of agrarian lands and goods. Bishops collected 20 *soldi* in Egna (in modern-day South Tyrol), after citizens gained the right to buy and sell

a money of account in certain parts of Italy, equivalent to four *taris* (2.78 grams of gold). In Western Europe, it was a multiple of 12 silver *denarii*. Curzel and Varanini, *La documentazioni dei vescovi di Trento*, p. XXVI; Grierson and Travaini, *Medieval European coinage*, p. 473, 466.

[98] Mueller and Lane, 'The first coins and moneys of account,' p. 108.

[99] Kelleher, 'From the Commercial Revolution to the Black Death (c.1150–1350).'

[100] Edbury, 'Warfare in the Latin East.'

[101] The florin weighed approximately 3.54 grams and had a diameter of 20 mm. The Venetian gold ducat was heavier—3.56 grams. Kelleher, 'From the Commercial Revolution to the Black Death,' p. 139–145; Vauchez, Dobson, and Lapidge (eds.), *Encyclopedia of the Middle Ages*, p. 418, pp. 420–421; Porteous, *Coins in history*, pp. 45–47.

[102] Garipzanov, 'The image of authority in Carolingian coinage,' p. 208, footnote no. 47.

Fig. 2.3 Miners working in a smelting factory with overshot wheel, a scene from *Anna Metercia* (A.D. 1513). A miner revolves the charcoal burning in a container placed at the bottom of a hearth, while another miner breaks up a lode of matter resembling brown coal or peat. The scene comes from a religious panting depicting the Virgin and Child with Saint Anne, patron of miners, displayed at the Church Assumption of the Blessed Virgin, in Rožňava, Slovakia. A Jesuit and 'experienced missionary,' Matthias Sámbár sponsored the idea of displaying religious art with mining images in the Church. His goal was to allure the inhabitants of the village into the Church through 'ideas familiar to them' as to leave Lutherans and Calvinists with no souls to prey upon. Institute for Material Culture, University of Salzburg

property in the *subburgii*.[103] In another rent agreement, a well-to-do vassal of the bishop paid 25 *soldi* for usufruct rights pertaining a building in Bolzano, an amount of money that was to be paid *omni anno in kalendis marcii ad husum domorum burgi de Bolçano*.[104] The annual *fictum* paid by the dean of the village of *Comaio*, in Lomaso and Bleggio, was much higher—30 Veronese pounds, in addition to *XV castronos*.[105] Lands leased by *Enricuso & Riprandus* in Ala also paid 25 *solidi*.[106] In Fiemme, the *iscla de sanctum Martinum* yielded some rent, but only from half of its *iscla*, the *one-half quanta pars fuit roncata*. After A.D. 1339, the *iscla* of Lidorno, located to the south of the urban quarter of Trent, and the *isclas* of Campotrentino and Spini in the northern side were leased and segregated at a price of four *grossi per piovo*. Each *piovo* was equivalent to approximately 3382 square meters, suggesting increasing concentration of land for agrarian use in the fourteenth century.[107] Even the *tera vacua*, land worked during certain months of the year and left unimproved for long periods of time, paid rents.

Rents priced in silver coins figured prominently in leases involving hydraulic works. *Samuele*, son of the late *Gualcone* of *Roubatasca*, declared to return to the bishop a fief consisting of a *domus murata* located at the end of the bridge built in the Adige River, a watermill, and the one-tenth of Muralta; Samuele declared that he received 500 Veronese pounds, an amount of money to be restituted to the bishop after 'the son of Samuele' inherited the fief. The agreement took place in November 2010, after a purge against some rural lords who had threatened the first years of the government of Wanga. In another agreement, the bishop enjoyed income rights over a watermill in Calavino, which he granted to *Gisla*, wife of *Galiciano*, for a period of two years, on May 30, 1216. Another large sum of money appeared in relation to a watermill mentioned on December 27, 1208. Located in Borgonuovo, near the center of power of the bishop, the mill was mortgaged for a loan of 200 Veronese pounds. A *runcus* in Borgonuovo near Fersina River also paid 12 *soldi* of Veronese *denarii* as rent. This sum seemed sufficient to cover expenses of the journey of the

[103] Curzel and Varanini, *La documentazione dei vescovi di Trento*, pp. 191–194.
[104] *Idem*, pp. 487–488.
[105] *Idem*, p. 528.
[106] *Idem*, p. 562.
[107] *Idem*, p. 135; also, Vaj, *Notizie storiche della Valle di Fiemme*, p. 268.

bishop to the court of King Otto IV, before clashes between the king and Pope Innocentius III crushed all imperial aspirations of the king.[108]

A year later, Wanga faced a controversy over a watermill worked by *Gando* of the *Porta oriola*. *Gando* was by no means intimidated by the *gastaldia* of the bishop when he claimed his usufruct rights over the mill. He only acknowledged the administrative authority of the bishop over the watermill conditioned to receiving 600 Veronese pounds in compensation for restoring the watermill.[109] Wanga purchased a watermill in Calliano, according to a declaration of property undertaken on January 8, 1211. Wanga paid 900 *denarii*, an amount of money that ensured his rights over Beseno Castle.[110] *Ludovic* of Strassolo, acting on behalf of his wife and sister-in-law, daughters of the late Enrico of Manzano, and brothers *Federico* and *Ulrico* of Caporiacco, sold the mill. The Manzano family was part of the local nobility that exercised rent rights for the plains east of Vallsugana. The same mill appeared in A.D. 1212, in a document that confirmed the transaction done by the bishop a year earlier.

Not only bishops bought and sold assets priced in coined metals, but they sought to increase economic advantages by coining and minting money. Bishops obtained rights of coinage and minting, *regulandi monetam*. These rights were confirmed by Emperor Frederick I on February 9, 1182.[111] Numismatic evidence available today confirms that bishops minted silver *grosso* up until A.D. 1220, albeit research is still needed on this matter.[112] It is possible that the Tassullo gold mine or *Taxulo* in the Non Valley reached considerable level of development.[113] Yet, Tassullo mine yields never fully displaced the role agrarian commodities played in rent and monetary relations. Monetization of rents was only possible because this rural economy produced agrarian surpluses and accumulated value. Italy was *la terre monétaire par excellence*, according to historian Philippe

[108] Curzel and Varanini, *La documentazioni dei vescovi di Trento*, p. 363.

[109] *Idem*, pp. 579–580.

[110] *Idem*, p. 217, 285.

[111] Gorini, 'Aspetti della documentazione numismatica medievale nel Trentino-Alto Adige,' p. 240; Kink, *Fontes Rerum Austriacarum*, p. 432.

[112] Gazzoletti, *Della Zecca di Trent*, pp. 28–29; Gorini, 'Aspetti della documentazione numismatica medievale nel Trentino-Alto Adige,' p. 241.

[113] Tassullo is a commune that includes the villages of Rallo, Campo, Sanzenone, Pavillo, and Valer Castle. Piemonti situated the mine in the valley overlooking Tovel Lake, or the valley at the foothill of Peler Mount. In the classical work of Agostino Perini, the mine appears in the site of Mount Peller (*nel luogo detto Minerf*). Perini, *Dizionario geografico, statistico del Trentino*, pp. 516–517.

Wolff.[114] De Roover even once speculated that bank deposits began in Italy in A.D. 1200.[115] Historians agree that rulers anxiously enforced monetary ordinances, aware that advantages gained by coinage could not be taken for granted. The reason seems fairly obvious: mints competed for bullion with the rising manufacturing arts. To presuppose that *silbrarii* delivered silver and gold exclusively to mints, ignoring brisk demand for bullion from the defense or jewelry industry, is to ignore the profit-making force that drove producers in this period. Industries for the making of gilt spurs, 'a jealously guarded class privilege that distinguished knights from other riders,' silver-inlaid sword hilts and rims, ornamental armors and plaques, and other artifacts, demanded precious metals.[116]

None of the rents previously mentioned were determined by speed and volume of metal coins circulating in Trent. They were determined by the process of production of value itself. Metal coins had no special economic feature placing them above and beyond the world of commodity production to which they belonged. Neither Marx nor Smith, or Thomas Aquinas before Smith, or any of the famous scholastic thinkers who examined the question of 'just prices,' conceived of coined metals separated from the realm of commodity production.[117] Since coined metals were another commodity available in an economy producing agrarian surpluses, prices of land leases could be expressed in coined metals as well as agrarian commodities. Sums of coined money that appeared in the rent accounts of the bishops only expressed measures of relative values of intangible units

[114] Wolff, 'Monnaie et développement économique dans l'Europe médiévale,' p. 496.

[115] De Roover, *Money, banking, and credit in medieval Bruges*, p. 247.

[116] Nickel, 'Arms & armors,' p. 13; also, La Salvia, La Salvia, *Iron making during the migration period*; Precopi Lombardo, 'Artigianato ebraico dei metalli preziosi nella Sicilia medievale.'

[117] Adam Smith centuries later summarized and synthesized foundational ideas on prices and value in one of his most celebrated statements: 'It was not by gold or by silver, but by labor, that all the wealth of the world was originally purchased; and its value, to those who possess it, and who want to exchange it for some new productions, is precisely equal to the quantity of labor which it can enable them to purchase or command.' Cannan and Lerner (eds.), *The wealth of nations*, p. 76; also, Baldwin, *The medieval theories of the just price*, pp. 27–29; Carpintero Benítez, *Justicia y ley natural: Tomás de Aquino y otros escolásticos*; De Roover, 'Scholastic economics: survival and lasting influence from the sixteenth century to Adam Smith'; 'The concept of the just price: theory and economic policy'; Johnson, *Predecessors of Adam Smith The growth of British economic thought*, esp. pp. 239–247; Monsalve, 'Scholastic just price and current market price: is it merely a matter of labeling?' pp. 9–14; Schumpeter, *History of economic analysis*, pp. 74–107.

transferred to ratios of tangible quantities.[118] One must take for granted that money transactions required separating the unit of accounting money from the real means of exchange or the coined *denarii*.

However, agrarian commodities also served as means of exchange. They were a means of purchase and a means of payment. The fact that rents were paid in coined metals and agrarian commodities means that both commodities fulfilled money functions.[119] This feature made of Trent a rural economy fully immersed in the commercial revolution of times in which cash and 'barter' transactions coexisted at all levels of society. Bishop Wanga banned the pawnbroking business that naturally developed in taverns and blacksmith shops near Monte Calisio. This ban indicates that *tabernarius* and *ferrarius* accepted all sorts of pledges as security for small-scale loans (which most likely were also given in a range of commodities including cereals and meat). It is possible that shopkeepers added an extorting interest, moved by the general principle that small-scale businesses made small profits but quick returns.[120] By their very nature, places like taverns and blacksmith shops had warehousing functions. Miners brought articles such as *ferros*, *funes*, and *fegas* (weapons, iron tools, and knives) to be pawned and which shop owners stored as inventory.[121]

In the world of high commerce and money-lending, merchant houses were also versed in the making and accepting payments in agrarian commodities as well as coined metals.[122] Enjoying unrivaled commercial advantages in the Levant, Genoese merchants frequently specified in their contracts that payments were accepted in *libras*, *solidi*, and *denarii*, and agrarian goods of equal value or *seu valens*. They commonly quoted prices

[118] Flynn, 'Six monetary functions over time,' p. 21.

[119] Adam Smith observed the money functions of 'useful and plentiful commodities' in various historical periods including the eighteenth-century world economy. 'The armor of Diomede, says Homer, cost only nine oxen; but that of Glaucus cost a hundred oxen. Salt is said to be the common instrument of commerce and ex-changes in Abyssinia; a species of shells in some parts of the coast of India; dried cod at Newfoundland; tobacco in Virginia; sugar in some of our West India colonies; hides or dressed leather in some other countries; and there is at this day a village in Scotland where it is not uncommon, I am told, for a workman to carry nails instead of money to the baker's shop or the ale-house.' Cannan and Lerner (eds.), *The wealth of nations*, p. 67.

[120] Marx explained this idea in Marx, *Capital, vol. 3. The process of capitalist production as a whole*, p. 370.

[121] Kink, *Fontes Rerum Austriacarum*, p. 446.

[122] De Roover, 'Characteristics of bookkeeping before Paciolo,' p. 345; Reynolds, 'Origins of modern business enterprise: medieval Italy,' p. 351.

of silver currencies in goods, indicating that both commodities functioned as reserves of means of payments. Commodities found their money function only in the realm of circulation. A Genoese contract in A.D. 1147 defined the price of 100 pounds of Genoese *denarii* as equivalent to a one-quarter of its value in pepper, another one-quarter in bark (used for making dyes), another one-quarter in a highly prized wood, and only a one-quarter in the *denarii* currency.[123] The commune of Genoa borrowed 200 *libras* in pepper (no amount was specified), in a transaction in A.D. 1162. The fact that these examples come from Genoese merchants, the capitalists par excellence of the European economy, and when Genoa minted its own currencies, suggests that what happened in Trent was fully consistent with the progress of the medieval commercial revolution.

The rapid rise of monetized rents was but an expression of the rise of agrarian surpluses. Trent was a rural economy that offered 'very few possibilities for an object to be considered irrelevant.'[124] Even 'worn out' goods were of value, as medievalist Mariana Romani concludes. Inventories of goods that appeared in wills reveal an economic mentality that privileged the reuse and circulation of commodities like clothes, linens, furniture, pots, pans, and other inexpensive goods besides luxury items. *Gastaldia* officers prepared inventories of resource stocks useful for estimating agrarian wealth and thus fiscal revenues of land. It is true that coined metals allowed lords to liberate mortgaged resources. They possibly facilitated the rise of bank deposit, albeit there is no evidence prior to the beginning of the fourteenth century.[125] But the idea of coins 'safely locked up' in chests because they stored all value produced by an agrarian economy is unrealistic given the money-trade relations at stake. First, merchants used currencies in their chests to finance trade, because specific coins originally placed on deposit needed not be returned, only their equivalent value in any currency available. Coins had no superior value when compared to other valuables such as jewelry, caskets, ornamental swords, and other items in the coffers of Italian money-changers. They simply allowed bailees or depositaries to further interchange valuables at ease, and for a profit.

[123] Casaretto, *La monete genovese in confronto con le altre valute mediterránee*, pp. 3–14. The rest of the paragraph borrows integrally from this work.

[124] Romani, 'Denaro, monete-merce e merci-moneta,' pp. 170–171.

[125] De Roover, *Money, banking, and credit in medieval Bruges*, pp. 247–249. The rest of the paragraph borrows heavily from this work.

Second, prices of all commodities including coined metals depended upon circumstances beyond the control of lords. Commodity prices depended first and foremost upon production costs. Thomas Aquinas and other Fathers of the Church who distilled Aristotelian and Roman principles of prices argued that prices were generally agreeable to the parties of the transaction. 'It is necessary that a price should be agreed upon, for there can be no sale without a price.'[126] 'And the price must be fixed and certain.'[127] Aquinas argued that a certain 'freedom of bargaining' exists between buyer and seller, determined by abundance or scarcity of commodities. It was this condition which governed intrinsic value of all commodities, according to medieval thinkers.[128] These ideas expressed transformations occurring in European lands. Although the full analytical possibilities of these notions were still in the making, economic thinkers then saw prices as a social phenomenon determined by the community rather than imposed by rulers. The price of a commodity could be fixed either by the 'estimation currently arrived at in the market' or *secundum aestimationem fori occurrentis* or by public authorities for the common good.[129] The first was the natural price; the second, the legal price. The legal price did not affect the real value of the commodity in question.

Studying the history of silver-based money, monetary historian Dennis Flynn has discovered three additional conditions that determined commodity prices, namely transit routes; 'end-markets'; and rate of change of available stocks on a world scale.[130] All of these conditions were at stake in the world economy of the long thirteenth century. Despite the prevailing

[126] De Roover, 'Monopoly theory,' pp. 496–497, esp. footnote 1; Stark, 'The contained economy: an interpretation of medieval economic thought,' p. 7.

[127] Sandars, *The Institutes of Justinian*, 3, 23, p. 363. The Institutes stated that 'the price should consist in a sum of money.'

[128] Baldwin, 'The medieval theories of the just price: Romanists, Canonists, and theologians in the twelfth and thirteenth centuries,' pp. 27–29; De Roover, 'Monopoly theory prior to Adam Smith: a revision,' pp. 496–497; Monsalve, 'Scholastic just price and current market price: is it merely a matter of labeling?'

[129] De Roover added: 'Aquinas tells the story of a merchant who brings wheat to a country where there is dearth and knows that others are following with more. May this merchant, Aquinas asks, sell his wheat at the prevailing price (*pretium quod invenit*) or should he announce the arrival of fresh supplies and thus cause the price to fall? The answer is that he may sell his wheat at the current price without infringing the rules of justice, although, Aquinas adds almost as an afterthought, he would act more virtuously by notifying the buyers.' De Roover, 'The concept of the just price,' pp. 422–423.

[130] Flynn, 'Six monetary functions over five millennia: a price theory of monies.'

silver standard with its theoretical weight, or the 'legal price,' commodities only found their real prices in the context of exchange. All commodities circulated in the northern European silver-standard area, where prices were expressed relative to the value of silver. Once commodities left the market of Trent, they were priced in different coins, never losing intrinsic values. This was especially the case of individual coins. Susceptible to wear and tear, merchants in 'end-markets' rejected clipped or damaged coins, lowering prices for these coins in comparison to prices of freshly minted coins. Merchants carried scales and weights to markets when they were making or receiving payments.[131] The custom of evaluating the extent of wear and tear of individual coins before accepting them as payment was so widespread that there was frequent mention of scales for coins and weights for precious metals in *post-mortem* inventories.[132] Lords knew well that 'high-quality silver coinage with a well-maintained weight standard' was not enough to support feudal power.[133] Stamps and elaborated iconography they impressed on their minted metal coins did not increase or decrease real purchasing power of coins independent of intrinsic values determined by the conditions described earlier.[134]

Third, conversion of land values into silver-based prices had already emerged in medieval Europe. Agrarian land value could fluctuate, especially when floods suddenly affected production, forcing silver-based prices to change accordingly. Lords took part in price-setting relations not as primary agents of historical change, but as subordinates of the invisible hand of economic change. They guaranteed that weights measured value in accordance to the accepted coined money standard, in the same way in which they guaranteed weights and standards for agrarian commodities. *Urnas*, *galetas blave*, *galetas anone*, *sexstarios blave* were accepted units of measurement for wine, grains, and cereals. They expressed a general assessment of value and *lucrorum* or valorizations built in improved lands and which satisfied the 'necessaries and conveniences' of life. Lords and merchants exchanged coins as they exchanged agrarian commodities, by relying on weights and standards to ensure that the expected quantity of the given commodity was bona fide *sine fraude*.

[131] For scales and weights, see: Arhin, 'Gold mining and trading among the Ashanti of Ghana'; Feugère, Depeyrot, and Martin, 'Balances monétaires à tare fixe: typologie, métrologie, interpretation.'

[132] Romani, 'Denaro, monete-merce e merci-moneta,' p. 181.

[133] Woods, 'From Charlemagne to the Commercial Revolution (c.800–1150),' p. 98.

[134] Romani, 'Romani, 'Denaro, monete-merce e merci-moneta,'' p. 187.

Fourth, ongoing land development and absence of pandemics exempted Bishop Wanga from the need to guarantee food supply by controlling agrarian prices. There is no evidence in *Codex Wangianus* of implementation of controls on agrarian production or distribution, analogous to agrarian-market restrictions that appeared kin other regions before and after the thirteenth century. The first 'necessity of life' was not wheat but the produce of livestock. On account of the economic geography described earlier, fixing agrarian prices could not be easily put into effect. In the absence of market controls, one must conclude that coinage gave no power to control value and prices of 'the necessaries' of life.

Coined metals if anything allowed lords to increase the 'time-value' of money. But this advantage was something no lord could monopolize. Rather, it was a situation imposed unto the rural society by the invisible hand of economic change. The rise of long-distance credit instruments, such as bills of exchange, offered merchants opportunities to use interest rates to inflict profit losses and extract gains. Merchants negotiated bills of exchange based upon an agreed exchange rate. An exchange rate was an assessment of value of the time lag that separated the geographic point where the bill of exchange was issued from the point where it was destined for settlement. Frequently, each exchange included a specific *usance* or maturity period, which referred to the number of days that the specific bill was expected to take after it was issued or drawn. Maturity varied, depending mainly upon geographic distance and transport costs. But the 'time-value' function of bills of exchange forced merchants to rely either on commodity function of silver currencies or on the monetary function of agrarian commodities in order to open and close transactions. The interest charge that compensated a lender for the time-value of his money relied upon the commodity function of silver currencies insofar as 'the same currency pair was quoted at different rates at each end of the transaction.'[135] The form of payments accepted in long-distance trade transactions could rely upon monetary functions of goods. We come back full circle to the money role those agrarian commodities played in medieval societies.

Finally, land lease contracts show an important sequence of money operations involving bishops. The terms *dedit*, *pignoravit*, investiat, and *solvunt* emphasized lending and borrowing relations, suggesting that money including monetary commodities changed hands at a relatively high speed

[135] Bell, Brooks, and Moore, '*Cambium non est muttum*: exchange and interest rates in medieval Europe,' p. 375.

within the upper class including well-to-do free vassals.[136] What is certain is that rise of monetized rents was faster than changes in the social conditions of the agrarian peasantry. The majority of the population remained legally dependent upon lords, indicating that agrarian surpluses allowed lords to tighten authority over *macinatae* and *familiae*.[137] However, contradictions embedded in the rise of agrarian surpluses acted as destabilizing forces that pressured Bishop Wanga and competing lords in the direction of accelerating the pace of land improvement. It was not uncommon to find rural lords who remained highly dependent upon the agrarian production of their vassals. Andrea Tomedi describes how the lords of Mezzo in Rotaliana Valley forced agrarian peasants to use their grinding mills under quite onerous conditions, yet the lords heavily depended upon vassals for their own sustenance.[138] Finally, there were the men and women living in open and uncultivated lands located far away from the nearest *mansus*. In those cases, the open land was contested territory between lords and *homines*. These contradictions transformed Germanic feudalism into competitive land and labor relations that continually challenge feudal powers, as Italian medievalists insist.[139] They were the forces that triggered rapid rise of monetized rents. From the thirteenth century onward, the 'partial rent' lease flourished, whereby peasants paid one-quarter, one-third, or one-half of the value of land in agrarian produce. Although these formulas changed according to the burden of expense absorbed by peasants, especially for vine cultivation, the general pattern was the introduction of money rents in lands that produced high levels of marketable surpluses.[140]

The 'Wet Ores' of *Mons Arçentarie*

Silver 'functioned as benchmark against which to compare relative values of all non-silver commodities.'[141] Because it sustained value of all available silver stocks, the 'wet ores' of Monte Calisio became the target of Bishop

[136] Kelleher, 'From the Commercial Revolution to the Black Death (c.1150–1350)'; Romani, 'Denaro, monete-merce e merci-moneta.'

[137] Franceschini, 'Castelli e campagne in area trentina,' pp. 199–202.

[138] Tomedi, 'Tra nord e sud. Le signorie rurali in valle dell'Adige, nella piana Rotaliana.'

[139] Italian medievalists have coined the term *condominium* to describe feudalism as a phenomenon of multiple layers of jurisdictions. See, for example: Franceschini, 'Signorie in un'area di strada'; Landi, 'Non solo vescovi e imperatori. Dinastie comitali e attività mineraria in area trentino altoatesina'; Stenico, 'Signorie rurali e risorse economiche: forme di prelievo e di gestione.'

[140] Stenico, 'Signorie rurali e risorse economiche,' p. 228.

[141] Flynn, 'Six monetary functions over five millennia: a price theory of monies,' p. 16.

Wanga. The bishop intuitively knew that high montane pasture stations and Alpine grass lands, *runcus*, cultivated lands, and toll roads generated rents based upon different combinations of land, labor, and capital. He soon discovered that mining was unlike any other form of land improvement, and where land and labor seemingly conspired against the basis of feudal power. In the early stages of development, mine improvement demanded minimal capital stocks. But such condition had much to do with geology, which made it 'easy to dig through rocks.'[142] Locally made iron pickaxes and chisels were the valuables of labor. An ordinary pickaxe measured 'three-quarters of a foot long [about sixteen inches], a digit and a half wide, and a digit thick.'[143] A wooden handle inserted through the eye of the iron-head and at an angle of approximately ninety degrees allowed for an easier handling of the tool. It was smaller and lighter than picks used by farmers to remove unwanted grasses. Its head had a broad and square upper and a lower pointed end 'so as to split the hard rocks and veins with its point.'[144]

The advantage of Monte Calisio geological endowments can best be understood when one considers that the norm in districts north of Venice was to use hydraulic rock-breaking techniques. Miners dug holes on the surface of ore-containing rock, filled them with water, and waited for water to freeze for ice to create fissures into the rockwalls that facilitated the breaking of the rock.[145] It is possible the Monte Calisio miners also used this technique in Winter seasons. However, soft limestone formations described earlier made it easier to break and cut through rocks. Archeological evidence confirms that miners preferred fire-setting techniques to break rock walls. Fire-setting techniques were fairly common across mining districts of the medieval world. Miners placed 'really dry wood sticks' in targeted zones of the mineralization body to set the sticks on fire. They splashed water unto the fire, forcing rocks to give in to sudden thermal changes, separating ore-bearing veins from rockwalls.

Prospection methods also require minimal capital expenditures. They demanded, however, laborious and patient work. Mineralization of the region consisted of common base metal sulfides, such as galena, sphalerite,

[142] Martin Straßburger, 'About Monte Calisio' Zoom video-meeting and emails to Jeannette Graulau, September 9–10, 2024.

[143] Hoover and Hoover (transl.), *Georgius Agricola, De re metallica*, p. 50.

[144] *Idem*, p. 150.

[145] Zammatteo, 'Le antiche miniere di Faedo,' p. 7; Weisgerber and Willies, 'The use of fire in prehistoric and ancient mining,' p. 134.

arsenopyrite, chalcopyrite, and blende.[146] Experienced miners coming from 'galena basins' north of the Alps were acquainted with nature of various metal sulfides. However, the matrix of Monte Calisio mineralization body was dolomite ankerites, a mineral formation commonly associated with baryte (a barium sulfate) and small quantities of other minerals. Baryte veins in turn had argentiferous galena ores.[147] This relation among minerals was possibly first observed by eighteenth-century French geologist Déodat Gratet de Dolomieu, whose name the Dolomites proudly bear today.[148] Monte Calisio miners prospected the plateau looking for signs of baryte veins. Most likely, they were attentive to signs of old mining works in the landscape and mineral dust in rock formations. But assuming that miners could easily spot baryte veins, assessing silver content of veins required digging, extraction, and smelting works.[149] This condition anticipated land and rent relations different than agrarian land and rent relations, as discussed in the following chapter.

The course maintained by baryte veins, whether regular or winding, determined the direction and shape of prospection shafts. Miners built drifts or tunnels that reached 200 meters in length, in the borders of the plateau. Tunnels were the form enclosures took in this ore-yielding land. The goal was to encircle the mineralized deposit. Drifts not only allowed miners to follow the direction of coveted mineral veins, but to attack the mineralization zone from all possible directions. It was a mine enclosure like no other. It suddenly gave miners the opportunity to exploit the deposit without deranging or thinning the mineralized region—a problem that miners confronted in other geological landscapes.[150] Baryte veins were flat strakes of silver-yielding galena that ran into the mountain, as if dipping into the inner core of Monte Calisio. The mineralized lode ran vertically, in

[146] Bianchini, Natali, Ferretti et al., 'Trace-element distribution on sulfide mineralization in Trento.'

[147] At nearby sites, miners dug galena-bearing chalcopyrite at Belluno in Imperina Valley east of Trent. Further away, in Monte Rusiana northeast of Trent, miners extracted silver from galena ores containing calamine. Tizzoni, 'Le scorie della riduzione di minerale argentifero dal Monte Calisio,' p. 284. For more on the subject, see: Braunstein, 'Les entreprises minières en Vénétine au XVe siècle,' p. 535, p. 540; also, D'Achiardi, 'La miniera del Bottino nelle Alpi Apuane'; Garlandini, Micheletti, and Poggio (cur.), *Il patrimonio storico industriale della Lombardia*; La Salvia, *Iron making during the migration period: the case of the Lombards.*

[148] For an excellent history, see Gardien, *Deodat Gratet de Dolomieu.*

[149] Kernot, *Prospecting and valuing mines*, p. 76.

[150] See, for example, Simonin, *Underground life, or mines and miners*, pp. 404–407.

parallel to the direction of mountain orography. When miners encountered steep slopes or impenetrable rocks, they changed the direction of mining works by digging a horizontal tunnel fortified with wood girders from where other vertical or diagonal shafts were excavated[151] (Figs. 2.4 and 2.5).

Ore veins yielded other minerals besides baryte, indicating the need for ore smelting techniques.[152] This geological condition imposed expenditures of capital and labor, altering the initial costs of mine development. Ore smelting was the stage that determined the amount of silver that could be obtained from crude ores. It was a capital-intensive process, and the one that also opened the door for *silbrarii* to work the mines of Bishop Wanga. As such, it determined the rate of return (or silver yields) of mining works. Smelting was a series of operations performed by a technical specialist aiming at cleaning the ore from unwanted materials and recuperating silver from mined crude ores. The method required smelting silver-bearing lead ores to create 'de-silverization' of lead bullion and recuperation of silver. The first stage was to 'dress' the lead sulfide containing silver before the mined ore could be separated from other vein minerals and unwanted rock.[153] Evidence from other mining districts indicates that miners generally relied upon two options for the process of smelting. The first option required heating the dressed ore at approximately 600 and 800 °C. It recovered up to 75 percent of the metal, producing a lead-rich, gray slag. Oxygen was essential for inducing chemical reactions between liquids, gases, and solids. Boles were employed in this first step and only for smelting large pieces of ore. A bole was a 'windblown hearth fueled by wood and built on a prominence to catch the wind.'[154] Bole hearths created an oxidizing atmosphere for the needed chemical reactions to occur.[155]

Since the lead-rich, gray slag carried amounts of silver-rich lead, a re-smelting of the slag was needed for recovering as much silver as possible from the ore. Bellows-blown furnaces were the second smelting option. Extensively developed in Central Europe, they were also used for the

[151] Casagrande, 'Paesaggi minerari del Trentino,' p. 183.

[152] Weisgerber and Willies, 'The use of fire in prehistoric and ancient mining: firesetting,' p. 134.

[153] Gill, 'An outline of the chemistry of lead smelting.' The rest of the paragraph borrows heavily from this work, unless otherwise noted. For smelting experiments, see Bodmer and Aegerter, 'Ber Bergbau in Val Minor,' pp. 3–4; Tizzoni, 'Le scorie della riduzione di minerale argentifero dal Monte Calisio,' pp. 285–289.

[154] Rippon, Claughton, and Smart, *Mining in a medieval landscape*, p. 89.

[155] *Idem*, p. 90.

Fig. 2.4 *Virgula divinatoria* or prospection rod, in *De Re Metallica* (A.D. 1556), by Georgious Agricola. Two miners use divining rods or forked twigs for identifying the spot of land containing valuable ores. The fork is held in each hand in a way that the end of the twig points upward. Miners believed that the end of the twig was pulled downward by the 'inherent energy' of metals, indicating in this manner the spot of land concealing ore veins. The twig, some speculators added, could drive a miner dizzy by whirling round and round once it detected metals or water beneath the earth. Most experts agree today that it was only the magnetic needle the device that greatly enhanced the art and science of prospection. In any case, the method was more useful for prospecting grounds of valley floors and less efficient for prospecting Monte Calisio ores. ETH-Bibliothek Zürich, E-Rara

Fig. 2.5 Shaft and *cuniculus*, in *De Re Metallica* (A.D. 1556) by Georges Agricola. Agricola described vertical shafts of relatively moderate dimensions: 30 *passus* deep, or approximately 44 meters. The drawing shows useful timbering and vertical shaft designs. However, this mine geometry was by no means universal. It was impossible to replicate in Monte Calisio. ETH-Bibliothek Zürich, E-Rara

re-smelting of the slag. Bellows-blown furnaces required crushing and washing the slag for separating the lead-rich material from the waste. This operation added to the cost of mine improvement. It required heavy hydraulic machinery, such as waterwheels and horse-powered millstones that flourished in many mining towns. Sometimes miners built bellows-blown furnaces for re-smelting small ore pieces, sacrificing economic efficiency given that these machines consumed large quantities of charcoal. Costs of wood needed for making charcoal in situ, as well as charcoal transport costs, also increased capital and labor expenditures.[156] Transporting ores from the mines to ore-washing installations and smelting sites also impacted costs. Weighing and carting materials could also swell mine expenses. These calculations imposed the need for large allocations of capital and labor for an efficient production of mines and smelting sites.

Archeological evidence confirms this general picture of mine improvement in Monte Calisio. Marco Tizzoni and his colleagues conducted smelting experiments using slags discovered at Doss Le Grave and Fornace sites in Monte Calisio. Their evidence shows that ores contained high amounts of unwanted substances. Tizzoni and his team concluded that smelting required cupellation, as was the case of ores from most European mines.[157] Cupellation was a second smelting stage that transformed lead to litharge (or lead oxide) so that it could be separated from silver.[158] It was a 'high-temperature metallurgical operation aimed at refining the noble metals.'[159] In the process of creating litharge, the oxidized base metals reacted with metal oxides, producing fusible compounds. The process separated the noble metals that do not react with oxygen or lead oxide from the melt, and stayed as a discrete button. A smelter or technical expert employed a cupel for this metallurgical operation. A cupel was a small vessel made of ashes from calcined bone, a material not in scarcity in this Alpine valley. Ashes of horns and bones of ovicaprine livestock and cattle allowed for a 'neat separation' of silver since 'the mineral bone apatite does not react with the oxidized metals but mechanically absorbs them by capillary action.' Silver was then separated from the metal melt and was

[156] Stöllner, 'Montan-archaeology and research on old mining,' p. 13.

[157] Tizzoni, 'Le scorie della riduzione di minerale argentifero dal Monte Calisio,' pp. 285–286.

[158] Rippon, Claughton, and Smart, *Mining in a medieval landscape*, p. 98.

[159] Martiñón-Torres, Thomas, Rehren et al., 'Some problems and potentials of the study of cupellation remains,' p. 60. The rest of the paragraph, unless otherwise noted, comes from this work.

left relatively 'free' from impurities.[160] Digging and extraction works continued while smelters and assayers completed cupellation works and assessed the results of ore sampling. Such assessment was the very foundation of the estimation of mineral wealth of Monte Calisio.

Recent archeological studies of Faedo in Monte Calisio offer a glimpse of the mining environment. The mine had two galleries traversing the main prospection shaft in different points. From the galleries, miners dug ore-extraction shafts in different directions.[161] Size and shape of extraction shafts varied. Some were long, others were short, many were narrow, others were wide, depending upon direction and thickness of ore veins. Unlike mines in Saxony in the use of timber resources prevailed, miners fortified shafts using discarded rocks, especially gallery and shaft sections with heavier traffic of men and materials. Mine tunnels were very narrow since they were only used for connecting shafts and transporting materials. Most likely, miners 'had to proceed on their knees or crawling.'[162] Working independently, and using only a hammer and a chisel, a miner was able to 'build about ten meters of tunnel in a year.'[163] A team of archeologists identified approximately 150 mine entrances into *mons arçenterie*. Miners dug every zone they could, aggressively attacking the mineralization in all possible directions. The rationale was to save money, time, and labor, as to increase mine returns right from the start of operations. Such rationale, however, contained its own antithetical relations. Trying to 'empty' the mineralized mass, miners discarded 'good' rocks containing fair amounts of argentiferous galena.[164] The overall picture was one where mine improvement progressed at an accelerating speed. Miners transformed the entire mountain into a system of irregular caves built for the rapid extraction of mineral wealth (Fig. 2.6).

[160] Galena's density and compact nature facilitated the separation of wanted metals from gangue, the worthless minerals contained in an ore deposit. Oxidized lead, or PbO by its chemical name, was sometimes recycled for cleaning silver-bearing copper ores. The following equation describes the chemical reaction creating oxidized lead: Ore + Charcoal+ (Fluxes) + Air ↔ Metal + Slag + Dust/Gases (as CO, CO_2, SO_2). Craddock, *Early metal mining and production*, p. 205; Segers-Glocke, Witthöft, and Balck (eds.), *Aspects of mining and smelting in the upper Harz Mountains*, p. 54.

[161] Zammatteo, 'Le antiche miniere di Faedo,' p. 6.

[162] Casagrande, Päffgen, and Straßburger, 'Mining archeological research of medieval silver ore mining at Trento,' p. 187.

[163] This is a possibility archeologist Martin Straßburger discussed with the author, given the vast scale of mining workings in Monte Calisio. Martin Straßburger, 'About Monte Calisio' Zoom video-meeting and emails to Jeannette Graulau, September 9–10, 2024.

[164] Casagrande, 'Paesaggi minerari del Trentino,' p. 183; Tizzoni, 'Le scorie della riduzione di minerale argentifero dal Monte Calisio,' p. 284.

The overarching problem of mine improvement was shaft flooding. In an economy producing agrarian surpluses that triggered monetization of rents, 'wet ores' were a restraint to the creation of value. They lowered the mass of value that sustained economic development as well as profits and rents. As such, flooded shafts threatened to lower the value of all improved lands, altering along the way the land and labor relations that sustained feudal power. How to drain the 'wet ores' of the mountain, as to add this resource to the mass of agrarian wealth of the city, was suddenly a question of lordly power. In ordinary underground shafts described earlier, miners adapted Roman, Islamic, and Byzantine techniques to drainage operations that could reach 'colossal scales.'[165] This was the case of Iglesias in Sardinia in the fourteenth century, then a colony of the Kingdom of Aragon. Shaft flooding also occurred in fifteenth-century Kutná Horá in Bohemia. In these cases, miners built waterwheels adapted to mine drainage.

In the Levant, where Carolingian Europe established crusading posts and merchant colonies, Europeans witnessed many popular and efficient adaptations of the pre-Islamic *qanat* technique to drainage works.[166] The logic of the *qanat* was to tap water at the base of a mountain with a high level of water table and drive water away by means of a slightly declining slope.[167] Similarly, the *shādūf* and *sāqiya* wheels were adapted for mine-drainage purposes. 'At one end of the beam is a bucket, at the other end a counterweight.' The bucket was immersed in water, and lifted when 'the beam was rotated by the counterweight, so that the water in the bucket could be emptied into a cistern or supply channel.' The *sāqiya* or chain of pots drawn by animal power was a large vertical wheel 'erected over the water supply on a horizontal axle.' A gear-wheel was attached to the other end of the axle that engaged a horizontal gear-wheel with an attached driving bar. An animal was harnessed to the other end of the bar. It walked in a circular path rotating the gears and wheel carrying the chain-of-pots. 'The pots dip in succession into the water and when

[165] Angelakis, De Feo, Laureano et al., 'Minoan and Etruscan hydro-technologies'; Judson and Kahane, 'Underground drainageways in southern Etruria and northern Latium'; Wilson, 'Machines, power and the ancient economy,' pp. 17–20.

[166] The technique spread centuries earlier through Iraq, Syria, the Arabian Peninsula, and northern Africa. Hill, *Studies in medieval Islamic technology*, pp. 7–8, 26; also, Canto García and Cressier (comp.), *Minas y metalurgia en al-Andalus y Magreb occidental*, p. 11, pp. 185–186, about water in the Zukandar mine of Morocco, and drainage in Iberian mines, respectively.

[167] Al-Qazwīnī confirmed that 'the Sultan installs water wheels and water is raised until the mud appears.' The silver mines of 'Zakandar' [Zukandar?] were drained for his 'taking of the fifth.' Brooks, 'The "Vitruvian Mill" in Roman and medieval Europe,' p. 75. The rest of the paragraph comes from this work.

Fig. 2.6 A mining camp, scene from *Anna Metercia* (A.D. 1513). The scene shows all stages of mining including prospection and timber-cutting. An undershot wheel is moved by two horses, controlled by two workmen using horsewhips. A third workman inspects or waits for the lift to raise up from the shaft. In another shaft, a windlass is mounted and worked by one single miner. The painting is today at the Church of the Assumption of the Blessed Virgin, in Rožňava, Slovakia. Institute for Material Culture, University of Salzburg

they reach the top of their travel they empty into a channel.' It contained 'two hundred component parts.'

However, these hydraulic machines and techniques were very efficient in geographic settings radically different than Monte Calisio. The mining territory of Monte Calisio was located north east of the city, near lands long plagued by lordly competition for rent rights and privileges.[168] This situation added pressing political questions, such as what could happen if mining works attracted the attention of competing lords given that the

[168] Martin Straßburger, 'About Monte Calisio' Zoom video-meeting and emails to Jeannette Graulau, September 9–10, 2024.

city had then no fortified walls. At the same time, Monte Calisio offered peculiar advantages to Bishop Wanga. Silver-rich galena formations were found at the summit of Monte Calisio. The mountain defied the regular layout of most mining districts, where deposits spread through narrow valleys that facilitated fixing hoisting machines on the ground. Since the womb of the mountain concealed the prized ore veins, mining works had no reason to expand beyond the jurisdictional boundaries of the bishop. An independent mining town was thus less likely to emerge, regardless of intensity of mining works and size of population settlement. Indeed, specialists speculate that the medieval mining settlement was as large as Santa Colomba, a small area located near a lake by the same name offering prime access to Monte Calisio plateau.[169] Ore geography promised to bring a fresh stream of rent revenues and minimal disputes over 'profits of jurisdiction.'[170] At a time when the aristocracy and the nobility refused to back down in the competition for hegemonic power, the benefits of draining the mines of Monte Calisio outweighed any political cost.

[169] Ibidem.

[170] Adams, 'The judicial conflict over tithes,' p. 1937.

CHAPTER 3

Fighting the Bishop's Tax Charges

Taxation was an economic warfare waged simultaneously in two battlefronts: the battle for land 'as *source* of wealth' and the battle for labor 'as *cause* of wealth.'[1] They were two sides of one single coin: an intra-class struggle for jurisdictions of rent rights and privileges. Episodes of this struggle might seem separated from one another, but they reveal changes in the whole of a class-based society. Above all, they reveal shifts in relations and structures that bonded together the upper class. These shifts were by no means sudden. Rather, they were small and localized quantitative changes that over the long run altered the foundations and relations that sustained the upper class. Roman juridical notions had survived throughout the early Middle Ages in the rise of the class of an imperial or free nobility.[2] Bishop Wanga belonged to this class, and so did the Counts of Tyrol and other patrimonial families of the region. Dissolution of territorial jurisdiction of Merovingian monastic houses created the conditions for the rise of an imperial nobility that controlled the House of Canons of the Chapter of the Church of Trent.[3]

[1] I borrowed the phrase from Daniel Raymond, a nineteenth-century writer, cited by Johnson, *Predecessors of Adam Smith: The growth of British economic thought*, p. 246.

[2] Unless otherwise noted, this discussion borrows heavily and integrally from Maisse, 'Libertà fra tardo medioevo e prima età moderna: il mondo germanofono,' pp. 246–249.

[3] Kosi, 'The Fifth Crusade and its aftermath: crusading in the Southeast of the Holy Roman Empire.'

J. Graulau, *Medieval Mining and Power in Thirteenth-Century Europe*, https://doi.org/10.1007/978-3-031-99239-1_3

The juridical principle that legitimized the change at stake was the idea that a nobleman was 'free' because he possessed a certain freedom transferred unto him by his ancestors.[4] By virtue of this condition, a nobleman owned his own freedom, and thus was not subordinated to any lord. A nobleman also owned his allodium, a *curtis* or seat for the exercise of public authority, and a noble retinue. Assets transferred unto his legal personae were immune from constraint by royal authority. This condition presupposed that a certain equality united the Sovereign and the nobility. It presupposed resisting and combating claims that the Sovereign could advance against his property. This condition separated the privileges of class from the claims and privileges enjoyed by 'free vassals,' or those who depended upon a lord or nobility of feudal origins.

Legal freedoms and privileges that imperial and the new nobility enjoyed defined a rising bundle of property rights of this rural economy. With these freedoms came social rank and stratification within the upper class. Certainly, this was a rural economy in which farmers, shepherds, and miners formed the bulk of value-producing labor and the upper class consumed the value produced by labor. But the dynamic stratification of the upper class was remarkable. At the top of the social hierarchy were the patrimonial families and the imperial and old nobility of the region. What Braudel once called the 'predators of the jungle' were vigilant against the liberties gained by the new feudal nobility, as well as a significant group of free men of different ranks all of whom were socially superior than the free peasant. This last group included ministerials or administrators of immunity rights, and knights of non-free birth. The limited but significant social mobility within this upper class fueled competition for rent claims and privileges. This intra-class struggle at the top of the social hierarchy was the motor of historical change of this rural economy in the long thirteenth century, more so than class struggle from below. It was a hegemonic competition among lords, all seeking to grab higher surpluses of lands undergoing change by value-producing labor. The very basis of public authority, taxation, changed in response to military alliances, political negotiations, and wars between bishops and competing lords.

Ongoing land exploitation, however, dynamized the hegemonic competition within the upper class. Every additional unit of improved land created a monopolizable asset in the form of a new source of rent. The most important tax undergoing rapid change was the *bannum*. The *bannum* was

[4] Maissen, 'Libertà fra tardo medioevo e prima età moderna: il mondo germanofono.'

a fixed payment collected for purposes of building and repairing public infrastructure including parishes and monasteries. It represented *potestas* of a lord over a district. *Bannum persone et districtus* or the 'right of pursuit, constraint, and punishment.' In time, this right evolved into a public tax.[5] With consolidation of Carolingian power, bishops made alliances with local patrimonial families and feudal lords by granting *bannum* rights in exchange for loyalty and military aid. Such alliances nominally tied secular lords to bishops in lord-vassalage relations. Bishops sometimes granted this source of incomes to free vassals who in turn escalated in the social ladder to a low-rank knighthood or lower nobility title. Rooted in a struggle against the old aristocratic and patrimonial families of the region, this bundle of rights offered an opportunity for new noble families to enlarge rent claims especially jurisdiction over castles. A rising class of rural lords benefitted from the *bannum* in other ways, too. Through the jurisdictional privileges the tax entailed, lords alienated their vassals or *homines de masnada* from the cultural and political struggles deepening city freedoms that originated in the Guelph movement based in Lombardian communes and Verona.[6]

Predecessors of Bishop Wanga confronted and responded to these forces by granting rights over specific districts especially Garda in the south. No lord was exempted from the spillover effects of this competition, although the Tyrolean aristocracy enjoyed considerable advantages. The Counts of Tyrol owned extensive patrimonial possessions north and east of Trent, stretching into Austria, Carinthia, Styria, and Carniola. Members of this aristocracy were part of the House of Canons of the Chapter of the Church of Trent. They were tenacious in their quest for maintaining the territoriality of power of the Church. This feature made them a 'vibrant and belligerent aristocracy,'[7] precisely because they sought to enlarge the territoriality of their power. The family lost ancient rights in Trent, coinciding with the rise of immunity lands.[8] It waged war against competing lords, but also used rural communities against rising feudal powers.[9] This aristocracy played a dominant role in the politics of the Church of Trent. When the family of the Counts of Flavon was

[5] Reuter (ed.), *The New Cambridge Medieval History*, p. 51.

[6] Pacaut, *Frederick Barbarossa*, pp. 125–127; Pivano, *I contratti agrari in Italia nell'alto medio evo*.

[7] Tomedi, 'Vescovi e signori rurali nella regione trentino-tirolese tra XIV e XV secolo,' p. 256.

[8] Franceschini, 'Castelli e campagni in area trentina,' pp. 212–213.

[9] Tomedi, 'Tra nord e sud. Le signorie rurali in valle dell'Adige,' pp. 62–63.

extinguished, the *avvocatus* office was available for 'sale.'[10] Count Meinhard II of Tyrol assumed such role, in a move led to a 'bipolar world' favoring the old nobility allied with the empire. Officers of bishops as well as the Count exercised politico-administrative functions on behalf of one another in their respective territories.[11]

Struggles against the Tyrolean aristocracy came from all directions, and especially from bishops whose families came from the new nobility of the region. Many of these bishops responded to revolts by agrarian peasants by tightening alliances with military lords, deepening the divide between the new nobility and the old imperial nobility. When Bishop Adelpret confronted a 'private war' by a citizen of Trent in the second half of the twelfth century, he sought military aid from powerful lords of the Garda region. This citizen had headed south, and took refuge in an elevated *domus* located somewhere between Folgaria and Caldonazzo near Garda. Armed with his own militia, this citizen of Trent ravaged local villages, plundering and terrorizing settlements of *runcatores*. This kind of incident revealed the vulnerability of lords to agrarian rebellions from below. Even when agrarian peasants were not *milites*, and lacked warfare techniques and organizational capabilities, they could cause havoc in local villages. Bishop Adelpret knew that peasants could easily exploit the montane geography they knew well to gain support among local farmers.

With the intent of suppressing the rebellion, Adelpret made an alliance with lords from the Garda region. The bishop granted jurisdiction of Garda to a lord by the name of *Carlassario* in exchange for military aid. This alliance ran counter to the interests of noblemen from the city and especially detrimental to the economic interests of the Counts of Tyrol. As mentioned earlier, Garda was a strategic corridor of trade and a rich agrarian valley. To the south of Garda, the empire confronted quarrels against the League of Lombardy. The latter was 'made up of 16 cities, all of whom promised to fight for independence, not to make a separate peace, and to restore Italy to the happy state she had enjoyed under Herny V, Lothar III, and Conrad III.'[12] Garda had thus far functioned as buffer zone to resist the advance of the political revolution toward autonomy and citizenship coming from southern Italian communes. Memories and costs of a recent war against Veronese *milites* south of the Adige Valley were still

[10] Ferrandi, *L'Alto Adige nella storia*, p. 103; for a general history of *avvocato*, see Sarti, 'Tra mestiere e scienza giuridica.'

[11] Voltelini, *Giurisdizione signorile*, pp. 55–57.

[12] Pacaut, *Frederick Barbarossa*, p. 127.

Fig. 3.1 Searching for metals and precious stones. From *Tractatus de herbis et plantis* by Dioscorides. France, late fourteenth century. The illustrator portrayed a miner using a curved and long iron pick in a deforested patch of land and working on his own with no fellow miner in the field. The drawing was an idealized view of mining. Biblioteca Estense, Modena, Italy. Photo: Alfredo Dagli Orti. Art Resource, N.Y.

haunting Trent citizens. Then, Veronese lords had sieged the Rivoli Castle, prompting Emperor Frederick I to grant the investiture of the Garda district to the bishop of Trent in A.D. 1167[13] (Fig. 3.1).

[13] Cortese, 'L'Impero e la Toscana durante il regno di Federic Barbarossa.'

One year had barely passed when Bishop Adelpret granted Garda in *beneficium* to Carlassario. Adelpret sought to use Veronese connections and loyalties Carlassario had, against his own enemies within the Chapter. Carlassario promised to provide *milites* and *fidelitas* or loyalty to Bishop Adelpret, including the *ius aperturae* or right of access to Garda Castle.[14] This incident was only the tip of the iceberg, revealing unsolvable contradictions inherent to hegemonic competition. Indeed, the Garda donation was one among many enfeoffments of rent rights that altered class relations and lordly power. The bishop donated other rent-yielding assets, when in desperate need of *werrae* (war and military aid). Those offering military aid promised *negocia* or alliances, building along the way an overlapping but shifting layer of lord-vassalage relations. Bishop Adelpret gave away jurisdictions of rents in exchange for and he also enfeoffed the Beseno castle to *Carbonio* of *Povo* in the Arco region. The *Povo* family had an important past in the history of the territory.[15] It changed its name to

[14] Bishop Adelpret expected that if his enemies in Trent made *securitates* or agreements with lords from cities of the March of Verona, Carlassario and his *milites* would consider them as their own enemies and wage war against them. The bishop understood the agreement as binding Carlassario in a promise of loyalty to all citizens of Trent. However, Carlassario saw the agreement in a different light, based upon the documents studied by Curzel. Carlassario limited his promise of military intervention only to the Garda region, rather than all *Tridentinae partes.* Moreover, Carlassario also stipulated that his military aid was to be provided twice a year only, and for a total period of two months. Only upon explicit request, his *milites* would serve on behalf of the bishop for a longer period of time. Sustenance of *milites*, which included wages in coined money, expensive goods, military equipment, and food provisions, was the sole responsibility of the bishop of Trent. Carlassario also demanded the obligation by Bishop Adelpret to compensate him for losses suffered at war. Curzel, *Il capitolo della cattedrale di Trento*, pp. 57–61.

[15] Carbonio was the son of Pellegrino of *Povo*, who was Patriarch of Aquileia in A.D. 1131 (and after intercession by a bishop who came from the Carinthian aristocracy who knew the father of Pellegrino in Arco). *Povo* was a locality on a hill east of Trent. The son of Pellegrino, Carbonio, abandoned the name of Povo for *Beseno* sometime in the last quarter of the twelfth century. Carbonio was in Venice in the Summer of A.D. 1177, during the negotiations of the 'the truce of Venice,' presumably in the entourage of Bishop Salomon. In August of the same year, Carbonio and his son Otto witnessed two acts relating to a dispute that had reached the imperial court in appeal, over a dispute between the Patriarch of Aquileia and the Veronese monastery of S. Maria in Organo. Another son of Carbonio was member of the entourage of Bishop Albert of Campo, and also the entourage of Emperor Frederick in A.D. 1186. These were events that most likely played a role in the election of Bishop Conrad of Beseno as successor or Bishop Albert. A third son of Carbonio, Pellegrino, witnessed the imperial *laudum* in Germany that the emperor proclaimed in defense of the Counts of Eppan and other episcopal vassals, and against 'illegitimate' alienations of rents rights done by Bishop Albert of Campo (who was already at his deathbed). *Idem*, p. 492.

Beseno. A few years later, the family gave Trent one of its most unscrupulous bishops, Conrad of Beseno. The Beseno Castle was located in Volano, northwest of modern-day Nomi and Pomarolo. Rights over the castle exacerbated lordly competition in the south, this time involving the Castelbarco lords at a high cost to the bishop. The Castelbarco lords possessed an imposing castle in Lagaro, a village facing Volano in Lagarina Valley. Suddenly, the 'Beseno' lords held rent rights and privileges that encroached upon the lands of interest of Castelbarco lords, as well as lands claimed by the Counts of Eppan. Competition for rents reached its heights when Bishop Adelpret was assassinated in the Cathedral. The assassination of the bishop was a well-planned plot involving the Arco and the Castelbarco lords.

Meanwhile, the lords of Arco assiduously built alliances with local lords. They secured imperial confirmation of jurisdictional rights over Garda, benefitting from the schism between the empire and the Papacy. Rights to 'confirm tutors, curators, and procurators,' 'emancipate vassals,' and 'approve contracts' in their territories made them a powerful nobility in the south. They sustained loyalties and wars with Veronese lords at different times. The sources of rents that sustained this nobility were twofold: duties for the Torbole Pass, and typical agrarian rents. Both were fiercely contested by neighboring lords, including in time Bishop Wanga. The villages of Ledro, Bono, and Condino were part of their territoriality of power. Despite internal family conflicts, the Arco lords increased the number of *villae* and *curtis* in their jurisdiction, reaching villages in the Giudicarie. Banale, Bleggio, and Lomaso, in the Rendena Valley of the Giudicarie, also paid rents to this family.

Along with Beseno and Castelbarco lords, the Arco lords were protagonists of the most enduring wars against the fiscal power of the bishops of Trent. The Castelbarco family later claimed the Beseno Castle, from where they collected custom duties from caravans of trade crossing the valley in east-west direction. The family also demanded customs on river driving services—*navis per quam fit transitus ultra Athesim*—of the Adige River near Calliano. The Arco lords were the protagonists of an insurrection against Bishop Wanga that lasted for two years until A.D. 1210, in a series of events that decisively impacted the political orientation of the rule of Bishop Wanga (Fig. 3.2).

Fig. 3.2 Wanga Tower. A view of Wanga Tower and part of the city walls of Trent. According to legend, the tower had the inscription *Montes argentum mihi dant, nomenque Tridentum*. Courtesy of Martin Straßburger, Mining Archaeology Consultancy

Paving the Way for the Rule of Bishop Wanga

After Adelpret, bishops defended the jurisdiction of rent rights and privileges of the Church. They built military alliances with surrounding feudal powers, guaranteeing access to castles. Not always, however, they favored the Counts of Tyrol. Bishop Conrad was the most notorious, for he accumulated debts with many money-changers, and left the coffers of the bishopric in deficit. Son of *Carbonio* of Beseno, Bishop Conrad donated rent rights and privileges not only in exchange for military alliances but also for ready cash. Like Adelpret before him, Bishop Conrad had powerful enemies among the group of citizens and burghers of Trent. Feeling the pressure of his debts, and facing increasing hostilities within the curia, the daring bishop planned a siege to attack the city of Trent. Conrad hired the *milites* of Briano of Castelbarco. Negotiations between the bishop and the Castelbarco lord took place in May A.D. 1201, when the bishop donated Ala to Briano in exchange for military aid. Castelbarco spent the Summer months recruiting a *conducta* or contingent of 500 armed men, including well-equipped knights, *pedites* (warriors on foot), and *arcatures* (bowmen). He provided food and supplies. Hundreds came from the southern lands including Verona, hoping to make money in the war venture. However, *milites* had no time to move northward. Castelbarco received news from one of his Veronese contacts in Trent that some canons and the Count of Tyrol arranged for *Rubeo* or *Rosso* of Breganze (from Vicenza) to provide military assistance to the city. Indeed, Rubeo left Castelbarco no time to act, when his soldiers occupied the city, forcing Bishop Conrad to desist from his plans. The episode created greater hostility against Bishop Conrad. Still, a year later he returned to Trent from Riva, seemingly endowed with full powers of government. By then, he was in an untenable position, surrounded by enemies in the Chapter of the Cathedral and the city.

Meanwhile, lawyers had to respond to Castelbarco, who waged a legal battle against the city over Ala. Castelbarco also demanded compensation for expenses incurred in the planning of the military operation. Narrated in detail by Curzel, the episode illustrated the many dimensions of the ongoing and fierce competition for larger jurisdictions of rents. In the arbitration dispute that followed, Bishop Conrad even suspected that Castelbarco had secretly planned the entire Rubeo operation in advance. The humiliated bishop thought that Castelbarco wanted to gain the rents of Ala with little effort. The political advantage of Castelbarco lied less in the milites and more in the infamous government record of the bishop. Conrad had encouraged the lords of Campo to defend their rent claims for pasture stations in Breguzzo, against the Verona bishop. This rent conflict was part of a longer dispute that had spillover effects beyond the region, when Pope Celestine III (A.D. 1105–1198) threatened the Campo lords with excommunication.

Bishop Conrad had ignored the old threat, and confirmed the donation in favor of the Campo lords, seeking much-needed allies in the south. Also, Bishop Conrad granted customs of the Torbole Pass on the northern shore of Garda Lake to the Arco lords in A.D. 1200. Situated between Monte Baldo mountain and the Sarca plain, the pass was a trade advantage soon exploited by the Arco lords, when they charged duties to merchants crossing the northern lake route. The route was strategic to the circulation of surpluses, because it also included the traffic that crossed through Ballino, Banale, and the Giudicarie. The Arco lords enjoyed unrivaled control of the port of Riva, a settlement commercially and culturally tied to the territories of Verona, Brescia, and Lombardian communes. They strengthened their geostrategic advantage particularly when a peace treaty between the *podestà* of Verona and Oldorich of Arco, on the one hand, and Bishop Conrad, on the other, forced the bishopric to surrender rents rights to the Arco lords in A.D. 1204.

The double burden of debt and litigation forced the old and the new nobility to reorient their strategies for taking back what they thought belonged to the Church. Coinciding with the coronation of Philip of Swabia in A.D. 1205, the Count Albert of Tyrol wasted no time and rapidly relaunched an expansionist campaign in the region. Along with allies in the city, the Count forced Bishop Conrad to resign. The group forced the bishop to accept a recommendation not to elect one of his allies within the House of Canons as his successor. Vested in protecting the Church against the political rebellions of the south, Pope Innocent III confirmed the decision in May 1207. From St. Georgenberg monastery in the Inn Valley, and humiliated, Conrad attempted but failed to return and take over the city. Little he knew his nefarious politics had paved the way for the rise of Frederick Wanga. Wanga certainly had the necessary upbringing to aspire to the seat of Prince-Bishop, as described earlier. The Count of Tyrol and his allies in the canon of the Chapter of the Church did the rest, by gathering support for the election of Wanga as bishop of Trent. The newly elected bishop was to govern a city in political turmoil. The lords of Arco, Beseno, and Castelbarco contested jurisdictions of rent rights in the south. Citizens demanded centralization of revenues and taking back rent rights and privileges (Fig. 3.3).

Fig. 3.3 Gold mining. From the manuscript *Tractatus de herbis et plantis*, by Dioscorides. France, late fourteenth century. The lonely miner in the drawing comes from the medieval French copy of the book about medicinal properties of plants and other substances. Its author wished to portray medical uses of gold. Most likely, this spontaneous but patient prospection of soils took place by the side of large scale mining works. Biblioteca Estense, Modena, Italy/Alfredo Dagli Orti/Art Resource, N.Y.

This scenario of turmoil, however, created strategic opportunities for Bishop Wanga. First, some local lords had rent-seeking strategies that proved useful to centralization of public authority.[16] Such was the case of the Campo and Lodron lords.[17] The lords of Campo moved up in the social hierarchy by building military alliances and monopolizing rights for castles scattered through Chiese Valley including the Campo Castle.[18] The Campo lords held jurisdiction over Breguzzo near Monte Calisio; 17 men were *sue iurisdictionis.*[19] In A.D. 1211, *Armanno* of Campo swore loyalty to the lord of Toblino, *sicut vassallus facit suo domino.* He obtained in exchange a fiefdom with vassals from various villages. He owned *homines de macinata* from Toblino, along with lands, farmhouses, and a mill. By A.D. 1234, *Armanno* of Campo and *Cognovuto*, his nephew, paid Count Udalrich of Ultimo the amount of 2000 Veronese *denarii* in exchange for lands and men in Tione and Preore.[20] The Lodron family was the military power par excellence of the Giudicarie. It came from the class of free vassals, but accumulated jurisdictional rights in many *villae* and *curtis* of the Giudicarie.[21] The Lodron lords appeared in relation to the mines of the region when the Count of Eppan 'donated' the mines of Monte Calisio to Bishop Adalbert (r. A.D. 1184–1188).[22]

Even when these allies transferred rent rights to their vassals, continually negotiating loyalties with the big lords of the region, their competition for rents posed no threat to Wanga. *Graziadeo*, son of *Albertino Longino* of Campo, obtained confirmation of rights over land vassals in Favrio previously granted by the Counts of Flavon. *Graziadeo* confirmed

[16] Cagon, 'Le Giudicarie e la val Vestino,' p. 122. The rest of the paragraph comes from this work.

[17] Varanini, 'Itinerari commerciali secondari nel Trentino bassomedievale,' pp. 107–108.

[18] Villages in the dominion of the lords of Lodron included Carbié, Fiavé, Stumiaga, Favrio, Curé, Dasindo, Lundo, Poia, Godenzo, Comano, Vigo, Lomaso, Seo, Stenico, and Banale.

[19] Cagol, 'Le Giudicarie e la val Vestino: i Lodron e i da Campo,' pp. 134–135.

[20] They enjoyed *plenam potestatem dandi et iurisdictionem faciendi inter ipsos homines illius plebatus racionem tam maleficiorum quam de aliisquestionbus, dandi sentences et estates et omnia facere que ad iurisdictionem pertinent.* Cagol, 'Le Giudicarie e la val Vestino: i Lodron e i da Campo,' pp. 132–133. The rest of the paragraph borrows integrally from this work.

[21] Stenico, 'Signorie rurali e risorse economiche,' pp. 228–229.

[22] The donation included rights over vassals from the villages of Breguzzo, Bondone, and Tione, except the villages under the jurisdiction of *Galapino* of *Ludrun* [Lodron]. Curzel and Varanini, *La documentazione dei vescovi di Trento*, pp. 172–174; Kink, *Fontes Rerum Austriacarum*, pp. 438–439.

to a certain *Bonomo di Favrio* some properties that he had granted to his father *Ognibene*, on the condition that 'he and his male heirs born from legitimate marriage would render account only before him, that he would recognize himself as a man *sue iurisdictionis (…) tamquam esset civis romanus et pater familias* ["he would serve him as his father had always done"].' Despite the fact that they never reached the stature of their northern Tyrolean neighbors, they acquired a large number of rent-paying villages surrounding the Campo Castle.

Second, regardless of the conflicts each had with the Tyrolean aristocracy, smaller patrimonial families remained generally favorable to the government of Bishop Wanga. Such was the case of the counts of Flavon and Eppan in the Giudicarie. A member of the family of the Counts of Flavon was *avvocatus* of a bishop of Trent a century before Wanga came to power.[23] A Count of Flavon appeared again in Sonnenberg as *avvocatus* of Wanga, but also exercising political roles on behalf of local aristocratic families.[24] Such a title emerged nowhere else except in northeast Italy.[25] Rooted in Germanic feudalism, *avvocatia* was a judicial office representing ecclesiastical lords in imperial secular courts. Further to the north, the lordships of Thun, comprising Bragher and Castelfondo, collected lease rents from settlements located in Non and Sole valleys. The Telve lords became Telve-Castellalto. They had interests in the silver mines of Monte Calisio. *Riprando* of Telve was one of the four *silbrarii* named in a mining contract dated A.D. 1185, *ab argentariis qui solent appellari silbrarii.*[26] Besides, the family owned allodial lands in Telve, Torcegno, and Roncegno, southeast of the urban quarter of Trent. It also extracted rights from agrarian peasants in Civezzano and Fornace, on the eastern edge of Monte Calisio plateau.

Third, lord allies of Wanga controlled the lucrative tolls and montane passes, with the exception of the lords of Arco and their hold of Torbole Pass. The Castellalto lords collected *pro muda antiqua*, a tax equivalent to eight *soldi* and four *denarii* for every 100 pounds of wool entering from the territory of *Giacomo* of Caldonazzo in Valsugana *in allienis partibus.* They collected the same amount for wool exports from Ivano Castle, *in*

[23] Bishop Adelpret had *Arpone avvocatus* from the Flavon dynasty in A.D. 1124. Castagnetti, *Governo vescovile, feudalità, 'communitas' cittadina*, p. 28.

[24] *Idem*, p. 29.

[25] Voltelini, *Giurisdizione signorile*, p. 47.

[26] Stenico, 'Signorie rurali e risorse economiche,' pp. 242–243.

partibus superioribus. The Spaur family, lords of Flavon Castle, collected tolls in money on a road crossing the right bank of the Noce Valley toward the Adige valley. In the Atesina Valley north of Trent, the lords of Mezzo and Firmiano held local jurisdictions of rents useful to Bishop Wanga. They remained allies of the bishops of Trent until the mid-thirteenth century.[27] Atesina Valley afforded easy east-west communication, linking Avisio and Noce valleys. The hydrology of the Rotaliana plain, which was frequently impassable due to floods, forced a regime of cooperation between the bishops and the Counts of Tyrol that had paradoxically benefited these small rural lordships. The Mezzo and Firmiano lordships exploited this condition well. The Mezzo family emerged in the second half of the twelfth century, holding jurisdiction of villages in Livo, in the upper Non Valley. It obtained the castle of Monreale (renamed Königsberg) as a fief from the bishop of Trent in A.D. 1183.[28] The Mezzo Castle allowed its lords to dominate the Rotaliana plain northwest of Trent. The lords Germanized their surname to *Metz*.[29]

The Mezzo lords owned hydraulic works in Mezzolombardo and Bugnana as well as half of the rights over the Zambana bridge and half of the duty collected on the Nave San Rocco bridge. Their scattered jurisdictions of rent rights were the outcome of the territorial expansion of the Counts of Tyrol, who displaced them from strategic lands in exchange for pockets of rights in the region. The Firmiano family obtained feudal rights in the upper Adige Valley starting from *munitio Formicaria* in the twelfth century. They held feudal rights and owned castles including *Formicaria* Castle, beyond the Adige valley, in Cembra, Fiemme, Giudicarie, Non, Sole, Valsugana, Venosta, and the upper Garda Lake region. Other local allies included the lords of Caldes. These came from a family rooted in the village of Cagnò in the upper Non Valley. The Corona lords posed no major threat to Wanga either. They owned land-usufruct rights in the region, and remained loyal to bishops because their land was a fief of the Church of Trent.[30]

[27] Curzel, *Il capitolo della cattedrale di Trento*, p. 480.

[28] Bettotti and Landi, 'Signorie rurali, coscienza nobiliare e autorappresentazione,' p. 303.

[29] The Mezzo lordship lasted until A.D. 1465, when Giovanni Mezzo died. He was the last male heir of the family. Ten years later, his only daughter, Dorotea Mezzo, married Nicolò Firmiano, whose family inherited the Mezzo patrimony in the Rotaliana plain. Ibidem.

[30] The territory of Mezzocorona was encompassed by Noce River, from the Alpine mountain to the confluence of the Adige River, and from there to the Church of Mezo or *Punchelmandel*. It is possible the nobles of this land were of Italian stock, but later in the fourteenth century German migrants became dominant. Mor and Schmidinger, *I poteri temporali dei vescovi in Italia*, p. 209; Reich, 'Documenti di Mezocorona,' pp. 6–9, 17–18.

With allied powers encircling most of the district, Bishop Wanga aggressively founded settlements and courts everywhere. As expected, enlarging jurisdictional claims required donating streams of rents. Wanga confirmed toll rights to the monastery of Saint Bartolomeo in Romano, near Tonale Pass, in the westernmost fringe of the district. The monastery was a station for pilgrims and merchants on their way to the Garda Valley. The bishop organized the population in *plebes*, the natural space of market activities. He tightened the economic nexus between the parishes of Lomaso, Bleggio, Banale, and Tione in the Giudicarie, and the city of Trent. Also, *gastaldia* or tax officers gained a wider spatial realm of action. As mentioned earlier, *gastaldia* were secular agents who functioned like the 'fearful tithe collectors' Georges Duby found in medieval France, with one significant difference.[31] The *gastaldia* of the episcopal city needed not to replace the old feudal *curtis* it found everywhere in the valleys surrounding Trent. It tolerated and even usurped functions of the feudal *curtis*, while marking the juridical frontier between rights and privileges of immunity lands of the bishop and rent claims of competing lords.

This fiscal dualism was only possible because up to the eleventh century, the *curtis* flourished in Alpine lands. As the preeminent feudal tithe-collecting institution, the *curtis* organized agrarian relations between lords and peasant farmers. It was the space where tithes and declaration of land yields took place on behalf of feudal lords. Lords demanded that vassals delivered rent payments to the *curtis*. In many jurisdictions, the *curtis* gained other administrative functions in response to challenges lords confronted with surplus appropriation. It provided 'administrative and patrimonial linkages' between allodial and feudal lands.[32] In other cases, the *curtis* was the political space where free vassals gained some rights. In many cases, however, it was an instrument for the exercise of lordly power, especially in villages where the right of representation in judicial and criminal matters remained in the hands of lords.[33] In isolated agrarian villages, the *curtis* still retained its old fiscal functions but on behalf of episcopal lords.[34] The tendency was for *gastaldia* to slowly take over fiscal functions of the *curtis*.

[31] Duby, *The three orders*, p. 36.

[32] Castagnetti, *Uomini e civiltà agraria*, p. 34; Pivano, *I contratti agrari in Italia nell'alto medio evo*, p. 11.

[33] Leicht, *Studi sulla proprietà fondiaria nel medio evo*, p. 35.

[34] In those cases, the *curtis* paid generally a one-fifth of wine and six days of labor per year. *Idem*, p. 36.

Gastaldia in some villages was also 'estate manager,' a role the *curtis* failed to provide. It was common to find *gastaldia* of bishops exercising oversight of sales of produce and animals in rural villages.[35] A *gastaldionibus* named *Ambrosio* was responsible for general oversight of mining works.[36] This officer collected taxes and settled disputes among *silbrarii* concerning drainage works. His duties included periodic visits to *mons arçenterie* for the purpose of checking the state of shafts and appraising mine yields. Miners challenged his jurisdiction, forcing Wanga to impose a fine of 25 pounds of Veronese *denarii* against miners refusing this fiscal oversight.[37] Cheating on this payment could result in a heavy fine (*C solidi*).

In northern lands, *gastaldia* enjoyed ample administrative rights beyond tax collection. This officer also exercised judicial functions and was responsible for settling trade disputes as well as cases of homicides in Egna. The *gastaldia* of Rendena, Fiemme, and Sole Valley had analogous roles. In Non Valley, *gastaldia* was responsible for income and population surveys. Officers prepared detailed accounting of quantities of millet, grains, and animals that each curia paid to the bishop.[38] In A.D. 1260, the *gastaldia* of Monreale had *iurisdictio* and guard of a castle located in Faedo, north of the Adige Valley. In other villages of Rotaliana Valley under the jurisdiction of the Counts of Eppan, *gastaldia* had more limited roles. Mezzocorona was governed by *gastaldia* of the bishop, until Count Meinhard II (A.D. 1258–1295) of Tyrol acquired the land.[39] The *gastaldia* of Firmiano Castle or *Formicaria* exercised limited jurisdiction in Bolzano and Fiemme in the northern limits of the district. Levico in Rotaliana Valley north of Trent was *iurisdictio gastaldia* in A.D. 1258.

In some villages, *gastaldia* paid dues to the bishop, delivering essential commodities and possibly money when needed by the bishop. It was not uncommon to find *gastaldia* administrators delivering a fixed amount of

[35] For a discussion of the development of *gastaldia*, see Drew, 'The Carolingian military frontier in Italy,' p. 439; Malfatti, 'I confini dei Principato de Trent,' p. 6; Jansen, Drell, and Andrews (eds.), *The Middle Ages series: medieval Italy*, p. 554; Voltelini, *Giurisdizione signorile*, p. 46, pp. 49–50.

[36] Kink, *Fontes Rerum Austriacarum*, p. 443.

[37] Curzel and Varanini, *La documentazione dei vescovi di Trento*, p. 352.

[38] Each curia paid tithes for a period of three weeks, and one and a half weeks in the summer and the same in the winter. The court of Cles and Romeno delivered produce covering expenses for one week every Summer and one week every Winter. Ossana and other farm lands were responsible for furnishing produce to the religious holidays in honor of San Vigilio. Voltelini, *Giurisdizione signorile*, pp. 60–62.

[39] Reich, 'Documenti di Mezocorona,' p. 5; Reich, 'Toponomastica storica di Mezocorona.'

linen cloth and one horse to furnish bishops with everything they needed to complete pilgrimage trips to Rome.[40] In Valsugana east of Trent, a *gastaldia* administered incomes from Civezzano and Fornace. Fiscal power of *gastaldia* in southern lands was more incoherent when compared to northern lands. In Tenno, a castle captain and not a *gastaldionibus* exercised rent-collection functions in A.D. 1211. Only in the last decades of the thirteenth century, *gastaldia* performed administrative duties in villages of Garda and Giudicarie, specifically in Ledro, Bleggio, Lomaso, and Tignale. A *gastaldia* was responsible for agrarian surveys and tax collection in Banale, Preore, Tione, and Rendena, in the Giudicarie. Again, one finds a *gastaldia* exercising limited roles in Beseno Castle in A.D. 1234. This tax-collector only held civil jurisdiction responsible for *inter homines episcopi*; the bishop of Trent only exercised criminal jurisdiction. Nonetheless, this officer carried out administrative duties pertaining to the guard of the castle. Only the *gastaldionibus* of Riva was an important officer, given the strategic importance of *Rocca di Riva* or Garda Castle owned by the bishop and situated in the heartlands of the powerful Arco lords.[41]

Feudal castles mattered for taxation, too, as they were the places of residence of *gastaldia* officers.[42] Surrounded by highly populated villages, castles had thus acquired distinctive functions on behalf of competing lords. They provided territorial unity to the fiscal functions of the Sovereign power of bishops. Unlike his predecessors, Bishop Wanga reclaimed general administrative functions over strategic castles enforcing the *ius aperturae* and *ius custodiae*. These rights, which were his prerogatives as Prince-Bishop of Trent, were particularly important in his policy toward the dissident lords of the Garda region.[43] Wanga also relied upon the *curtis* of competing lords, in ways that strengthened his rule of law in allodial

[40] Voltelini, *Giurisdizione signorile*, p. 67.

[41] *Idem*, p. 53.

[42] Cusin, *I primi due secoli del Principato Ecclesiastico*, p. 20; Reich, 'Toponomastica storica di Mezocorona,' pp. 70–71; Voltelini, *Giurisdizione signorile*, pp. 60–62, p. 67.

[43] Bishops granted castles under the condition that these assets remained 'open' for *negocia* and *werrae* or war when bishops so demanded. Castagnetti, *Governo vescovile, feudalità, 'communitas' cittadina*, pp. 112–114.

and feudal lands scattered in the Giudicarie and Garda and Lagarina valleys, as described later.[44]

Everywhere, *gastaldia* was a dynamic institution, deeply immersed in a world of agrarian surpluses. Its functions and roles truly took off only at the local level, where it was directly engaged with the agrarian wealth of the district. Thus, it possibly played its part in the rise of monetary functions of agrarian taxes. Administered by *gastaldia*, the *fodrum* was an agrarian tax based upon an estimation of incomes of agrarian lands. It was essentially an agrarian census that only appeared in Alpine cities, 'an authentic fiscal novelty,' in the words of Mainnoni.[45] Because it was an assessment of land incomes, *gastaldia* officers fixed the *fodrum* based upon a census or survey of land and evaluation of land yields. This condition was only possible in society that had imposed economic barriers to ancient 'common rights' of patrimonial lords. From the thirteenth century onward, the *fodrum* was a loan that northern Italian city-states drew from well-to-do citizens. In time, the *fodrum* changed into *taglia* or *dacia*, a fixed amount of money aimed at preserving jurisdiction of lords but still based upon assessment of yield capacity of lands (Fig. 3.4).

Widespread diffusion of fiscal power never eliminated challenges to rent charges. If anything, the spatial reach of the fiscal power of Bishop Wanga was fuel to the flame of competition for jurisdictions of rent rights. Approximately one-fourth of rent-paying localities listed in *Codex Wangianus* were engulfed in legal battles, as the figure below summarizes. A religious house for the care of lepers located in Arco was under litigation. The local clergy openly defied the authority of bishops for approximately three decades starting in A.D. 1191.[46] The *arimmania* held by *Giovanni Piolo* in Fornace also challenged the jurisdiction of the bishop.[47] *Arimannia* were free vassals who provided military service to lords. A castle built by the vassals of the Count of Tyrol, located *supra villam Selsi*, near Terlan in south Tyrol, was a contested asset. The bishop held jurisdiction of rents in the locality. The asset was listed as property under litigation in A.D. 1185.[48] Jurisdiction over *Monte Cimone*, possibly located in Ala, was part of the assets under litigation between Briano of Castelbarco and

[44] Leicht, *Studi sulla propietà fondiaria nel medio evo*, p. 75.

[45] Mainoni, 'Fiscalidad directa e indirecta en la Italia medieval,' p. 152, 156, 160. The rest of the paragraph comes form this work.

[46] Curzel and Varanini, *La documentazione dei vescovi di Trento*, pp. 204–206, 225–229.

[47] *Idem*, pp. 232–234.

[48] *Idem*, pp. 166.

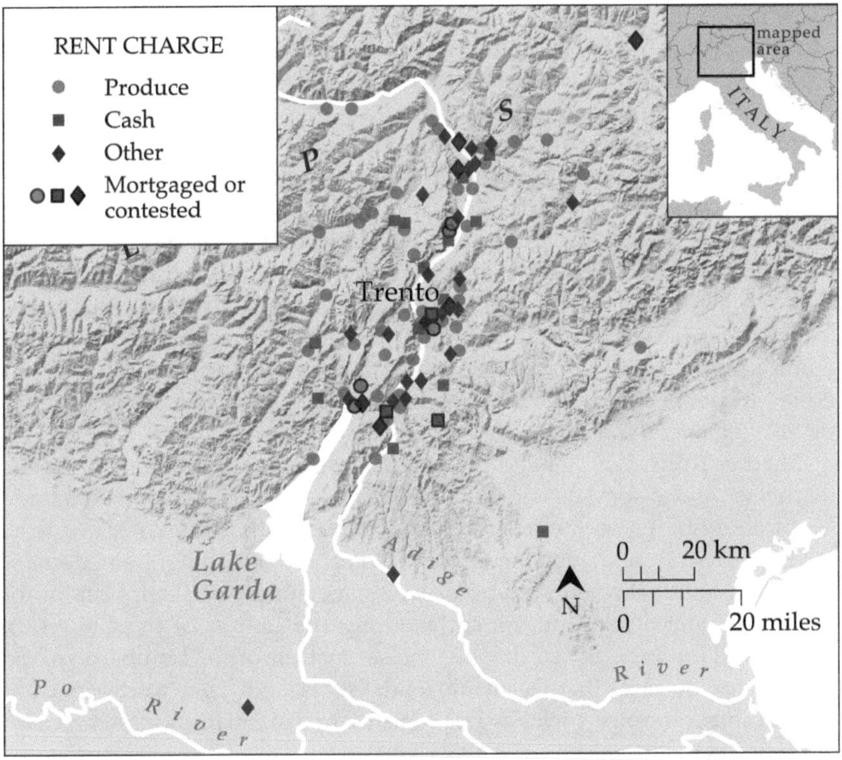

Fig. 3.4 Tax-paying localities under the jurisdiction of Bishop Wanga, by type of rent. Agrarian surpluses led to hegemonic struggles. Contrary to the general idea that prosperity brings peace because of its inherent spill-over effects, the case of Trent shows that land improvement and cultivation increased the appetite of lords for the profits of specialization. Besides patrimonial families such as the lords of Arco and the Counts of Tyrol, a new nobility of serf origins joined the struggle for agrarian surpluses. The result was a dynamic process of shifting rent jurisdictions, revealing the impulse with which lords sought to increase their dominions. Map based upon Codex Wangianus

the city of Trent.[49] Lands near the Fersina River, 'in the area indicated by *Amelrico* da Civezzano,' belonged in *rectum feodum* to *Andrea Borgonuovo*, even though the bishop remained as overlord.[50]

Patrimonial families also confronted litigations and challenges to its rent claims. The Counts of Tyrol held patrimonial rights and privileges in

[49] *Idem*, pp. 464–471.
[50] *Idem*, pp. 212–215.

Fiemme in Egna Valley since A.D. 1185, the same year when they appeared in a mining contract. The Count granted grazing rights to villages, claiming rents from pasture lands that legally belonged to the jurisdiction of the bishop of Trent. Predecessors of Wanga granted exemption from taxes to shepherds from different communities of the Egna Valley north of Trent. The policy aimed eroding the power of the Count of Tyrol in the region. This was a strategy to subtract vassals and rents from the Tyrolean aristocracy. Empowered by tax exemptions, herders refused to pay tolls for the transit of livestock through a montane road under the jurisdiction of the Count of Tyrol.[51] This was the beginning of a legal controversy that lasted a few centuries. Wanga exploited this condition to his advantage, when the community of Fiemme northeast of Trent accepted a settlement whereby it paid to the bishop 24 *arimannia* annually as the price for securing 'protection' against the Tyrolean aristocracy.[52]

Further south, Verona and the bishops of Brescia also weighed heavily in the struggles for rent rights.[53] Relations between Trent bishops and Veronese nobility were not limited to the problems Wanga had with the lords of Arco, Beseno, and Castelbarco. Veronese noblemen trained in law played an essential role in the bureaucratic machinery of Trent bishops for decades. Some figured prominently among the canons of the Church of Trent.[54] Many brought to the city the sophistication of Lombardian and Italian legal cultures that Germanic feudalism lacked. They were experts in the administration of ecclesiastical rents of Lombardian monasteries, and

[51] Reich, 'Documenti di Mezocorona,' p. 6.

[52] The Counts of Tyrol retained rights over pastures until A.D. 1499, when the legal dispute was finally solved. Curzel and Varanini, *La documentazione dei vescovi di Trento*, pp. 112–115; Vaj, *Notizie storiche della Valle di Fiemme*.

[53] For a history of the region, see Castagnetti, 'Enti ecclesiastici, Canossa, estensi famiglie signorili e vassallatiche a Verona e a Ferrara'; Corritore, 'Verona e Mantova nell'età comunale: Mercatum fori, granai privati'; Miller, *The formation of a medieval Church: ecclesiastical change in Verona*.

[54] Magister Romanus was a prominent canon under the rule of Bishop Adelpret. Fatolino, a notary from Verona, was also a member of the House of Canons, along with Odolrich of Arco, who worked with Bishop Adelpret in Riva. The bishop had vassals from Veronese villages, and had worked with two Verona men, one of whom had held the office of consul of Verona in A.D. 1144 and then in A.D. 1151, along with Carlassario. Moreover, a Veronese canon by the name of *Adriano* was present at Firmiano Castle when the bishop stayed in the castle in A.D. 1163, along with another Veronese man, Riprando, who was archpriest of the Chapter of the Cathedral. Castagnetti, *Governo vescovile, feudalità, 'communitas' cittadina*, pp. 107–108.

brought to Trent skills and knowledge needed for administering episcopal rents. A Veronese family by the surname *Bella* exercised criminal law in Trent from A.D. 1150 to 1225. Its members were secular judges working for the bishops.[55] It was *a potente famiglia*, in the words of Fabio Cusin, and which bishops kept close even if it meant sharing functions of political power.[56] Bishops owned various fiefs in the lands of the Chapter of the Cathedral of Verona, too. The Chapter of the Cathedral of Verona held rent claims over Bondo, Breguzzo, Bolbeno, and Zuclo villages by virtue of imperial diplomas obtained during the tenth and twelfth centuries.[57] It exercised rent rights and privileges over these villages until the last quarter of the thirteenth century, despite an attempted usurpation of lands and rights perpetrated by a branch of the Campo family in A.D. 1193.

The Monastery of Santa Giulia in Brescia held rent rights over forest in Lorina Valley and Mount Alpo, east of Storo. A female monastical culture flourished at Santa Giulia, in the service of Carolingian hegemony. Nuns were relentless in their exercised of rent rights, deepening lordly competition near the Garda region. The community of Storo contested forest rights held by the nuns, in a prolonged battle that lasted until the mid-eighteenth century, when the monastery agreed to transfer all contested rights to the community.[58] The commune of Brescia also enjoyed certain jurisdictional rights over vassals in Preore and Rendena in the Giudicarie, which it granted to the lords of Arco in A.D. 1186. Some of these rights originated in earlier processes of alienation of rights by villages attached to feudal *curtis*, which continued to unsettle the territoriality of power near Garda region, as the case of Preore illustrates. Preore paid rents to the commune of Brescia as well as the Arco lords (who administered justice in the community) still in A.D. 1319.[59]

[55] Mor and Schmidinger, *I poteri temporali dei vescovi in Italia*, p. 209.

[56] Members of the family of De la Bella appeared with high frequency as ministers and officers in the bishops' courts after the second half of the thirteenth century. Cusin, *I primi due secoli del Principato ecclesiastico*, pp. 121–122; Mor and Schmidinger, *I poteri temporali dei vescovi in Italia*, p. 210.

[57] Cagol, 'Le Giudicarie e la val Vestino: i Lodron e i da Campo,' pp. 115–116. Unless otherwise noted, the rest of the paragraph comes from this work.

[58] For more on female monasticism, see: Valone, 'Matrons and motives: why women built in early modern Rome'; West-Harling, 'Female monasticism in Italy in the early Middle Ages.'

[59] Curzel and Varianini, *La documentazione dei vescovi di Trento*, pp. 125–127; Malfatti, 'I confini dei Principato de Trent,' p. 17.

Competition for jurisdictions of rent rights was ongoing, shaping the class structure of society. At the top of the social hierarchy, lords competed against each other for grabbing higher shares of agrarian surpluses. At the bottom, a class of agrarian peasants and farmers, whose labor produced the surpluses that sustained the wealth of society, competed for distribution of surpluses. As seen before with the assassination of Bishop Adelpret, frequent episodes of violence were the norm rather than the exception.[60] The emperor denied the right to bear arms to monasteries in the region, which made parishes and monasteries of the Church of Trent more dependent upon the competitive dynamics that tied bishops to the Counts of Tyrol and the lords of Arco. Lords oftentimes 'acted from within' by infiltrating these communities, triggering contradictory political processes. Blood ties with vassals were a useful instrument in the warfare against bishops, exercised when aristocratic families 'infiltrated' rural villages by appointing illegitimate sons as lordly officers. As lordly officers but also vassals, their presence in villages prone to rebellions deepened lord-vassalage relations.[61]

The feudal institution of 'blood espionage' proved useful to other noble families besides the Counts of Tyrol. Mixing genetic pools with vassals was common in rural villages, according to Franceschini. After a major flood of the Sarca River in A.D. 1361, the community of Rendena relied upon Albert of 'the Campo Castle,' an illegitimate son of the Campo lord. This man finally settled the controversy. The lords of Lodron and Campo drew strength from rural communities which they infiltrated in various ways. They drew Alpine *rustics* for their military campaigns from their rural villages. Furthermore, bandits were prevalent in Rendena Valley in Giudicarie. They could be seen following the lords of Arco in their military campaigns against local noble families. Local sources studied by Franceschini referred to these bandits as *latrones et malefactores*, or men who spread terror in rural villages.[62] In sum, thefts, murders, kidnapping, and armed clashes never disappeared from the Giudicarie, where local rural lordly competition remained strong (Fig. 3.5).

[60] Franceschini, 'Castelli e campagne in area trentina,' pp. 203–204.
[61] *Idem*, p. 207.
[62] *Idem*, p. 204.

Fig. 3.5 Gold miner. From *Compendium Salernitanum*, by Matteo Platearius (c. A.D. 1161). In this fourteenth-century copy of the Compendium, a miner is portrayed wearing a colorful garb and mining for gold using a pickaxe. A distant cousin of the mattock, the pickaxe was personal property that could be pledged in rural pawnbroking shops in exchange for a small loan in coined money or its equivalent. The Morgan Library and Museum, N.Y.

The Intrusive Effect of Worldwide Economic Change

The invisible hand of economic change was propitious to the rule Bishop Wanga soon enforced unto the city and his competing lords. European population grew substantially from A.D. 1000 to 1347.[63] Alpine cities have nothing comparable to *Domesday Book* and its wealth of information on population growth rate, but historians have reached agreement on some useful numbers.[64] Grigg estimated that population increased in Italy from five million in A.D. 950 to eight million in A.D. 1300. Studying land clearance, rise of towns, and construction of cathedrals and parishes, he argues that population in France increased from 6.2 million in A.D. 1100 to 17.6

[63] Grigg, *Population growth and agrarian change: an historical perspective*, pp. 51–54.

[64] Fleming, *Domesday Book and the Law*; Jones, 'Domesday Book: an early fiscal, accounting narrative?'

million in A.D. 1328. More reliable figures for England and Wales show an increase from 1.5 million in A.D. 1086 to 4.5 million by A.D. 1340. Grigg concludes that annual average growth rate for continental Europe stood at 0.26 percent. His estimates seem consistent with numbers available for medieval pastoralist and agrarian settlements. Towns in coastal Flanders and Dender, Scheldt, and Lys valleys, whose inhabitants practice sheep farming, reached approximately 50,000 to 60,000 inhabitants in the thirteenth century.[65] Their rapid population growth imposed the need to expand the internal agrarian frontier. The need for land drove migration from southwestern Bavaria and Tyrol toward woodlands and valleys of Trent, Veneto, Friuli, and other Alpine valleys.[66] Immigration of *Welsches* or Germans to the region continued until the fifteenth century, when miners were allured by newly opened mines in the region.[67] Mining towns did not lag behind. They also experienced population growth in the thirteenth century. Kutná Horá or *Kuttenberg* in Bohemia had 18,000 inhabitants by the end of the century.[68] Towns in Germany experienced population explosion; there were over 200 towns in West German lands by 1200, of which 120 had gained 'embryonic urban character' a century earlier.[69]

Population figures for Lombardy show impressive growth. Milan, Venice, and possibly Genoa 'reached even 100,000 souls.'[70] Waves of migration contributed to demographic explosion in the region between A.D. 1000 and 1300—a high rate of growth second only to that of Holland and Flanders.[71] Available numbers show remarkable demographic expansion of Alpine and pre-Alpine settlements: 10,000 peoples spread between Treviso, Vicenza, Bergamo, and Novara. Higher numbers were possible in Verona and Brescia. By mid-thirteenth century, an estimated number of 30,000 to 35,000 inhabitants lived in Verona. During the demographic increase of the second half of the fifteenth century, there were 40,000

[65] Nicholas, 'Structures du peuplement, fonctions urbaines et formation du capital dans la Flandre médiévale,' p. 502.

[66] Barbiera and Dalla-Zuanna, 'Demographic systems of medieval Italy (6th–15th century AD),' p. 544.

[67] Braunstein, 'Les enterprises minières en Vénétie au XVe siècle,' p. 531; Irsigler, 'Rheinisches kapital in Mitteleuropäischen montanunternehmen des 15. und 16. Jahrhunderts'; Stromer, 'Nuremberg in the international economics of the middle ages.'

[68] Grigg, *Population growth and agrarian change: an historical perspective*, pp. 51–54.

[69] Dickinson, 'The development and distribution of the medieval German town,' p. 12.

[70] Postan (ed.), *The Cambridge economic history of Europe*, pp. 344–345.

[71] Curtis and Campopiano, 'Medieval land reclamation and the creation of new societies.'

inhabitants in the city. In Vicenza, the number increased by 15,000. In Brescia, the number of inhabitants increased to almost 50,000. In Trent, population increased by 5000 inhabitants in the same period.[72]

Income also expanded, deepening the integration of the continental European economy to Afro-Eurasian trade networks. Many decades ago, Carlo Cipolla remarked that income growth in the form of monetized rents led to 'real progress.'[73] Currency was abundant even when the silver content of the *denarius* fell from 1.7 grams of pure silver in the last years of the eight century to 0.35 grams in the early thirteenth century.[74] The stock supply of bullion was abundant, too, given the wave of mining booms that spread throughout European lands from the ninth to the fifteenth centuries. From the silver-bearing lead mines of Melle, which exploited an extensive galena deposit stretching over 47 square kilometers in Deux-Sèvres, western France, to the famous Goslar mines, ore-yielding lands joined the vast continental mosaic of reclaimed lands. Mints absorbed metals from the most fertile mines of the period.[75] Local and regional patterns of mining production and specialization tightened the nexus between income and population growth. Mining booms, more than crusading

[72] Varanini, 'Le relazioni istituzionali ed economiche fra città e montagna,' p. 126. For the enduring footprint of migration in the Adige region, see Coia, Boschi, Trombetta et al., 'Evidence of high genetic variation among linguistically diverse populations: a case study of the Italian Alps'; Destro Bisol, Anagnostou, Batini et al., 'Italian isolates today: geographic and linguistic factors shaping human biodiversity'; EAB, 'Effects of migrations: "closed holdings" on DNA of Alpine peoples.'

[73] Carlo Cipolla cited by Wolff, 'Monnaie et développement économique dans l'Europe médiévale,' p. 491, 495

[74] The number refers to the *denarius tournois*, which weighed 1.127 grams. Its fineness was less than 330/1000. The quantity of silver remained high (roughly 0.25 grams) for the *denarius* minted at Lucca and Pisa. Carlo Cipolla cited by Wolff, 'Monnaie et développement économique dans l'Europe médiévale'; Naismith, 'The social significance of monetization in the early Middle Ages.'

[75] Even if direct geographic and chronological relations between local mines and mints is still the subject of controversy. For case studies on the controversy, see: Allen, 'Silver production and the money supply in England and Wales, 1086–c.1500'; Dumas and Barrandon, 'Sur les traces de l'argent de Melle à l'époque carolingienne'; Wolff, 'Monnaie et développement économique dans l'Europe médiévale.' For Melle mines, see: Jeanne-Rose, 'Trouvailles isolées de monnaies carolingiennes en Poitou: inventaire provisoire'; Téreygeol and Dubois, 'Mines et métallurgie carolingienne à Melle (Deux-Sèvres): l'apport des charbons de bois archéologiques.' For Harz mines, see: Hemker and Burghardt, 'Medieval mining in Saxony—selected results from excavations'; Rehren, Bartels, and Schneider, 'Medieval lead-silver smelting in the Siegerland, West Germany'; Stöllner, 'Mining and economy.'

wars, proved detrimental to producers managing Banjahîr mines in north Kabul, Afghanistan, and the Shāmam mines in Najd in the Arabian Peninsula.[76] The progressive loss of productive advantages of these mining centers contributed to a reorientation of east-west silver trade routes, and related to hegemonic wars between the Mongol Empire and the Mamluks. New metal-trade routes in Cilicia in Lesser Armenia, Crimea, Cyprus, Egypt, India, and China increased world demand for European silver, adding further stimulus to income expansion in Europe. Furthermore, increases in the gold-silver ratio attracted a rush of silver (in various forms) to eastern Mediterranean markets and beyond.[77] This condition increased demand for European silver. 'Much of the silver which allowed Islamic mints to strike silver coins [in the thirteenth century] seems to have come from Europe'[78] (Fig. 3.6).

Population and income expansion were the most salient manifestations of a long-term cycle of capital accumulation under way, dominated by Genoese capitalists.[79] Genoese silver exports to Asia reached Seljuk rulers, who made consignments of European coins. Rulers ordered coins by weight rather than denominations. Merchants from Genoa shipped these coins from the port of Ayas to Sivas. Venetians also stamped ingots that arrived at Armenia, along with Bohemian silver that they exported to Cilician mints.[80] Seljuk Prince Levon established mints in Sīs, in the Tarsus region, which produced the tram, a coin of high silver content weighing 3 grams.[81] Mints in the Eastern Mediterranean imitated the Venetian silver grosso (weighing 2.18 grams), and some struck currencies of high silver

[76] Chaudhuri, *Trade and civilization in the Indian Ocean*, p. 39; Dunlop, 'Sources of gold and silver in Islam according to al-Hamdānī (10th century).'

[77] Bautier, 'L'or et l'argent en Occident de la fin du XIIIe siècle au début du XIVe siècle'; Lombard, 'Les bases monétaires d'une suprématie économique: l'or musulman du VIIe au XIe siècle'; Marchéville, 'Le rapport entre l'argent et l'or au temps de St Louis'; Noonan, 'The start of the silver crisis in Islam: a comparative study of Central Asia and the Iberian peninsula'; Watson, 'Back to gold -and silver.'

[78] Abu-Lughod, *Before European hegemony: the world system* a.d. *1250–1350*, p. 157; Smith, 'The silver currency of Mongol Iran,' pp. 16–17.

[79] For the role of Genoese capitalists in medieval cycle of capital accumulation, see Arrighi, *The long twentieth century*, pp. 86–129; Brătianu, *Actes des notaires génois de Péra et de Caffa de la fin du treizième siècle* offers rich of credit relations and 'wage-system' contracts that prevailed in Genoese colonies in the Levant.

[80] Sinclair, 'Some conclusions on the use of coins on the Ayas-Tabriz route,' p. 88, footnote 7; Smith, 'The silver currency of Mongol Iran.'

[81] Vauchez, Dobson, and Lapidge (eds.), *Encyclopedia of Middle Ages*, p. 418.

Fig. 3.6 Miners dig for rubies, in *Livre des merveilles du monde* (A.D. 1460). Marco Polo described the ruby mines of 'Balashan' or present-day Badakhshan, Afghanistan. 'The mines are embedded in the high mountains,' and the king forced his subjects to work them in 'the same manner as for gold or silver.' The portrayal of stylized bodies of miners, wearing immaculate white garbs, digging a spot protected by dragons, reveals the fascination with which fifteenth-century French artists absorbed of the book by Marco Polo. The Morgan Library and Museum, N.Y.

content (such as the gros of Tripoli, weighing 4.22 grams).[82] In the Rus Principality further to the east, cast silver bars known as *slitki* appeared as payments in international trade transactions. Merchants used *slitkis* as international form of payment from the twelfth to the mid-fifteenth centuries, after Novgorod ceased to cast silver bars in A.D. 1447.

Not only did money travel eastward, but circulated within the continental European economy where 'real progress' was in the making.[83]

[82] Papadopoulou, 'Betwixt Greeks, Saracens and Crusaders. Lusignan coinage and its place in the Eastern Mediterranean,' p. 484.

[83] Gunder Frank, 'The thirteenth-century world system'; Saccocci, 'L'introduzione dei grossi agli inizi del XIII secolo e la massicia esportazione di argento dall'Europa Occidentale ai territory islamici'; Wolff, 'The significance of the "feudal period" in the monetary history of Europe.'

Crusading wars contributed to this situation.[84] Outfitting and maintenance of armies was a costly enterprise. Some historians have estimated that between 8000 and 10,000 marks were needed annually to cover the costs of outfitting a contingent of 500 knight crusaders.[85] The sum included the value of horses, supplies, and wages, which from the twelfth century onward were paid in coined metals and goods instead of land donations. Money paid in wages returned to local markets, unleashing the intrusive effect of economic change. 'The northerners in general seem to have bought more goods from Italian merchants than they sold to them.'[86] Lasize, a commercial entrepôt in the southern shore of Lake Garda, received Asian goods sold by Venetian merchants who made a stop here on their way to Trent and Brescia. 'As early as 1140s and 1160s,' 'the Genoese could not pay or their imports from Sicily and southern Italy with the industrial products of northern Italy and transalpine Europe and had to pay for the majority of their imports in silver.'[87] Despite the negative balance of trade, Bolzano developed into a commercial city from its humble beginnings as a village founded by the bishops of Trent in the twelfth century.[88] Then, it was only a single market street, located in modern-day *rue des Portiques.*

European silver in ingots, bars, and coined traveled east and south of the continent.[89] But did so after finding markets in the mints that emerged in the period. Mints flourished in Bologna by A.D. 1219; Arezzo by A.D. 1250; Perugia in A.D. 1259; Messina in A.D. 1270; Milano, Piacenza, and Venice by A.D. 1300.[90] Pfennings struck at Friesach from silver of 'the first generation of thirteenth century mines,' traveled from the Bohemian kingdom to Venice during A.D. 1220 and 1241. From Venice, silver con-

[84] On war expenditures, see: Postan, 'Money, population and economic change in late medieval Europe,' p. 78. Dobb, 'The entrepreneur myth,' p. 69.

[85] Bird, Peters, and Powell, *Crusade and Christendom*, pp. 130–132, 139–140; O'Callaghan, *Reconquest and crusade in medieval Spain*, pp. 153–158; Maier, *Preaching the crusade*, pp. 123–134.

[86] Spufford, *Money and its use in medieval Europe*, p. 140.

[87] *Idem*, p. 146.

[88] Freschi, 'L'axe du Brenner,' p. 49.

[89] Spufford, *Money and its use in medieval Europe*, pp. 134–137.

[90] For an excellent summary of the literature of the period pertaining to metals, see Bork et al. (eds.), *De re metallica: the uses of metal in the Middle Ages*, pp. 327–343.

tinued its journey to Alexandria, Cyprus, Armenia, and Constantinople, in its way to Mongol-dominated markets in Central Asia. Asian merchants in the Black Sea accepted *virge sommorum argentari* that Italian merchants brought as payment for wheat, honey, wax, and slaves. The *sommorum* was a 'nearly pure silver bar' casted at the mints of Genoa and Venice with silver ores from Bergamo and weighed approximately 200 grams.[91] Genoese merchants in Messembria, Anchialos, Varna, Kaliakra, Vicina, Chilia, Licostomo, and Moncastro in the Black Sea exported these silver bars into Western Asia.[92] The southern and eastern European export route carried 'an immense flow of specie,' and accounted for large volumes of primary-commodity exchanges in Hungary, Poland, and northern Italy.[93]

European silver also followed a western continental route toward Central Asia. The route began with silver trades at the famous six fairs of Champagne. These bullion fairs 'followed one upon the other year after year.'[94] They functionally linked extractive hinterlands of Europe to the world of monetary exchanges.[95] Fairs attracted 'unminted' silver mined at the imperial fiefs of Styria, and Meissen, including Freiburg, and which traveled through Bruges and Cologne. Cologne became the principal bullion market of the twelfth century. Merchants in Cologne fairs paid in uncoined bullion known as *marc argenti de Ramesberch* in A.D. 1172–1178.[96] Silver also traveled to England through commercial dealings of merchants from Flanders, Brabant, and Cologne. Cloth and other goods traveled in the opposite direction, to Bohemia and Hungary, where merchants from Flanders and Cologne could be seen 'attending the fairs

[91] Mainoni, 'La politica dell'argento e del ferro nella Lombardia medievale,' p. 419.

[92] Day, 'Fiorentini e altri italiani appaltatori di zecche'; Grierson and Travaini, *Medieval European coinage*; Hernández Esteve (ed.), *Moneda y monedas en la Europa medieval*; Oberländer-Târnoveanu, 'The coinage of the Genoese settlements of the Western Black Sea shore and on the Danube'; Rogers, 'To and from, aspects of Mediterranean trade and consumption in the 15th and 16th centuries.'

[93] Spufford, *Money and its use in medieval Europe*, p. 136.

[94] Face, *The caravan merchants and the fairs of Champagne*, p. 3; Spufford, *Money and its use in medieval Europe*, p. 139.

[95] Mainoni, 'Fiscalidad directa e indirecta en la Italia medieval'; Saccocci, 'L'introduzione dei grossi agli inizi del XIII secolo e la massaccia esportazione di argento dall'Europa Occidentale ai territory Islamici,' p. 130, for a note about dual functions of thirteenth-century silver-coined metals; Watson, 'Back to gold-and silver.'

[96] Segers-Glocke, Witthöft and Black (eds.), *Aspects of mining and smelting in the Upper Harz*, p. 105; Spufford, *Money and its use in medieval Europe*, pp. 139–142.

at the mining-town of Golniczánya (Göllnitz) in Spiš (Zips).'[97] A third but less popular route was the open-sea specie route around the Iberian Peninsula. Galleys from Genoa, Venice, and Pisa traveled along the Mediterranean shores and journeyed northward, reaching England and Flanders. 'These brought specie from the north-west to Italy and their departures from Bruges in June and December were marked by *strettezza*, a scarcity of money.' Galleys in Flanders took advantage of the '*larghezza*, that is, money was easy to find in Bruges, in August and September, when merchants from Germany arrived in Bruges and brought in a flow of specie.'

Minting offered lords opportunities for additional gains. The Archbishop of Cologne, who had been chancellor of Emperor Frederick Barbarossa, enjoyed spectacular revenues related to the minting business. He mortgaged 'the income from his mints for a year for 1000 marks,' equivalent to an annual output of 'at least 13,000 marks.'[98] The number of new mints established by charter in this period is astonishing: around Freiberg, there were 25 mints by A.D. 1197, from only 9 mints in A.D. 1130, and reaching almost 40 by A.D. 1250. In A.D. 1135, only three cities had mints in the land belt stretching between the Alps and the Apennines. Seventy years later, the number grew to 12. Thirty-seven mints operated north of Rome by A.D. 1200, from only four mints in A.D. 1130. Most likely, old mints in northeast France and north Germany experienced a revival, as new 'semi-independent rulers' rose to power in Germany and France and 'usurped' coinage and minting rights (Fig. 3.7).

The relatively small size of Trent when compared to Genoa, Verona, or Milan was no impediment for the city to procure profits from regional silver-trade relations. Genoese and Lombard merchants frequently crossed the Alps through the Tonale and Duron passes on their way to northern European markets. Tuscan merchants traveled near Trent when reaching the fairs of Geneva, which were mentioned since A.D. 1262.[99] Silver from Monte Calisio possibly joined a popular trade route in the eastern boundary of the principality, which crossed the Tarvis Pass from Friesach. The route looks like a small circuit of trade but its effects on incomes cannot

[97] Spufford, *Money and its use in medieval Europe*, pp. 139–142.

[98] Jordan, *Goslar und das Reich im 12. Jahrhundert*, pp. 52–53, for the debt of gratitude felt by Henry IV to his hometown of Goslar; Wolff, 'The significance of the "feudal period" in the monetary history of Europe,' p. 81.

[99] Coativy, 'La montagne est-elle une frontière? Le témoignage de la circulation monétaire,' p. 43.

Fig. 3.7 Miners dig under the soil of Spain and attack demons, in *Livre des merveilles du monde* (A.D. 1460). Written in France, the book presents a mythical view of the East and the West, loyal to the spirit of the original book by Marco Polo and Rustichello da Pisa. The miniature shows miners digging deep under the earth and destroying demons planted into the land of Spain by Muslims. This xenophobic portrayal of Islam flourished in the Latin West, fueling the crusading zeal of the European ruling classes. In the left corner of the drawing, a miner digs a new shaft in land 'free' from demons. The Morgan Library and Museum, N.Y.

be underestimated.[100] The Patriarch of Aquileia north of the Alps imitated pfennings from Friesach when striking his own silver coins. Northern European silver traders reached Alpine cities following this trade route. They most likely bought silver from Monte Calisio and surrounding mines. Around the time of the Fourth Crusade, *Bernardus Teotonicus*, a merchant who bought silver from Alpine mines, 'had accumulated so much profit from the trade that he had become the richest foreigner in

[100] Spufford, *Money and its use in medieval Europe*, p. 136. The rest of the paragraph borrows heavily from this work.

Venice.' Moreover, Trent joined the heaviest Alpine-Lombardian trade route for bills of exchange in the fifteenth century, along with Cremona and Brescia. It was also a strategic city in the interregional trade route exploited by the Hanseatic League, and which connected Italy to Bolzano, Innsbruck, Augsburg, 'and from there over Würzburg, Eisenach, Goslar, and Brunswick to the Elbe and then toward Mollen and Old Lübeck' leading to Denmark and Scandinavian lands.[101]

Agrarian production in Trent added stimuli to silver trade networks. All sorts of commodities traveled through Alpine passes. *Parmigiani*, *lodigiani*, and *di grana* cheese, wine, salted fish, lard, olive oil, and timber crossed montane passes packed in barrels and containers made with local raw materials. Commodity traffic was so heavy that in many jurisdictions customs for dry goods were fixed based upon container and barrel weight rather than content, simplifying taxation on behalf of merchants.[102] As mentioned earlier, the Adige River itself was the shortest route connecting Bolzano to Verona, which speaks of 'the supreme importance which Emperors attached to having that city on their side.'[103] Only a 100-meter tract of navigable river waters separated Trent from Verona. Navigating from Castagnaro and Adighetto to the Gulf of Venice, where a channel was built in modern times, required only covering a distance equivalent to 200 meters.[104]

Marx wrote that commerce had 'everywhere more or less a dissolving influence on producing organisations,' but commerce deepened agrarian specialization in Trent.[105] The vibrant traffic of goods and people in these 'rugged and underdeveloped'[106] lands further stimulated specialization in livestock. Dependency upon imported cereals and foreign trade placed lords and vassals as participants in ever expanding local and regional divisions of labor. Trent sold livestock, hay, firewood, and timber from resinous trees, in exchange for cereals from the 'wheat basin' of the Po River plain.[107] Merchants from Bergamo, Brescia, Vicenza, and Verona domi-

[101] Gade, *The Hanseatic control of Norwegian commerce during the late Middle Ages*, p. 12.
[102] Pini, *Vite e vino del medioevo*, pp. 181–182.
[103] George, *The relations of geography and history*, p. 208.
[104] Massimo, *Corografia d'Italia*, p. 18.
[105] Marx, *Capital*, vol. 3 *The process of capitalist production*, p. 390.
[106] Lopez and Raymond (transl.), *Medieval trade in the Mediterranean world*, p. 95.
[107] Stenico, 'Signorie rurali e risorse economiche,' pp. 223–224.

nated grain imports. The *tesina* wool from Trent found local and regional demand. It was nevertheless of average and even low quality when compared to wool from Vicenza, Verona, and Padova, which was reputed to be of a superior quality well into the eighteenth century.[108] Uneven exchanges were pronounced in the last quarter of the thirteenth century, suggesting a cereal-production deficit that could not be solved without recourse to interregional trade networks. In A.D. 1482, the bishop of Trent negotiated a trade agreement with Venice whereby the bishop would buy grains from Veneto but Venice would deliver the grains to Riva in Garda. The terms were agreeable to the Doge of the Republic, since the bishop 'made the commitment to supply Venice with a quantity of saltpeter for the equivalent market value.'[109]

Bishops also responded to the ongoing 'commercial revolution' by promoting road and transport improvements. They inadvertently added a unifying economic element that sustained the ascent of marketable surpluses. Their goals were to attract traffic that generated toll revenues and strengthened the geopolitical role of the Imperial Church in the region. Roads provided safety to merchants and pilgrims alike. They also increased the value of real estate property including monasteries and churches, as Fiore describes.[110] Bishop Adelpret built a Romanesque church, expanding the installations of San Romedio Monastery near modern-day Sanzeno in Non Valley.[111] From 'a primitive chapel on the rock face, already an object of local veneration in the previous period,' the monastery underwent incessant expansion until the thirteenth century. Such was a good use to the *bannum* tax described earlier. The monastery attracted travelers that crossed the Brenner Pass heading to Verona and Lombardy. Emperor Frederick Barbarossa crossed this route in A.D. 1236, when on his way to Milan. Merchants crossed from Non Valley to Brescia and Lombardy through the road of the Church, in 'an area in which feudal possessions of the bishops were particularly dense and concentrated.'[112] Bishops also

[108] Varanini and Demo, 'Allevamento, transumanza, lanificio,' p. 282.

[109] Stenico, 'Signorie rurali e risorse economiche,' p. 224.

[110] Fiore, 'Luoghi sacri, pellegrinaggi e scambi tra i due versanti delle Alpi occidentali,' pp. 91–92.

[111] Perini, *Statistica del Trentino*, 2, p. 454.

[112] Fiore, 'Luoghi sacri, pellegrinaggi e scambi tra i due versanti delle Alpi occidentali,' p. 92.

improved secondary routes connecting the Adige Valley to Lombardy. This was especially the case from the twelfth century onward, when high volumes of traffic through the Brenner Pass demanded more functional arteries of trade in the region.[113]

The conditions above were the macro-regulators of the hegemonic competition that bonded the upper class together. These conditions did not lock lords into a path of self-destruction, nor they carved a wide opening of freedoms on behalf of the mass of value-producing labor. They surely added a progressive character to intra-class warfare, reorienting the interests of Bishop Wanga toward the ore-yielding lands of Monte Calisio. The intrusive effect of economic change had transformed Monte Calisio into a mountain of taxable wealth. Confronting fierce competition and dynamics of economic change he could not foresee, Bishop Wanga opted for digging the subterranean wealth of his district. The burden of debt and litigations left by Bishop Conrad forced Wanga to speedily focus on mining as a source of episcopal income.[114] An *invasione tedesche*, in the words of Carlo Cipolla, already laid the basis for his monopoly of mine gains, or so it seemed to Bishop Wanga.[115]

[113] To a large extent, this road policy reinforced the tendency toward disappearance of the *curtis* mentioned earlier, as roads promoted rise of market places. It is also possible that new transport demands revived some old market functions of the *curtis*, such as local storage and warehousing of agrarian commodities (especially oil). Leicht, *Studi sulla proprietà fondiaria nel medio evo*, p. 87.

[114] Kink, *Fontes Rerum Austriacarum*, p. 433.

[115] Cipolla, *Publicazzioni sulla storia medioevale italiana*, p. 253, footnote 1.

CHAPTER 4

Foreign Miners Battle Pit Waters

Miners found a world of opportunities in Trent. Allured by prospects of mining profits, German miners who settled in the Adige Valley were unlike any other form of agrarian labor. Undeniably, all labor produced value. But several historical conditions put miners above shepherds and peasant farmers. Miners had the benefit of accumulated experience and knowledge learned in other galena basins of Europe. They exploited mines in the Harz Mountains, Freiburg, Corvey, and Mansfeld in Saxony; Alsace in the Vosges Mountains; and various locations in the Sudetes in Poland.[1] Miners brought useful mining skills, ingenuity, and dexterity to war campaigns of the empire. Digging tunnels and trenches with the intent of besieging towers and building various *rotam* adapted to military scenarios were among the mining skills crucial to the success of armies. These men built 'formidable stone fortifications and ingenuous siege techniques' characteristics of European warfare.[2] Crusading wars against Islamic Andalusia, Eastern Europe, and

[1] Bailly-Maître and Benoît, 'Les mines d'argent de la France médiévale,' p. 34; Górecki, *Parishes, tithes and society in early medieval Poland*, p. 28; Graulau, 'Capitalist miners in feudal Europe: a commentary on Marxist agrarian history,' p. 598.

[2] *Idem*, p. 115.

J. Graulau, *Medieval Mining and Power in Thirteenth-Century Europe*, https://doi.org/10.1007/978-3-031-99239-1_4

Jerusalem and Palestine increased demand for men with these skills.[3] Relying upon men dexterous in the use of pickaxes and mills, aristocratic *milites* perfected the tactic of laying siege to cities.

A chronicle of the military campaigns of Emperor Otto I (r. A.D. 962–973) referred to the *terre Saxonica venas argenti aperverit.*[4] Possibly miners joined militarized groups not as conscripted labor despite their lower rank compared to the heavily armed mounted knights. Even if most miners went to war as vassals, their mining skills, ingenuity, and dexterity afforded a certain upward mobility.[5] Such limited mobility was rooted in the dynamic processes of class differentiation described earlier. *Milites* enjoyed autonomy, especially when *beneficium* was granted in reward for military service. The *Edictum de beneficiis* (A.D. 1037) by Emperor Conrad II granted *milites* juridical legitimacy.[6] This benefit consisted of alienation or privatization of public goods on behalf of members of *milites.* While *beneficium* increasingly disappeared from the twelfth century onward, it afforded certain privileges and liberties to military men.[7]

The triumph of a bellicose Carolingian Empire had placed a premium on mining labor. Along with this premium came a certain geographic mobility that agrarian labor lacked. Germanic emperors mobilized hundreds of *omni metallorii* from mining districts, sometimes by imperial decree. Imperial military campaigns put miners in contact with different landscapes dominated by *paludes et flumina* or marshes, swamps, and rivers, allowing miners to learn mining knowledge and skills. Moreover, in exchange for military service, Germanic emperors granted miners legal and political privileges, including the right to move freely in the territories of the empire. These privileges were not just rooted in complex relations of alliances, but in dynamic security threats built in a rural economy based upon monopolization of improved lands and rents. Kings and popes could

[3] Housley, 'European warfare (c.1200–1320),' p. 120.

[4] Knorn, *Dissertatio historica de metallifodinarum Hartzicarum prima origine et progressu*, pp. 6–7.

[5] Bradbury, *The medieval siege*, pp. 88–91; Cucini, 'Uno strumento da minatore dal territorio di Scarlino,' p. 732; D'Amato, 'Armi e strumenti di lavoro da Iasos,' p. 4; Squatriti, 'Digging ditches in early medieval Europe,' p. 18; Stiebel, 'Arms from the large Byzantine structure in area XV,' p. 157. For a discussion of Neolithic proto-types of the pickaxe, see Gógan, 'A perforated stone pickaxe from North East Louth.'

[6] Albertoni, *Vassalli, feudi, feudalismo*, p. 158.

[7] Bradbury, *The medieval siege*, pp. 88–91; Squatriti, 'Digging ditches in early medieval Europe,' p. 18.

mobilize large *milites*, increasing the premium on populations of miners who were 'employable' in times of war. This situation partially explains why Saxon miners were found everywhere in the military frontiers of empire, from Cracow to England, Hungary, France, Serbia, Bosnia, and as far as Scandinavian districts.[8] By the twelfth century, miners were found everywhere, building *vachum*, *actufus*, and *rotam* to exploit the subterranean wealth of the empire.[9]

Miners enjoyed advantages that originated in the rise of 'free mining towns.'[10] In no other historical period one finds such a strong European State backing of mining.[11] 'Free mining towns' granted rights and privileges to miners and their industry. Towns enjoyed 'rights to hold a market and to operate a mint.'[12] Economic functions of towns varied, as in the case of the *Siebenbürgen* or seven German towns west of the Transylvania basin. They attracted migrant miners and merchants who in time became town burghers.[13] Laws privileged 'pioneers' who colonized the most profitable ore-yielding lands by granting private rights to mining claims. Mining towns also emerged when emperors created 'new towns by imperial fiat.' Only in the Saxon side of the Erzgebirge range, 29 mining towns flourished during the twelfth and sixteenth centuries. 'As many as 54 percent of the towns founded there in the fifteenth and the first half of the sixteenth century were of mining origins,' noted Polish historian Danuta

[8] Fors, 'The limits of matter,' p. 110; Kovačević-Kojić, 'Les mines d'or et d'argent en Serbie et Bosnie'; Vergani, 'Lessico minerario e metallurgico dell'Italia nord-orientale,' pp. 55–56.

[9] Zammatteo, 'Le antiche miniere di Faedo,' p. 5, footnote 24.

[10] For more on this discussion, see: Hübner, *A history of Germanic private law*; Majer, 'Ore mining and the town of St. Joachimsthal/Jáchymov'; Molenda, 'Mining towns in Central-Eastern Europe in feudal times.'

[11] Spufford, *Money and its use in medieval Europe*, p. 75. See also: Bell, Brooks, and Moore, '*Cambium non est mutuum*: exchange and interest rates in medieval Europe'; Blanchard, *Mining, minting, and metallurgy in the Middle Ages, 3, Continuing Afro-European supremacy, 1250–1450*; Gorini, 'Aspetti della documentazione numismatica medievale nel Trentino-Alto Adige'; Patterson, 'Silver stocks and losses in ancient and medieval times'; Saccocci, 'L'introduzione dei grossi agli inizi del XIII secolo e la massicia esportazione di argento dall'Europa Occidentale ai territory islamici.'

[12] Spufford, *Money and its use in medieval Europe*, p. 75.

[13] The towns are Hermannstadt or modern-day Sibiu; Klausenburg or today's Cluj-Napoca; Kronstadt or Braşov; Bistritz or Bistriţa; Mediasch or Mediaş; Mühlenbach or Sebeş; and Sighişoara or Schässburg. Baedeker, *Southern Germany and Austria*, p. 331; Schröcke, 'Mining and German settlement in Slovakia,' p. 131; Steuer, 'Settlements in the southern Black Forest: castles and mining.'

Fig. 4.1 Miners dig a tunnel below a tower, a scene from *Confessio Amantis*, fourteenth-century copy, England. The legs of a miner can be seen while he crawls inside a shaft. Another miner looks at the King from the shaft entrance in the lower right corner of the illustration. A pair of 'happy feet' shown on the ground behind the tower suggests that a miner has comfortably crawled inside an inclined shaft. The Morgan Library and Museum, N.Y.

Molenda.[14] Although they were not all 'free towns,' they played vital economic and political functions on behalf of empire (Figs. 4.1 and 4.2).

Also, agrarian wealth of Trent was a magnet to miners seeking to escape economic crisis in towns north of the Alps. Intensive and long-term exploitation of agrarian land based upon the open field system led a

[14] Molenda, 'Mining towns in Central-Eastern Europe,' p. 175.

Fig. 4.2 St. Clare repulses the Saracens, a scene from the Diptych of St. Claire (ca. A.D. 1260), by Guido da Siena. The painting shows St. Claire displaying the Eucharist as a shield against Muslim soldiers. She is repelling their assault on the San Damiano castle, in Assisi, Italy. Soldiers and pickaxes fall from the tower, suggesting that mining tools and training were central to the rise of medieval warfare. Pinacoteca Nazionale, Siena, Italy. Photo Credit: Scala/Art Resource, N.Y.

'manuring gap' that lasted between 100 and 200 years in southwest Germany.[15] Populations in many German mining districts saw a drastic reversal of the conditions for social upward mobility that once characterized these towns. The adverse effects lasted between two and six generations, depending upon the town in question. Population expansion with its accompanying changes in land-tenure systems pushed families to leave their natal towns in search for better economic opportunities. Such migration trend had accelerated by the beginnings of the thirteenth century. Trent offered geographic and geological conditions that made it attractive to foreign miners. It was the periphery of autonomous and urban city-States of demographic weight, a condition that suggested openness and rural autonomy. Overall, miners escaping crises found in Alpine valleys a world relatively opened to migration and 'linking them to the larger urban world.'[16]

Lastly, Trent offered an auspicious legal and political climate for the growth of mining. Restoring unity to the episcopate by re-claiming rent rights and privileges was the goal of Wanga. Such a goal required a strong rule of law and politics. The bishop was determined to solve the debt crisis created by his predecessor.

Mining the Ore Veins of Monte Calisio Mountain

Much of the legal framework for the takeoff of mining operations was already built when Wanga came to power. As part of their legitimate exercise of public authority, predecessors of Wanga granted mining rights to free miners.[17] The mining laws contained in *Codex Wangianus* first mentioned *silbrarii* or free miners in reference to a contract of the year A.D. 1185, when the city was governed by Bishop Albert of Campo (r. A.D. 1183–1188).[18] The bishop most likely maintained extraction and smelting operations previously undertaken by his predecessor Bishop Salomon (r. A.D. 1173–1183). Evidence of the mining interests of Bishop Salomon

[15] Schreg, 'Late medieval deserted settlements in Southern Germany,' pp. 163–165.

[16] Lynch, *Individuals, families, and communities in Europe, 1200–1800*, p. 35.

[17] For *iura regalia*, see: Mainoni, 'La politica dell'argento e del ferro nella Lombardia medieval,' p. 422, footnote 20.

[18] Curzel and Varanini, *La documentazione dei vescovi di Trento*, pp. 122–127, 184–187; Kink, *Fontes Rerum Austriacarum*, p. 96; Sperges, *Tyrolische bergwerksgeschichte*, pp. 263–265. For a general commentary about *silbrarii*, see Braunstein, 'Les statuts miniers de l'Europe médiévale,' p. 42.

come from a document dated May 31, 1181, by which *Federicus*, Count of Eppan, and his brother *Enricus* renounced their allodial rights to the ore-yielding lands of Tassullo.[19]

The contract revealed the scale and magnitude of lordly competition for the gains of improved mines. Bishop Salomon had taken over the government of the city, after the scandalous events that led to the assassination of Bishop Adelpert. The emperor and canons loyal to the empire felt the urgency of bringing order and stability to a situation that undermined geopolitical interests in the region. The Tassullo contract settled a dispute between the bishop and the Count of Eppan. However, it did so to the benefit of the Count. It stated that Bishop Salomon paid 1400 Veronese pounds to the Counts for *vena auri fodienda in Tasule*.[20] The 'purchase' transaction meant that Bishop Salomon 'possessed' the investiture of the mine as part of his rights over the district. But in reality, the bishop granted the 'mining fief' of Tassullo to the Count, who gained feudal rights over the mine. Besides the confirmation of the investiture rights of Bishop Salomon over Tassullo, the bishop gained jurisdictional rights in Non Valley. Rights included unspecified rights over a castle 'situated over the rock of Grifenstein' and its annexed villages; usufruct rights for the Renon forest, with the exception of an ancient fief that belonged to the Counts; and jurisdiction over a feudal *curtis* in Vadena. The Counts of Eppan obtained in exchange confirmation of jurisdictional rights over Tassullo and other feudal lands they claimed under their dominions. The Counts of Eppan, however, retained access and jurisdiction of the castle, forcing a successor of Bishop Salomon to revisit this matter.[21]

The contract included the following warning to the Count of Eppan and his brother: 'If they do not put an end to the dispute and show to be satisfied, nor observe the articles of this agreement, the Counts themselves and their heirs are bound to pay a fine of 2000 Veronese pounds to the bishop and his successors; after the payment of the fine the agreement will be maintained and ratified.'[22] The Count and his brother consented to 'bring their children to swore oath [of fidelity to the bishop] when they reach the age of fourteen, if it were necessary.' The contract was a sale of

[19] Castagnetti, *Governo vescovile, feudalità, 'communitas' cittadina*, pp. 120–122; Curzel and Varanini, *La documentazione dei vescovi di Trento*, pp. 154–157; Kink, *Fontes Rerum Austriacarum*, pp. 41–42.

[20] Kink, *Fontes Rerum Austriacarum*, p. 432.

[21] Castagnetti, *Governo vescovile, feudalità, 'communitas' cittadina*, pp. 125–126.

[22] Curzel and Varanini, *La documentazione dei vescovi di Trento*, pp. 154–157.

mining rights in exchange for a one-time money payment. The sum of 1400 Veronese pounds suggests that Tassullo enjoyed a high market value, which included the mining labor premium mentioned earlier. By the year A.D. 1180, Tassullo had a church administered by the Dean of Cles in Non Valley and a court administered by the bishop of Trent.[23] This feature suggests that mineral profits and rents were high, corresponding to progress of improvement of nearby agrarian lands. Moreover, gold outputs of Tassullo possibly found their way to the metal trade flows described earlier, in which gold could be sold at a profit. Commercial relations between bishops and southern Italy and Islamic and Mediterranean 'gold-based markets' were unconstrained by religious orthodoxy.[24] The nobility and especially its entrepreneurial lords were familiar with the 'mixed system' in which silver- and gold-based currencies circulated side-by-side, and avidly sought to benefit from favorable market conditions.

New workings appeared when the Count of Eppan donated the mines of *mons arçentarie* or Monte Calisio to Bishop Adalbert. The Count ceded to the bishop his rights over mines and vassals from the villages of Breguzzo, Bondone, and Tione.[25] Dated August 27, 1185, the contract stated the following:

> In the name of God. On the day Tuesday, the fifth of August, and in the presence of *Arnoldi*, canons of Trent, lords *Ieremie* of Terviso, *Willelmi* of Calavino, *Zucolini* of Verona [...] and others. *Henricus*, Count of Eppan, irrevocably resigns and grants to Lord Adalbert, venerable Bishop of Trent, all that belongs to him in Breguzzo and Bondo and in all parishes of Tione, and declares that all that he holds or possesses within *Durun* [Duron Pass, near Campo Castle], wherever his possessions are located, in any place in the mountain and in the entire valley, and the silver mines and miners, with all rights and honors [...] and with the vassals that live in the said places, excepting, however, *Galapino* of *Ludrun* [Lodron], *Gumpone* of Madruzo and *Bozone* of *Stenego* [Stenico] and vassals who are his *milites*. For rescinding his rights [...] the said Bishop invests Count *Henricus ad rectum feudum* with his right to the one-tenth of the tithes of Laces [...] for the Count to enjoy and possess in perpetuity, with all rights and honors [...].[26]

[23] Curzel, *Le pievi trentine, trasformazioni e continuità nell'organizzazione territoriale*, p. 151.

[24] Kelleher, 'From the Commercial Revolution to the Black Death (c.1150–1350).'

[25] Curzel and Varanini, *La documentazione dei vescovi di Trento*, pp. 172–174; Kink, *Fontes Rerum Austriacarum*, pp. 438–439.

[26] Curzel and Varanini, *La documentazione dei vescovi di Trento*, p. 173.

The bishop agreed to advance 800 Veronese pounds in exchange for *argentariam et homines*. He pledged the curia of *Domo* and San Paolo of Eppan, which the Count would own *sine vi aut impedimento aliquo*. The price tag of 800 Veronese pounds for jurisdictional rights over Breguzzo, Bondo, and Tione was by no means an immodest amount of money. Along with the price paid for Tassullo, these sums of money indicate high capital valorizations rising from ore-yielding lands. Vassals of the villages swore loyalty to the bishop. They promised to defend the bishop and his property against enemies. The grant confirmed the right of the Church of Trent to execute imperial sentences dictated against dissidents or vassals 'unwilling to declare loyalty to the empire.'[27] The bishop, however, had no right over the *familia*, feudal vassals, *milites*, and property of *Galapino*, *Gumpone*, and *Bozone*. Just like the Tassullo contract, this act revealed the world of hegemonic competition that paved the way for the spectacular growth of mining. The bishop gained mining rights, but the secular lord asserted territoriality of power through the *ius pignoris* right mentioned in the document. The *ius pignoris* was the right to hold a non-possessory interest, in this case over courts and rents of *Domo* and Saint Paul. By virtue of this clause, the agreement was a transfer of asset management from one lord to the next without the need to transfer ownership, and 'without recourse to violence or imposition.'[28] It was a debt incurred by the bishop, which explains why *fideiussores* or creditors from Cagnao and Firmiano were mentioned in the document.

Drainage works appeared in mining acts immediately after Bishop Wanga was elected Prince-Bishop in A.D. 1207. Grouped under a total of four contracts titled *carta de postis argenterie et montis*, this was the first set of private rights granted by Wanga to a *consilium suprascriptorum wercorum* for improving Monte Calisio mines.[29] The first contract in this group is an extensive agreement that contains 22 items and which defines rights and obligations of *silbrarii*. Under the pressure of ongoing changes in territoriality of power in the south of the district, Wanga had no time to waste. *Silbrarii* were members of *consilium wercorum* or mining corporation that exploited Monte Calisio mines. Their membership in the *consilium* required a sworn oath, which in turn supported the citizenship status

[27] Voltelini, *Giurisdizione signorile*, p. 26.

[28] Verhagen, 'The evolution of *pignus* in classical Roman law, *Ius honorarium* and '*ius novum*,' p. 51.

[29] Curzel and Varanini, *La documentazione dei vescovi di Trento*, pp. 350–351.

of all *socii affidati* of the corporation. Such was the intent of the following legal formula added to the act: *omnes werki, qui haben rotas et qui ad rotas laborant arçenterie, debeant habitare in civitate et cives Tridentini esse.*[30] This requirement shows the progressive spirit of autonomous communes crawling into the mining laws of Wanga. Such was unavoidable impact of the ongoing and troublesome relations between Trent and the rest of the Lombardian world. Represented in the phrase *sea, sea, sea, silbrarii* proclaimed the oath in the presence of noblemen and canons who served as witnesses to the legal act. The legal phrase was for all intents a promise to keep peace in territories under the jurisdiction of the bishop. It represented the feudal mode of building the juridical foundations for the rise of mineral profits and rents but also the alienation of the mass of value-producing labor from these gains. In exchange, *silbrarii* obtained ample rights and liberties. It was not a relation of vassalage, but a commercial relation between a lord and entrepreneurs that nominally guaranteed gains for both parties in the form of rents for the former, and profits and political retribution for the latter.[31]

Once a *silbrarius* joined a corporation, his main obligation was paying for the running expenses of mining and smelting on a weekly basis. This meant sharing the costs of infrastructure repair, mine improvements, and ore extraction and smelting, revealing a remarkable business organization.[32] At the top of the business hierarchy there was the group of *silbrarii* members of the *consilium* and owners of mining shares. Subordinated to *silbrarii*, chief engineers were responsible for deciding over matters related to mine geometry and infrastructure works. They most likely received payment in currency. These engineers came from the group of *omni werki* or free miners of Germanic lands. Engineers were responsible for ensuring that mining works ran smoothly. They communicated directly with *silbrarii* and also built hydraulic structures such as drainage ponds and ore-stamping mills. Although documentary evidence is scanty, it is safe to assume that their experience, skills, and technical knowledge made them long-term employees of the *consilium*. As such, they were a small but important group of miners whose high labor cost added to the expenses of the *consilium*.

[30] *Idem*, p. 352.

[31] Decades later, Italian merchant and banking houses of the Bardi and Peruzzi followed the same tradition in 'foreign' territories. De Roover, *Money, banking, credit in medieval Bruges*; Sapori, *Studi di storia economica medievale.*

[32] Braunstein, 'Les statuts miniers de l'Europe médiévale,' p. 42.

The bulk of labor-sustaining capital valorizations gained by the business stood below the privileged group of skilled miners. It included skilled and unskilled laborers who performed the various processes needed for improvement of mines. Working under the supervision of foremen or *scaffiatore*, a group of miners dug and sank *xafetus* or shafts and tunnels. This group of miners did the mining work per se of extracting crude ores, which necessarily entailed different degrees of specialization and skills. Miners possibly worked extraction shafts for five to six days per week, in two daily shifts, each of eight-hour duration. Such was the practice in other mining districts.[33] The most skilled miners among this group were essential to the operations of the *consilium*. At the bottom of the hierarchy, there was a diverse group of workmen, from miners to shovelers, windlass men, ore-washers, ore-hammerers, ore carriers, smelters, and other laborers performing manual tasks. *Laboratores* were part of this group. They were most likely seasonal labor, and thus remained bonded to other economic activities besides mining. This group included craftsmen but also local *rustici* needed for guarding the transport of ore from mines to local smelting sites and from there to local and regional markets. The task of guarding cargoes was especially relevant considering the frequent episodes of violence integral to the competitive dynamics of this rural society. This diverse mass of value-producing labor stood at the bottom of the social hierarchy. Its alienation from economic gains and privileges enjoyed by *silbrarii* was the basis of the mining business.

The most significant characteristic of the mining *consilium* was its shareholding structure. The *consilium* divided each mine into 16 *partem* or shares, each share representing a fixed amount of money invested by *silbrarii* in a specific shaft or section of a mine. Calculated on a weekly basis, the cost of 16 shares equaled the total expenditure in mining works.[34] Suddenly, improvement of ore-yielding lands introduced a method for estimating gains possibly borrowed or developed alongside the world of high trade. Just like Lombardian *societates* specializing in grain trade and Genoese merchant houses monopolizing long-distance silver trade, the *consilium* defined its own rules pertaining to share ownership. This economic and legal autonomy revealed a genuine interest in guaranteeing longevity of the mining enterprise. If *silbrarii* delayed or neglected payments for his share of expenses and other members had to cover the bill,

[33] Graulau, *The underground wealth of nations.*
[34] Curzel, *Il Codice Vanga*, pp. 172–173, 184–187, 350–354.

he was responsible for reimbursing expenses. Depending upon specific circumstances, this could end his participation in mining works. However, defaulters had 15 days to bring their shafts into production and settle debts with the rest of the corporation—*et qui per XV dies non bareitaverit, et partem suam raitungi tenuerit laboratoribus, cadat a sua parte.*[35] A shareholder could rescind from participating in further investments but could only do so after canceling his debts to the *consilium*. Outstanding debts led to share transfers among members of the *consilium*.

Silbrarii calculated prices of mining shares based upon expenses of the mine. The latter included costs commonly known as 'lost to the mine,' such as permanent damages to infrastructure created by unforeseen events such as wars. Assuming that mine costs in Ardesio (located between Garda and Cuomo Lake) represented the general price tendency, each mining share reached a minimum cost of 25 *denarii*. The figure comes from a census done in A.D. 1217, by the bishop of Bergamo. The bishop of Bergamo owned the mine of Ardesio since A.D. 1077–1080, after purchasing mining rights from the local lords of Martinengo.[36] He had ordered that any man holding a mine claim for a period of six months was mandated to pay a *fictum* of one ounce of silver or its equivalent in market price (25 pounds of the Veronese mark).[37] Assuming that shareholders paid 25 *denari* each, after deduction of mine expenses, the bishop collected 400 *denari* as rent. This sum was by no immodest amount of money. Still, the number only represents expenses of production, and says nothing of the level of profits for the entire Bergamo region.

Estimating real costs of production were less problematic than grasping the value generated in the bundle of economic relations that governed prices of shares. Albeit rooted in the world of commodity production, shares were not commodities. They were notarized documents that represented quantities of value. As such, shares became legal tenders of value, ultimately dependent upon the success of mining operations. What made a shareholding business lucrative was this peculiar

[35] Curzel and Varanini, *La documentazione dei vescovi di Trento*, p. 352; Kink, *Fontes Rerum Austriacarum*, Doc. No. 239, p. 448.

[36] Zammatteo, 'L'arte mineraria sulle Alpi centrali e la diffusione delle idee nei secoli XII-XIV,' p. 42.

[37] The law was 'consistent with *consuetudo Ardesii*.' Mainoni, 'La politica dell'argento e del ferro nella Lombardia medieval,' p. 435.

economic function, which allowed producers to benefit *simultaneously* from demands and supplies of currency as well as demands and supplies of minerals. In the case of Monte Calisio, most likely minerals included lead besides silver ores. Demand for money came from the fact that a share represented an anticipation of profits redeemable at a specified time, specifically after miners extracted, smelted, and sold silver ores. Trade profits allowed *silbrarii* to estimate the money value of each share, which was equivalent to the credit value of each share (minus the time-function profits that amounted to a fixed percentage determined by money lenders, as mentioned earlier). This estimation was also the basis for buying and selling the mine claim represented in the share. On the other hand, demand for commodities came from the fact minerals were the produce of an improved mine, thus, they were the economic basis and ultimate source of value of each share. This peculiar function of shares suggests that *silbrarii* belonged to a world dominated by commodity-trade dealers and money-changers, besides silver mines.[38] These conditions strengthened the economic autonomy of *silbrarii* with respect to local feudal laws, but deepened their vulnerability to the invisible hand of world economic change.

Also, shareholding relations strengthened internal capabilities of small businesses exploiting local comparative advantages. One of the most significant business advantages was that members of the *consilium* handled ore sales. Because ore trade was the sphere of monopolies, *silbrarii* had opportunities to profit from bullion arbitrage. Mining laws of Bishop Wanga had this monopoly bias built in the definition of rights and obligations of the *consilium*. The corporation retained jurisdiction in matters related to digging through *fulumberg* and ventilation shafts.[39] Certainly, Bishop Wanga imposed general restrictions in areas of mine geometry, ore sales, and oversight of mining works. Ten *passus* was the minimum distance required between shafts if miners wanted to avoid the penalty of *L libras* (50 pounds). The law required miners to open slits in shafts prune to be affected by flooding and poisonous vapors. When disputes emerged over mining traffic in tunnels connecting shafts, miners had to reach

[38] De Roover, *Money, banking and credit in medieval Bruges*, pp. 13–14. For more on this point, see Cameron, 'Banking in the early stages of industrialization'; Sapori, *Studi di storia economica medievale*.

[39] Curzel and Varanini, *La documentazione dei vescovi di Trento*, p. 354.

agreement on their own. If miners failed to reach agreement, the *gastaldia* of the mines settled the controversy but miners paid a fine of *XXV libras.*[40] They also paid *C soldi* to the *gastaldia.*[41] Wanga also prohibited miners from carrying *fraudulenta arma* or weapons to mine workings. The bishop prohibited ore sales outside the designated market of the city and at night when *gastaldia* was off-duty. An exception was made for cases where drainage works required *silbrarii* to stay in Monte Calisio. Violations to trade regulations incurred a severe penalty: loss of silver ores. If and when caught, the ore buyer paid a fine of 10 Veronese *denarii.* The ore seller paid a fine of 100 *soldi.*[42] A *silbrarii* that refused to pay these fines faced 'extreme punishment.'[43] Furthermore, shareholders accepting money in advance for metal outputs were bound to sell to those who made such payments. Under no circumstance, the original shareholder could rescind from the sale of his share once he collected payment.

It was in the realm of production where *silbrarii* built the monopolies that sustained the exclusive privileges of mining corporations. The first monopoly pertained to drainage works. Evidence of a monopoly of drainage works only survived because of a dispute that emerged between *silbrarii* working the *mons Vace* extraction site of Monte Calisio. In A.D. 1213, the *actufus* or drainage works owned by *Gandi et Odolricis societatis* prompted the bishop to intervene to settle the controversy. The contract mentioned *discordie apparerent inter dnos de actufo Vace.*[44] The text explains none of the reasons for the disagreement that divided *silbrarii.* However, it states that the *consilium* that invested in drainage works was dissolved, and a new *consilium* was formed taking its place. *Silbrarii* members of the new *consilium* included residents from *Dosso*, and a man surnamed *Calespergarium*, among others. They agreed to drain *mons Vace* as part of exploratory excavation works in an area to the 'right side of the transport tunnel of the mining works,' as to induce a 'proper transfer of water from the flooded area into a drainage adit to be sunk at a lower level.'[45] The contract contains no further observations about transferring

[40] Kink, *Fontes Rerum Austriacarum*, Doc. No. 238, p. 446.
[41] Kink, *Fontes Rerum Austriacarum*, Doc. No. 237, p. 444.
[42] *Idem*, p. 435.
[43] *Idem*, p. 448.
[44] Kink, *Fontes Rerum Austriacarum*, Doc. no. 241, pp. 450–452.
[45] Kink, *Fontes Rerum Austriacarum*, Doc. no. 240, pp. 449–450.

water outside the mine. However, it added several technical conditions that allow one to see how *silbrarii* building drainage works had the last word. The bishop warned the old *consilium* against any damage to drainage works. The law prohibited following ore veins in the direction of the planned drainage canal, especially mining works of the old *consilium*. The bishop warned the old *consilium* that extraction shafts that interfered with function and construction of the planned drainage canal were forbidden. Any *silbrarii* that hampered the planned drainage canal faced severe punishment (Figs. 4.3 and 4.4).

The goal of the contract was to protect the new private drainage works *in integrum*. For this purpose, Bishop Wanga added that *silbrarii* owning mining claims in the mountain enjoyed the right to use the drainage canal of the new *consilium*, but such right was conditioned to maintaining the drainage tunnel in good state and operations. This astonishing condition meant that anticipating and responding to water-structural issues affecting the operations of the drainage canal was a shared obligation of all miners. The latter nominally exempted the new *consilium* from recurrent expenses

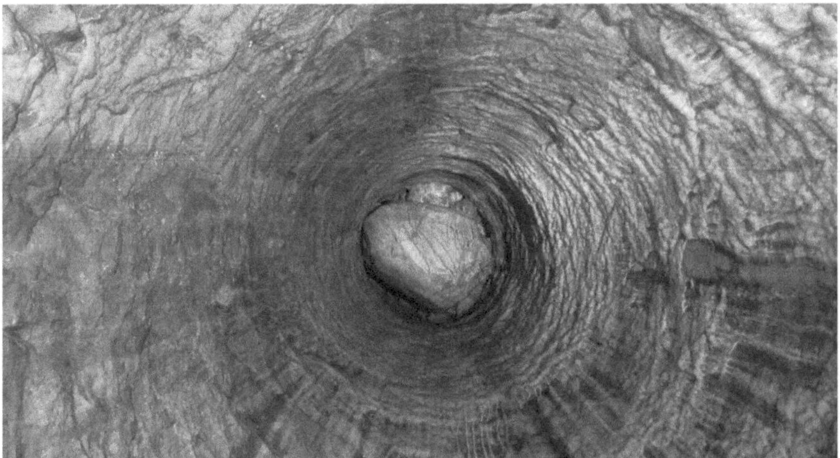

Fig. 4.3 The Pozza di Damocle shaft, Canopa delle Acque mine, Monte Calisio. Upward view of the shaft, which is blocked by a large rock. Courtesy of Martin Straßburger, Mining Archaeology Consultancy

Fig. 4.4 A shaft in Doss del Cuz mine in Monte Calisio. Upward view of the vertical shaft. Miners carved double lamp niches out of the rock near the bottom of the shaft. Courtesy of Martin Straßburger, Mining Archaeology Consultancy

associated with safeguarding tunnel drainage operations. The bishop also prohibited sinking shafts near the drainage canal if these blocked access to the drainage site. He ordered new shafts to keep a distance of three *pasus* from the drainage canal, which was needed for the transport of miners and crude ores.

The contract also prohibited miners from abandoning a section of the mine that required drainage for the sake of pursuing newly discovered veins in different areas of the same mine. Violators faced an astonishingly high penalty -*CCC libras denariorum veronensium*, revealing the importance of drainage works. The contract also mentioned a tribunal of technical experts whose duties included settling controversies related to drainage works.[46] It is not an exaggeration to claim that *silbrarii* developed the prototype of this tribunal, and the contract legitimized its presence. The tribunal was not intended as at enlarging the jurisdiction of the bishop, but rather provided a political instrument to reduce inherent antagonisms

[46] Curzel and Varanini, *La documentazione dei vescovi di Trento*, p. 448.

and tension of capital. The contract also stipulated that the bishop was entitled to receive a fixed revenue (as a specific amount of ores delivered to the city), but only after technical experts appointed by the *consilium* assessed silver content of ores. The bishop had no role to play in appointing these experts.

The second monopoly that enlarged mining profits was smelting works.[47] As described earlier, smelting was an economy that relied upon spatial concentration of productive activities. More so in a polarized rural society where hegemonic competitive for land and rents triggered violence from *milites* and bandits alike. Maintaining smelting and cupellation factories fully supplied, and operating above 'natural' market prices, was a precondition for mining production. Fertility of mines depended upon well-running smelting factories. The castles that surrounded Monte Calisio were the safest refuge for furnace and smelting equipment. They were a comparative capital cost advantage that this rural economy granted to the mining industry, in response to the ongoing integration of this economy to worldwide economic change. Archeological and documentary evidence indicates that Valsugana castles on the eastern side of Monte Calisio were employed as smelting sites. These castles included the Bosco Castle, located south of the village by the same name; Telvana Castle, a modest fortification that had a tower reaching 26 meters of altitude; Vedro Castle further north, near modern-day Civezzano; and Roccabruna Castle in Fornace.[48] Archeologists believe that these sites were built in the villages of Montevaccino and near Fornace Castle. The toponym 'Fersina' suggests that the riverine valley once hosted furnaces used for lime burning.[49] Near the Fersina River, a village named *Slacche* also suggests a history of smelting activities.[50] The castles were fortifications built at high altitudes, offering the additional advantage of defense. Their relatively small size when compared to Tyrol Castle imposed adaptations to smelting and fur-

[47] *Idem*, p. 433.

[48] Cavada and Pasquali, 'Aspetti di cultura materiale medioevale a Castel Bosco presso Civezzano (Trento),' p. 141, footnote no. 3.

[49] Cortese, 'Opifici idraulici per la lavorazione del ferro nel comprensorio del Monte Amiata'; Farinelli, 'Le risorce minerarie,' p. 42; Jannon and Trento, *Manufatti e fabricatti legati all'antico uso dell'acqua*, p. 9.

[50] Martin Straßburger, 'About Monte Calisio' Zoom video-meeting and emails to Jeannette Graulau, September 9–10, 2024.

nace equipment. Most likely, the *rotam* built in castles for ore-grinding purposes were relatively small, but with enough energy output as to sustain the growth of Monte Calisio operations.[51] Castles became factories that produced not only refined ores for different markets but also reused and recycled unwanted minerals needed for the making of irons, knives, blades, arrow heads, hooks, rings, and other inexpensive goods. This vital economic function also enhanced the value of castles, tightening the nexus between mining and land development. The weighty matter of lordly competition was at stake in each castle employed in mining operations. Mostly in ruins today, the Bosco Castle belonged to a vassal of the Campo lords since A.D. 1187. It offered a politically safe space for *gastaldia* to estimate silver yields of mining works, and collect taxes due to Bishop Wanga. The bishop confirmed investiture rights for the Bosco Castle to brothers *Giacobino* and *Ottolino* of *Bosco* in A.D. 1213.

Gains of drainage and smelting works were consolidated when Bishop Wanga mortgaged the *gastaldia* of the mines the following year. An act on January 7, 1214, established that Bishop Wanga mortgaged the *gastaldia* of the mines for the amount of *duobos mille libris denariorum veronensis monete* (2000 pounds of Veronese *denarii*) to *Albertum de Selano*, *Riprandinum Otonis Richi*, and *Odolrico Rambaldi*.[52] Wanga promised to pay back the loan in installments of *CC libras* (200 Veronese pounds) every year from *ficto montis et rotarum* or mineral rents from Monte Calisio. *Silbrarii* granted this loan because profits were high, and the turmoil of political competition restricted the power of the bishop to impose a monetary or credit policy that could hinder their profits. The transaction meant that the bishop 'sold' certain functions of *gastaldia*, but in no way Wanga renounced his jurisdictional rights over Monte Calisio. The contract added that the bishop had the right to impose fines 'whenever he wishes and it pleases him,' and punish *gastaldia* 'at his own will, if he finds them committing fraud.' *Silbrarii* had no freedom to extort the bishop either, at least nominally. The contrast was explicit that 'the lord bishop should not give them any more that what is owed to them, except to lord Albert of Selano, to whom the bishop is bound [...] for the wine that the

[51] On the subject, see: Jannon and Trento, *Manufatti e fabricatti legati all'antico uso dell'acqua*, p. 20; Molenda, 'Technological innovation in Central Europe between the XIVth and the XVIIth centuries,' p. 67; Munro, 'Industrial energy from water-mills in the European economy,' pp. 234–242; Reynolds, 'Medieval roots of the Industrial Revolution,' p. 125.

[52] Curzel and Varanini, *La documentazione dei vescovi di Trento*, p. 481.

said Albert gave to the lord bishop.'[53] The transfer of *gastaldia* to the trio mentioned above was based on the *posessionem pignoris* right that also emerged in dealings with castles and agrarian rents, and which meant transference of usufruct rights only. Later in the same year, the bishop confirmed an investiture of *ficto rotarum arceterie* to *Wisca* from *Casalino* in Pergine (right on the eastern border of the city). The *fictum* was equivalent to 100 *soldii.*[54]

The fact that *silbrarii* knew conditions of production and organization of works gave them an unrivaled advantage that they exploited only under the economic conditions at stake. Knowing about technical and organizational aspects of mining was not enough to command monopoly power over the gains of mines. Trade and money relations in the business circles in which *silbrarii* operated, in the context in which increasing agrarian surpluses including money commodities had positive impacts in the general levels of prices, were all factors that conspired to restrict the political choices available to Bishop Wanga. Appropriating mine surpluses by relying upon *milites* was not an option available to Wanga, especially when closeness and business secrecy of commodity-trading houses such as the *consilium* led to 'continuous refinement' of production strategies.[55]

In his last mining act on July 20, 1214, Bishop Wanga assumed a stronger interventionist role in the rising mining industry of Trent. He established that *concii sociorum* who died without heirs relinquished all mining shares to the bishop. This condition applied to mining works of Trent.[56] Attempting to stop what already was business conduct among *silbrarii*, Wanga warned the *consilium* against claiming ownership of those shares. He added that any *werco* holding 'illegitimate' mining shares had the obligation of the payment of the *fictum* retroactively for the section of the mining works represented in such shares. The act established a legal process for the transaction. A *werco* caught in this unfortunate situation had three days from the moment the bishop claimed ownership of shares, to submit a written declaration of ownership of mining works related to the shares in question. The bishop mandated that such document had to include a statement by three witnesses confirming ownership of the

[53] *Idem*, p. 482.
[54] *Idem*, p. 491.
[55] Reynolds, 'Origins of modern business enterprise,' p. 352.
[56] Curzel and Varanini, *La documentazione dei vescovi di Trento*, p. 498.

disputed claim. The burden of seeking witnesses was on the shoulders of *silbrarii*. Nonetheless, this was beneficial to the business of the corporation because it meant that miners could legally challenge mining claims by the bishop. If a miner failed to produce witnesses, the disputed shares belonged to bishop.[57] Above all, the act stipulated that management and administration of mining works were in the exclusive hands of foremen designated by the *consilium*, conditioned to the payment of the *jus custodiae*. The feudal tax however gave *silbrarii* exclusive rights of oversight of mining operations.

Contracts confirmed in A.D. 1208, 1213, and 1214 leave no doubt about the benefits Bishop Wanga gained from mining works. First, his mines were drained and improved. This meant progress in the development of mineral rent and the extractive frontier of Trent. Second, improved mines effectively shortened time needed for the bishop to enjoy mineral rents, even though exact nature of the rent of mines was a contentious relation, as described below. Third, Wanga gained creditors and a line of credit from the mining profits of the *consilium*. By protecting legally the business of *silbrarii*, Wanga put himself in a situation of entitlement for special concessions from the *consilium*. Besides advancing ready cash when the bishop needed, there were intangible gains. Prestige, favor, and influence came to Wanga the moment he decided to deal with *silbrarii*. The guarantee of mine returns was a source of pride against competing lords including allies of the Wanga. Fourth, mining had positive spillover effects in the general economy of the district, enhancing economic options of the bishop even if at the expense of feudal power. Wanga and his successors possibly gained some tangibles from the dissolution of the *consilium*. No information about this matter can be found in the mining contracts described above. One can assume that the *consilium* dissolved its partnership when the mine reached diminishing returns. If and when it happened, the corporation distributed gains and losses in the best form, not without paying the bishop for political favors granted. This scenario is conceivable because the law conditioned mining claims to keeping mines in continuous operation. In practice, it is possible that *silbrarii* consolidated gains among fewer partners and moved their capital into other mining ventures in neighboring lands.

The political cost of such gains was nonetheless high. Success of mine-drainage works deepened the contradictions embedded in clashes for jurisdictions of rent rights. It is astonishing that mining acts criminalized

[57] *Idem*, pp. 498–499.

accumulation of water in mines, as a way to guarantee efficient operation of private mine-drainage works. The last contracts imposed fine of 50 pounds against miners whose works 'fraudulently' led to shaft flooding—*vel aquam fraudulenter intus vergerit contra statum montis*.[58] At the same time, the bishop encouraged miners to accelerate the pace of extraction. Evidence also lies in the last contracts, where the bishop ordered that in cases when miners confronted hard limestone that slowed down digging works, miners had to identify soft limestone formations or *falumberg* and break and cut through it without damaging drainage adits.[59] The *consilium* effectively forced the bishop to rely upon its private mine-drainage works for the enjoyment of mineral rents. It is remarkable that in the same way that reclamation of *iscla* by agrarian peasants resulted in erosion of old feudal structures of agrarian power, mine reclamation works also eroded effective exercise of hegemonic feudal power.

Hydraulic Works and the Productive Powers of *Mining* Labor

Drainage techniques built in Monte Calisio were a remarkable innovation in mine improvement. Unlike drainage infrastructure built in other districts, Monte Calisio works were energy-saving structures built in the mountain itself, maximizing capital valorizations of mine works. Miners collected waters in retention basins and narrow canals cut below the working areas of the mine. These hydraulic structures allowed miners to solve the problem of flooding by acting as water-deposition ponds in which gravity did most of the work. This technique was only possible because miners discovered in Monte Calisio natural cave formations resembling 'extension clefts.'[60] Caves provided relatively easy access to mineralized zones of the deposit but also functioned naturally as water-collecting basins. Miners dug and enlarged some of these basins, adding these formations to the infrastructure of mining works. Canals or 'drains' permanently trapped subterranean waters inside the mine. Such ingenious technique exempted miners from building long pipes or tunnels for pumping water outside the mountain. If the old Roman *actufus* worked alongside topography, then the Monte Calisio *actufus* worked alongside geology. This

[58] Kink, *Fontes Rerum Austriacarum*, Doc. no. 239, p. 448.

[59] Kink, *Fontes Rerum Austriacarum*, Doc. no. 238, pp. 445–447.

[60] Martin Straßburger, 'About Monte Calisio' Zoom video-meeting and emails to Jeannette Graulau, September 9–10, 2024.

adaptation dispensed with the need to build windlasses and hoisting devices. A Schumpeterian instance of 'creative destruction' was at play here, suggesting that a more intrusive and ecologically destructive technique such as forcing the mountain to swallow the waste of mining operations efficiently solved the problem of flooding. The hydraulic technique triumphed over the fury of waters (Figs. 4.5 and 4.6).

Fig. 4.5 Drainage tunnel in Canopa delle Acque mine, Monte Calisio. View in direction of the workings. Miners built the tunnel for draining the lower workings of the mine system. Miners drove the tunnel 'completely by hand,' according to Martin Straßburger. Thick layers of flowstone are visible on the floor, accumulated on rocks that miners transported through the tunnel. Courtesy of Martin Straßburger, Mining Archaeology Consultancy

Fig. 4.6 Drainage tunnel in Canopa delle Acque mine, Monte Calisio. View of the entrance. Rocks block this side of the tunnel. Courtesy of Martin Straßburger, Mining Archaeology Consultancy

Carving water-retention basins and canals was a labor intensive process. It depended upon miners and their ordinary labor instruments. Once expended in the construction of these basins, this mining labor gave its value to the mine. Drainage canals were fully operational and demanded little maintenance costs. For this reason, they increased extraction rates of mining labor. Miners enlarged the area of the mineralized body 'available' for extraction. They dug new drainage ponds and grooves to reach deeper levels of the mineralization body. Their labor proved that there was nothing so secure to private mining claims than the subterranean progress against pit waters. Monte Calisio became a frenzied silver-mining factory, in which miners, pickmen, assayers, ore sorters and washers, ore carriers, and *tabernarius* and *ferrarius* joined an army of mining labor. At the site of the Faedo mine mentioned earlier, archeologists discovered relics of huts 'with interlocking logs' built outside the entrance of the mine.[61] Huts were depots for the tools employed inside the mine. It was possibly a workshop for the making of iron nails and repairing tools, adding

[61] Casagrande, Päffgen, and Straßburger, 'Mining archeological research of medieval silver ore mining at Trento.'

economic stimulus for geographic agglomeration of activities where capital found growth opportunities.

Labor productivity also increased in proportion to efficient solutions to problems of mine ventilation, lightning, and poisonous gasses. Miners opened air passages by digging shafts connected to extraction shafts. Ventilation shafts were hydraulic breakthroughs that cleared extraction areas from smoke and fumes. Archeologists Casagrande, Päffgen, and Straßburger discovered stone lamps and kindlings in various extraction sites at Monte Calisio.[62] Stone lamps weighed as much as 5 kilograms. They stood at lower level shafts. 'Walking or crawling on his knees, a miner held a bundle of bright wood between his teeth, a frequent use even in the houses,' or he created small bowls of raw clay, 'filled them with fat and put the wick, and left them in place once the fuel was consumed.'[63] Miners also used some basins as rock-deposition sites. Built to divert water away from mine workings, canals turned into rock-deposition sites blocked no access to extraction areas. The dual function of water-retention basins persevered in subverting the legal principle of private ownership of mining claims. As seen earlier with the dispute pertaining to the *actufus* of *mons Vace*, it was precisely the utility of this hydraulic structure the factor that triggered competition and litigation for the gains of mines.

Monte Calisio drainage basins compared favorably to hydraulic techniques prevalent in other mining districts. Even if relatively cheaper, windlasses were efficient only under specific conditions.[64] A windlass consisted of a shaft mounted on two braced posts, from which four 'spindly arms' radiated; a miner standing upright pulled its rams.[65] A rope ran over a

[62] *Idem*, p. 189.

[63] Martin Straßburger, 'About Monte Calisio' Zoom video-meeting and emails to Jeannette Graulau, September 9–10, 2024; Zammatteo, 'Le antiche miniere di Faedo,' p. 6.

[64] Brooks, 'The "Vitruvian Mill" in Roman and medieval Europe,' pp. 2–29; Macini and Mesini, 'Hydraulic pumps of Agricola's *De re metallica*,' p. 1051; Matthies, 'Medieval treadwheels: artists' views of building construction,' p. 512, pp. 517–518; Hirt, *Imperial mines and quarries in the Roman world*, p. 78, footnote 137; Grau Fernández (ed.), *Ars Mechanicae, Ingeniería medieval en España*, p. 99, pp. 203–215, for Mediterranean hydraulic machines in the Iberian Peninsula; Reynolds, *Stronger than a hundred men: a history of the vertical water wheel*, pp. 108–121; Rossi, 'The precursors of Leonardo Da Vinci's studies,' pp. 3–4, contains useful iconographic information on mechanical devices before the times of Da Vinci; Wilson, 'Machines, power and the ancient economy,' pp. 7–15.

[65] This design was different than the crank-type windlass. It consisted of a waist-high shaft mounted on a triangular wooden frame. Matthies, 'Medieval treadwheels: artists' views of building construction,' pp. 517–518.

T-shaped crane, used for hoisting a single basket. Miners added a flywheel to the crank for 'smoothing out irregularities of impulse and get over "dead spots".'[66] To increase strength, miners inserted a series of revolving levers into one or both ends of the roller, 'like the steering wheel of ships.'[67] They attached a large wheel at the end of the windlass, and wounded up a rope to the wheel, for raising water from a flooded shaft.[68] The machine endured further adaptions.[69] In some cases, a vertical treadwheel attached to one end of the roller allowed a man to climb up one side of the wheel turning it with his weight. The general design had a rim connected to a thick central shaft with various configurations of struts and spokes.[70] Pulleys were made of iron or bronze, strengthening the capital cost advantages of smelting and blacksmithing sites.[71] A large wheel reaching up to 16 feet in diameter, a *magna rota*, could be seen in prosperous mining districts in the sixteenth century. Two men could walk side by side the treadway inside a *magna rota*. 'Oxen, horses, mules, asses, dogs, goats and bears have all been used to propel these wheels and to raise water by

[66] Cited by Matthies, 'Medieval treadwheels,' p. 518. For energy output, see Allen, *The Industrial Revolution: a very short introduction*, p. 233, for a note on horse-power versus steam-engine; Cascio and Malanima, 'Mechanical energy and water power in Europe,' pp. 5–6; Munro, 'Industrial energy from water mills in the European economy, 5th to 18th centuries,' p. 228.

[67] Matthies, 'Medieval treadwheels,' p. 524, 526, 529.

[68] Ewbank, *A descriptive account of hydraulic and other machines*, p. 73.

[69] Sometimes, miners combined a series of pulleys to the windlass. *Idem*, pp. 69–71.

[70] Two general types appeared in between the thirteenth and sixteenth centuries: the 'compass-arm' and the 'clasp-arm.' The first type had 'spokes driven directly into the shaft,' 'in a greatly magnified version of the wagon wheel.' It was this type the one that appeared consistently in thirteenth-century manuscripts according to historian Hewett. In the clasp-arm treadwheel, arms were built as chords to the wheel rim. The primary pairs of arms 'flanked a square portion of the shaft and reach across the wheel's diameter.' The second pairs of arms 'extend from struts that brace against the primary arms near the shaft.' This allowed the struts to be used as handholds for the laborer walking the treadway. The rope coiled to the round profile of the shaft. *Idem*, p. 526, 529.

[71] Pulley supports became more sophisticated structures, such as the *verna* used in some regions. The later consisted of a stout vertical shaft mounted on a building and carrying a 'pivoting horizontal beam called the "hawk" or "falcon" with the pulley secured at the end.' Double treadwheels appeared or machines with one wheel at each end of a single axle. They were especially useful in ports for unloading ships. Sophisticated cranes were employed for 'loads heavier than normal,' albeit evidence of miners adapting jib-arm and slewing cranes to drainage operations is virtually nonexistent. *Idem*, p. 524, footnote 40, pp. 529–531.

them.'[72] Furthermore, windlasses eliminated the need for a high number of workers, but increased production costs. However, they were adapted only to vertical lifts. Proper inspection of water-raising works also demanded certain organization of daily operations to prevent accidents or vandalism.

Water-retention basins were also highly efficient when compared to waterwheels or *rotam*.[73] There were two basic designs of the waterwheel: the 'undershot or stream wheel' and the 'overshot.' The undershot version had flat radial blades attached to wheel circumference. In its simplest model, the impact of a water flow pushing under the wheel against the submerged blades triggered its motion. The wheel rotated only in one direction relative to the direction of the water flow. Nonetheless, it required a stream with enough water running at a moderate speed, or an open but confined channel of water. None of these conditions favored its use in Monte Calisio. The 'overshot' wheel was more 'efficient and practical' but also more expensive.[74] It had buckets built into the circumference of the wheel. 'There, the weight of water, rather than its impact, turned the wheel, with each bucket discharging its water at the bottom of the wheel and returning empty to the top to being the cycle anew.'[75] Usually placed above a stream or river, the overshot wheel was supplied with water from an elevated water channel or *rogge*, as it was known in northern Italy. The goal was for water to flow in from the channel or *rogger* and fill the buckets at the top of the wheel. Gravity did the rest. The wheel rotated around its central axis when the gravitational weight of water pushed the water-filled buckets down, making the empty buckets on the other side of the wheel lighter. Laborers could interrupt the movement of the wheel by changing the direction of a nozzle or *secèla* placed at the end of the water channel for this purpose. Italians introduced a *roggia bastarda*, a small

[72] At the silver mine of Chemnitz, in the Carpathian Mountains, there were three machines that consisted of three pumps. According to Agricola, 'it lifted the water from the lowest sump to the upper one and to the drains of a tunnel.' These pumps were 'turned by ninety-six horses; these horses go down to the machines by an inclined shaft, which slopes and twists like a screw and gradually descends.' Allen, *The Industrial Revolution: a very short introduction*, p. 233; Ewbank, *A descriptive account of hydraulic and other machines*, p. 74; Hoover and Hoover (transl.), *De re metallica*, pp. 194–195.

[73] Reynolds, 'Medieval roots of the Industrial Revolution,' pp. 122–125. Unless otherwise noted, the paragraph borrows integrally from this work.

[74] Munro, 'Industrial energy from water-mills in the European economy,' p. 232.

[75] Reynolds, 'Medieval roots of the Industrial Revolution,' p. 122. The rest of the paragraph borrows extensively from this work.

watermill built in front of a large one to take advantage of the excess of water flow from the first wheel.[76] Adapted to ore milling purposes, an overshot wheel crushed large pieces of mined ore into smaller pieces, which could be pulverized by further action of a watermill.[77]

However, a watermill required large capital expenditures. The machine demanded expert construction. An ill-built machine compromised delivery of the maximum energy possible. Building the aqueduct for a waterwheel sometimes required changing the course of a stream or a river. Carpenters preferred mature oak trees to the woods of *Castanea* or chestnut, *Kousa Cornus* or dogwood, and other woods available in pre-Alpine markets.[78] Oakwood meant high prices, since it enjoyed brisk demand as construction material of cathedrals and official buildings. Wrought iron was the preferred material for the pistons and bearings of waterwheels. It was inexpensive if and when miners exploited the economies of scale that smelting made possible.[79] Olive oil, used for lubricating iron parts of these machines, was among the most efficient lubricants employed in Mediterranean Europe. Its high viscosity and oiliness made it more efficient than tallow and grease, and easy to work with because it was spread manually and thoroughly onto the needed surfaces. However, it also required access to olive oil producers who supplied low-acidity olive oil obtained from the first press or before olives were left to ferment.[80] This condition potentially increased the cost of watermills.

Lastly, windlasses and watermills increased the demand for miners in situ, suggesting that considerable investments were at stake in a smelting site.[81] More so given that windlasses and also overshot wheels could only handle small volumes of water.[82] Undershot wheels also responded adversely to seasonal variations in water levels. This was a problem that

[76] Jannon and Trento, *Manufatti e fabbricati legati all'antico uso dell'acqua nel territorio del GAL Prealpi e Dolomiti*, p. 18.

[77] Wilson, 'Machines, power and the ancient economy,' pp. 22–24.

[78] Jannon and Trento, *Manufatti e fabbricati legati all'antico uso dell'acqua nel territorio del GAL Prealpi e Dolomiti*, p. 18; Squatriti, *landscape and change in medieval Italy*, pp. 74–77, 174–180.

[79] Muendel, 'Friction and lubrication in medieval Europe,' p. 375.

[80] *Idem*, p. 388.

[81] Molenda, 'Technological innovation in Central Europe between the XIVth and the XVIIth centuries,' p. 68.

[82] Cascio and Malanima, 'Mechanical energy and water power in Europe: a long stability?' p. 5; Jannon and Trento, *Manufatti e fabbricati legati all'antico uso dell'acqua*, p. 18; Reynolds, 'Medieval roots of the Industrial Revolution,' p. 122.

'could either swamp the mills or leave them with insufficient water.'[83] The man-made drainage basins of Monte Calisio were the natural responses miners gave to the real obstacles to production entailed in existing hydraulic machines. Monte Calisio drainage works indeed created quantitative change, altering the relation between labor and capital, with consequences for the rent of mines.

The Problem of Mineral Rents

Water-retention basins not only increased labor productivity on behalf of *silbrarii* but also increased the value of land. Bishop Wanga expected rents in proportion to such increase. This situation confronted the bishop with a singular fiscal problem: how to assess value of ore-yielding lands. If pastoralism produced value in proportion to productivity of land, and agriculture yielded rents in proportion to productivity of land and labor, the pressing question was about the real source of wealth of Monte Calisio. Mining produced value in proportion to the changes to the mountain that value-producing labor made possible. But the bishop understood this value as originating in the coupling of land and labor, whereas *silbrarii* understood value as the product of capital. The mineral *fictum* entailed thus antithetical relations. First, it was a grant of usufruct rights. The text of document reads as follows: *de cetero omnes wercos, qui per fictum voluerint laborare ad rotas aliorum wercorum, libere laborent et plenam habeant potestatem laborandi.*[84] Second, the mineral *fictum* was also a 'gift' that *silbrarii* granted Bishop Wanga. It was in exchange for obtaining the 'grace and favor' that allowed them to build profits from Monte Calisio *ad lucrum devenerit.*[85] The phrase implied that any gift was conditioned to the making of profits by *silbrarii*. This condition applied to the gift in the form of *fictum* or rent but also the *subsidium* owed to the bishop in cases of 'imminent necessity.'

The bishop expected the value of the 'gift' to increase in proportion to profits won from ores exposed as well as prospective profits to be gained from extending the extraction works beyond the zone of ore exposures. In the early contracts, Wanga demanded a one-ninth of mine

[83] Munro, 'Industrial energy from water-mills in the European economy,' p. 231.

[84] Curzel and Varanini, *La documentazione dei vescovi di Trento*, p. 352.

[85] Collatera and Primerano, *Un vescovo, la sua cattedrale, il suo tesoro*, p. 22; Kink, *Fontes Rerum Austriacarum*, pp. 434–435.

incomes; a one-tenth of total mine revenues on behalf of the Archbishop; and a fixed share over the total revenues of metal sales.[86] The corporation also paid a tax of two talents for each *Werhe* or mine specialist employed in its mining business.[87] It paid *II talenta* for each *Xaffar* or mine foreman; two for each *Waffar* or ore-washing laborer; *I talentum* for the Master of the *Waffar*; two for each *Smelzer*; and *X soldi* for mining operations, twice every year. The talent or *talentum* was the 'august biblical choice' used by the bishop to designate the mark, following other medieval rulers of the period.[88] An additional tax was imposed upon the *consilium* set at one tub of extracted ore every week, from each one of the sixteen mining shares. A tub was an open flat-bottom container used for ore-packing and storage, with a volume capacity of almost one hundredweight.[89] *Silbrarii* also had the obligation of *subsidium*, which possibly refereed to economic or military assistance. However, this tax disappeared in the last contracts confirmed by the bishop.[90] Wanga eliminated that provision and confirmed instead that *silbrarii* were not to be coerced into the payment of the *subsidium*. In exchange, the bishop received 10 percent of the final sales price of mining shares.[91]

These high fines reveal much more than the unflagging energy of a bishop seeking mineral incomes. They denote the high fertility of Monte Calisio mines. Archeometallurgical studies confirm that the ores of the region produced between 35 and 247 ounces of silver per ton of lead.[92] The number is significant when one considers that the average amount of silver in galena ores varies between 20 and 200 ounces of silver per ton of lead.[93] The majority of galena ores today contain 50 ounces of silver per ton of lead, or 0.15 percent of silver, with the most improved techniques for metal recuperation. An ore containing eight ounces of silver per ton could be considered profitable, and Monte Calisio ores clearly exceeded

[86] *Si vero diius episcopus, necessitate imminente, ab ipsis subsidium aliquod exigeret* (...). Poggi, *Discorsi economici, storici e giuridici*, p. 496.

[87] Kink, *Fontes Rerum Austriacarum*, Doc. No. 236, pp. 441–443.

[88] For an interesting discussion, see Kinkade, 'Money in the Poema De Mio Cid: a reassessment,' p. 116.

[89] Braunstein, 'Les statuts miniers de l'Europe médiévale,' p. 41.

[90] Kink, *Fontes Rerum Austriacarum*, Doc. No. 236, pp. 441–442.

[91] Salvioli, *Manuale diritto italiano*, p. 395, footnote 1.

[92] Martin Straßburger presents figures in kilograms, in Martin Straßburger, 'About Monte Calisio' Zoom video-meeting and emails to Jeannette Graulau, September 9–10, 2024.

[93] Forbes, *Metallurgy in Antiquity*, p. 180.

expectations. Mining works also generated marketable by-products such as lead and copper, which most likely found demand in construction and armor-making industries. It was clear that private mining works created capital valorizations unconstrained by diminishing returns or exhaustion of ore veins.

Silbrarii, however, understood fertility of mines and the *fictum* differently. They saw mine yields increasing in proportion to additional units of capital and labor employed in the mines. As such, *silbrarii* emphasized the capital expenditures that they provided in the fight against the 'old classical devil of diminishing returns.'[94] Diminishing returns refer to progressive depletion of the ore source of a given mine.[95] Assuming slow increases in metal demand for the long thirteenth century (as David Ricardo assumed constant demand for agrarian produce), constant rate of ore recovery at Monte Calisio, and constant rate of technological development, there could only be two manifestations of diminishing returns. First, diminishing returns occurred when capital flew away from a prospective land because it found another land offering minimal rent, good geography, or cheaper inputs. The situation was present when capital found mines that could be worked at lower costs. This situation also took place when bullion imports in a given locality forced capital to retreat from land in that same locality, effectively liberating capital to go elsewhere. This was possibly the case of northern European mines that *silbrarii* left behind when they reached the Adige Valley. None of these circumstances, however, had anything to do with ore exhaustion in Monte Calisio. If they took place, they were the result of worldwide economic development mentioned earlier. When these situations occurred, they offered no major problem to capital but a significant challenge to lords, who had to quickly respond to capital flight by extending privileges to citizens with money to invest in old mining lands.

Second, diminishing returns occurred when capital costs increased in proportion to decreases in output of mine produce at a given time. This situation was a problem to capitalists. The problem capitalists confronted in this scenario was how to substitute factors of production by introducing

[94] I borrowed the phrase from Rostow, *The stages of economic* growth, p. 155.

[95] Einaudi, *La rendita mineraria: origini e basi*. For contemporary debates, see: Fraser, 'On the neutrality of the resource rent tax'; Frechette, 'Scarcity rents and the returns to mining'; Lackman, 'The classical base of modern rent theory'; Murray, 'Value and theory of rent, part one'; Nnate Nwoke, 'World mining rent: an extension of Marx's theories.'

new hydraulic and smelting techniques. *Silbrarii* confronted this problem every time they created new water-collecting ponds and smelting oremills aiming at increasing silver recovery rates in Monte Calisio. Opening shafts in new areas of the mineralized body enclosed by drifts represented increases in units of capital to solve problems of decreasing ore yields in older shafts. This was a problem of ore exhaustion in specific zones of the deposit and not of the entire mine. In this case, there was no increase in quantity of land. As such, diminishing returns has nothing to do with exhaustion of a 'natural' supply of ore in a given quantity of land, but exhaustion of ore in a specific section of the mine. Fertility of mines, then, was theoretically possible without increasing units of land brought into production or lessening fertility of land itself.

Both views of diminishing returns presented antagonistic relations between *silbrarii* and Bishop Wanga. *Silbrarii* sought to grab higher shares of surpluses increasing the area covered by their mining claims. Claiming new areas of the mineralization body was relatively easy given that territorial limits of claims were imprecise. There was no fencing of mining claims, no *clausurae* similar to the fencing that demarcated agrarian lands. This feature led to speculation and episodes of litigation, as discussed earlier. *Silbrarii* also increased their gains by selling mining shares, and acquired new claims targeting different zones of the mine. Moreover, quantity of physical output produced in each mining claim did not correspond to size of extraction sites. Lack of congruence between size of territory and amount of mine produce imposed weighty questions about ore-yielding land rights that this rural economy failed to solve. The response of the medieval society to this contradiction was to condition ownership of claims to continuous operations of mining works. Such response, however, presupposed the supremacy of mining works in relation to all other extractive activities on neighboring surface lands.

Fiscal instruments rooted in monopolies of *agrarian* landed property by no means guaranteed a monopoly of the gains of mines on behalf of Bishop Wanga. The mineral *fictum* presupposed full disclosure of mine incomes on the part of *silbrarii*, whose entire business relied upon their ability to exploit trade and investment conditions. The bishop could not use his *gastaldia* to build *taxatio* or a census of the produce of mining claims that dotted the whole underground of Monte Calisio. Estimations of volumes of produce necessarily relied upon the commercial arithmetic calculations done by *silbrarii*. Direction of baryte veins, amount of unwanted minerals per pound of ore, lead output per tube of ore smelting, and redeeming prices of shares were among the economic circumstances that determined the turn-over rate of the capital invested in Monte Calisio. These circumstances were economic arguments that set an entry barrier to the world of *silbrarii*. Cross-checking the accuracy of these arguments was impossible for *gastaldia*, unless these tax officers were familiar with actual condition of mining claims. Certainly, *gastaldia* possessed a heavy dose of economic intuition. Experience in the valuation of surpluses of livestock and agriculture taught tax officers invaluable lessons. But only *silbrarii* knew quantities of inputs or stocks laid in the mines. This economic bond did not translate into a bond of solidarity and cooperation among *silbrarii*. Members of the *consilium* trusted or distrusted each other enough as to insist on 'detailed inventorization' of expenses and profits.[96] Their control of subterranean works afforded a range of possibilities about when and how to act honestly but also dishonestly against Bishop Wanga (Figs. 4.7 and 4.8).

If fiscal institutions for the exercise of lordly power relied upon the capacity of lords to impose sanctions given ownership of landed property, then the story of Wanga is paradoxically a story of failure. Monte Calisio mines were taxable wealth in the jurisdiction of rent claims of Bishop Wanga. However, the share of incomes due to the Sovereign was defined on a case-by-case basis and with agreement by *silbrarii*. Even the right of Bishop Wanga to a monetary *subsidium* depended upon consultation with *silbrarii*. The bishop could not compel them to provide this tax. The array of diverse mineral taxes also suggests the attempt to rapidly secure incomes from Monte Calisio on the part of the bishop. It also suggests that lords felt the need to adapt fiscal instruments of power to the economic organization of mining. Successes of agrarian land reclamation required adapting taxation to new forms of taxable wealth. A similar process was at stake with the mines of Monte Calisio. The historical process that had transformed land into an abstraction, and made it a 'lord's monopoly of a piece of the earth' in Marxist terms, paved the way for the rise of monopolizable mining surpluses.[97] To the advantage of Bishop Wanga, none of the struggles Wanga had with rural lords had negative spillover effects over Monte Calisio. This paradox suggests an early rise of capitalist valorizations of

[96] See, for example, Mills, 'Early accounting in northern Italy'; Yamey, *Essays on the history of accounting*.

[97] 'Even though the capitalist mode of production itself does not exist,' Marx added. Marx, *Capital*, 3, pp. 759–760, 762–763.

Fig. 4.7 A windlass hoist worked by two miners, in *De re Metallica Libri XII* (A.D. 1556), by Georges Agricola. Simple drainage machines such as the windlass formed an integral part of the medieval mining economy. However, machines embedded antagonistic relations between lords and miners for the gains of mines. What share of mine produce originated in the 'natural' fertility of land versus productivity of labor became the mineral rent problem of the times. A windlass was efficient for raising ores and water from shafts. Two miners rotated the axle by turning the winches attached to both ends of the horizontal cylinder. In this way, they winded the rope onto or off the cylinder, lifting the bucket attached to the rope. This type of windlass was employed in Freiburg by the mid-thirteenth century in draining shafts that reached a depth of 45 meters. ETH-Bibliothek Zürich, E-Rara

Fig. 4.8 An improved version of the windlass, in *De re Metallica Libri XII* (A.D. 1556), by Georges Agricola. Adaptations of the windlass suggest that miners figured out ways of saving time and labor in drainage works. Rotating the windlass required three 'level workers' or 'windlass men.' The wheel attached to the horizontal cylinder allowed miners to apply more energy in lifting heavier loads. Successive improvements of the machine led to contentious relations between lords and miners over the 'just price' of land. ETH-Bibliothek Zürich, E-Rara

ore-yielding lands that indirectly benefitted the upper class as a whole. It is safe to conclude that private drainage works had developmental consequences to the bishop and his city.

Competition for the gains of improved mines never went away. This continual contradiction fueled the rising capitalist class of miners, sustaining a rapid expansion of mining works in Trent as well as neighboring lands in the next century. Various conditions suggest that profits margins of the mining business of *silbrarii* were high. As mentioned earlier, Bishop Wanga demanded that *silbrarii* paid double the amount of *fictum* due to the second furnace these had added to ore-smelting works. The *fictum* for two furnaces was *L librarum denarium veronensis.*[98] The payment had to be made in due time so as to avoid additional fines.[99] Astonishingly, the bishop threatened *silbrarii* with the shutting down of the second furnace. This aggressive move shows that *silbrarii* found a way to increase value from crude ores without the burden of taxation. Second, Bishop Wanga imposed a high number of fines, antithetical to the spirit of 'freedom' that the first mining contract granted *silbrarii*. Fines, however, indicate that Bishop Wanga sought to enlarge his share of gains from mines while creating new jurisdictional areas pertaining to subterranean works. The bishop benefited but failed to monopolize the gains of Monte Calisio mines. His laws turned mine yields into monopolizable asset, but he failed to hold absolute ownership of these profits. Finally, *silbrarii* moved in an economic world that discouraged bad investment decisions and large-scale transactions. Medieval business firms had a high mortality rate and many ended sooner or later in bankruptcy, according to De Roover. This situation reinforced the tendency toward centralization of production and investment decisions, in a way that made it difficult for Bishop Wanga to regulate the profits of the mining business.

In addition, bookkeeping and accounting were crafts controlled by businessmen. It is impossible to argue that this development played no role in the economics of mineral rents. Italian merchants kept books and extensively developed the science of 'commercial arithmetic.'[100] The *consilium* belonged to this commercial world, and possibly adjusted the best accounting practices of the times to the needs of the mining enterprise. After all, the business of private mine-drainage works relied upon 'credit, partnership, and agency,' essential elements for the development of accounting.[101] We know also that similar mining *consilium* kept separate records of transactions containing all changes that the 'common capital' of the enterprise underwent.[102] Each record probably contained simple

[98] Kink, *Fontes Rerum Austriacarum*, Doc. No. 241, pp. 451–452.

[99] Curzel and Varanini, *La documentazione dei vescovi di Trento*, p. 352.

[100] Reynolds, 'Origins of modern business enterprise: medieval Italy,' p. 353.

[101] De Roover, 'Characteristics of bookkeeping before Paciolo,' p. 145.

[102] Ibidem.

entries, starting with the first entry or original expenses of building and repairing waterwheels. It is possible that a scribe working for *silbrarii* stroke across this entry when the gains of mining claims came in. Every time there was an expense, in the form of cash payments, there was an entry for that expense, which the scribe stroke across when debt was canceled. The scribe also recorded expenses, payments, and losses due to accidents, vandalism, or adverse weather. Copies of records were in the possession of all interested parties. This indicates that notes of entries recorded by *silbrarii* were documents that could be used against Bishop Wanga in case of disputes concerning mine yields.

Mineral rents represented value of improved ore-yielding lands. Comparisons of values of mining and agrarian lands are only approximations derived from everything else but price of land, as historian Michele Turner commented once.[103] 'We do not have land prices sufficient to tell a story about comparative land price trends in Europe, and although we have agricultural prices, there are doubts over whether they can be converted to a standard measure to allow transnational comparisons.'[104] His observation is valid also for the case of Trent, despite the copious diplomatic and legal documents that have survived for Trent. Statistics available for value of patrimonial lands are scanty. Assets of the Principality of Trent stood at 100,000 marks in the year A.D. 1250.[105] Annual income of the bishop then was approximately 10,000 silver marks. The sum was lower than that of the Count of Tyrol, valued at 19,770 silver marks in A.D. 1300, but not insignificant.[106] One can speculate that numbers included leases of agrarian lands and the profits of a well-drained Monte Calisio mountain.[107] Given the relatively compact size of the district, it is fair to say that mine development added value to agrarian lands of Trent, despite the problem of mineral rents.

Cementing the advantages gained in the economic organization of production, *silbrarii* sought to increasingly alienate the bishop from the subterranean wealth of Monte Calisio. They responded to rent charges by

[103] See for a general discussion, Braudel and Spooner, 'Prices in Europe from 1450 to 1750'; Dygo, 'Land prices and crises: Central Europe from the 15th to the 17th centuries,' p. 547, 549, 551, 556; Turner, 'Comparative land prices in Europe, 1500–1800.'

[104] Turner, 'Comparative land prices in Europe, 1500–1800,' p. 534.

[105] Mor and Schmidinger, *I poteri temporali dei vescovi in Italia e in Germania nel Medioevo*, p. 222.

[106] Ibidem.

[107] Montanari, *L'alimentazione contadina nell'alto medioevo*, p. 30.

adapting the logic of production to wider economic circumstances such as fluctuations in prices of bullion in different 'end markets' as well as local conditions such as prices of charcoal, oil, timber, and iron, among other goods. They were keen to exploit differences in prices, extract value from labor, and fix estimations of value owed to Bishop Wanga as to appropriate higher shares of mineral gains. *Silbrarii* operated under profit expectations different than the rent horizon of the bishop. This situation does not mean that *silbrarii* always enjoyed the conditions to extract profits from arbitrage. It suggests, nonetheless, that conditions related to growth and contraction of distant silver markets determined progress of mineral rents and profits in this rural economy.

CHAPTER 5

The Mines of the Bishop

Bishop Wanga benefitted from his drained mines. The 'hyperactivity' of silver production and trade, coupled with the economic gains of agrarian surpluses, sustained the wealth of Bishop Wanga. We lack exact figures about the incomes that Wanga had at his disposal for personal consumption. But evidence shows that the rule of Bishop Wanga was wholly tied to the subterranean wealth of his district. First, the bishop expanded public infrastructure works in the city. He built the Wanga Tower (A.D. 1208–1212), with its imposing bell eager to roar citizens and peasants alike when the bishop wanted to gather all. The *domus murata* built in the lower part of the tower protected and defended the Adige River bridge. It was a costly public infrastructure work that suddenly revealed to neighboring Alpine districts the power of solvency of the Prince-Bishop. The *domus murata* was a large, imposing, two-level structure, measuring approximately 10 by 11 meters.[1] Completed almost two decades after the government of Wanga, the wall protected the bridge leading to the urban quarter of the city. Along with Wanga Tower, the *domus murata* guarded the western side of the city that led to the Sarca Valley.

Wanga also sponsored construction works for the expansion of the Cathedral of Saint Vigil, hiring Master mason *Adamo* of *Arogno* for the project. Arogno came from the Diocese of Como. His apprentices continued to work in a project that spanned for 25 years from its

[1] Giovanni and Parenti, 'Torre Vanga a Trento,' p. 69.

J. Graulau, *Medieval Mining and Power in Thirteenth-Century Europe*, https://doi.org/10.1007/978-3-031-99239-1_5

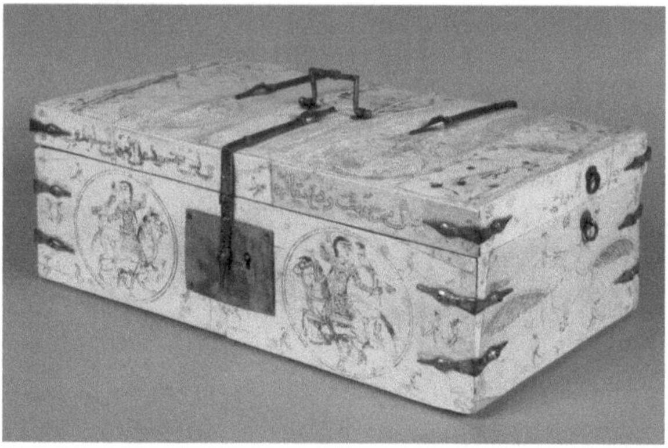

Fig. 5.1 Ivory casket purchased by Bishop Wanga, possibly of Sicilian manufacture, twelfth century. Museo Diocesano Tridentino

beginnings in the month of February of the year A.D. 1212. The Master mason left his indelible signature on an engraved stone cut that was originally placed near the main apse of the Cathedral of Saint Vigil. On permanent display at Museo Diocesano Tridentino, this handsome stone cut has an engraved Latin inscription bearing the signature of Adamo of Arogno. The Cathedral that was the 'silent witness' of the assassination of Adelpret, and the canon conclave against Conrad, became a potent symbol of imperial power in the region. Centuries later, it hosted the Council of Trent, the assembly that decisively altered the history of the Latin Church (Fig. 5.1).

Mineral incomes sustained the expensive taste of the bishop. Wanga acquired luxury goods useful for symbolic and propaganda purposes. The bishop obtained a fine ivory casket from Sicily, richly decorated with Islamic motifs in the best Sicilian tradition, as the above figure shows. Artists had decorated the casket with love verses written in splendid Arabic calligraphy, from an Egyptian version of the book of *One Thousand and One Nights*.[2] Why an imperial bishop felt attracted to this object is not difficult to understand if one considers that Sicilian love lyrics, which 'tapped into the poetics inherited from their Muslim forefathers,' had captivated

[2] I borrowed the description from the Museo Diocesano Tridentino. https://www.museodiocesanotridentino.it/articoli/manifattura-arabo-sicula.

the court of Emperor Frederick II.[3] Political pride and ambition moved Wanga to acquire other luxurious objects, such as a gorgeous trio of Liturgical Books that was carefully crafted to his taste. The Liturgical Books showed excellent gold and silver craftsmanship. The Lectionary is a superb work of art. Its crafters employed different gilding and goldsmithing techniques to produce splendid plates that served as front and cover for the book. The front plate offers one of the few artistic drawings of Prince-Bishop Wanga that have survived to these days. The artists chose silver for this plate, signifying a relation between Wanga and the silver mines of the district. The back plate depicted the figure of St. Paul, made of gold. The metalwork came from a workshop at the service of the bishop, in which scribes, illuminators, and goldsmiths of different cultures worked together to please the aristocratic taste of Wanga.

Beyond expanding public works and personal consumption, mineral incomes had significant developmental impacts. First, they sustained money relations of the bishop. The documents contained in *Codex Wangianus* allow one to build a general account of the monetary transactions of Bishop Wanga. The account reveals the weight of silver moneys in the riches of the bishopric. Money payments suggest that silver mining afforded Bishop Wanga resources to largely expand monetary transactions, when compared to his predecessors. Figure 5.2 summarizes the monetary transactions of Wanga and his predecessors (Fig. 5.2).

Second, bishops struck and coined silver currency. As described earlier, Trent sustained its coinage business for a long period of time after the city established its mint between A.D. 1130 and 1200. A fine specimen of the *denarii grosso* minted during A.D. 1236–1255 and conserved at Museo Diocesano Tridentino suggests that bishops tightened the nexus between mining and minting, possibly aiming at increasing money supply.[4] The museum also holds a *denarii piccolo* minted in A.D. 1182–1235. Of lower silver content, the 'small' *denarii* found a local market in rural villages where livestock and agrarian commodities enjoyed wide circulation. Small denomination coins like the *denarii piccolo* enjoyed demand in livestock production centers of Non, Sole, Rendena, Fiemme, Primiero, Tesino, Piné, and Folgaria-Lavarone.[5] These valleys exported livestock products in

[3] Carpentieri, 'Love poetry as a social practice: on the function of medieval Sicilian love lyric in Arabic and Italian,' p. 765.

[4] Collatera and Primerano, *Un vescovo, la sua cattedrale, il suo tesoro*, p. 168.

[5] Stenico, 'Signorie rurali e risorse economiche,' pp. 234–235.

Years	Asset	Amount
Wanga	Buying castle & house in Pradaglia	2,200
	Buying incomes in *loco de Warta*	700
	Repair watermill-works	600
	Buying incomes in Nanno & Don	500
	Buying part of Beseno Castle	--
	Buying incomes in Tesimo & land in Eppan	100
	Buying b*roillum* in Piedicastello	80
	Mortgage, *gastaldia* of mines	2,000*
	Mortgage of watermill in Borgonuovo	200
	Mortgage loan, St. Giustina in Bolzano	--
Conrad	Buying land & incomes in Corona	150
	Buying land in Egna	35
Albert III	Buying land & incomes in Eppan	1,100$^{\Psi}$
	Mortgage loan, land & incomes in Albiano	200
Salomon	Buying land & Tassullo gold mine	1,400
	Buying land in Caldaro & Eppan	400

NOTE: * The creditors were *Albert* of Seiano, who was 'very close to Bishop Wanga'; a member of a dynastic family of Arco, *Riprandino* of *Ottone Rico*, and Ulrich of Rambaldo. Curzel, *Il capitolo della cattedrale di Trento*, p. 477; Schneller, *Quellen und forschungen zur geschichte*, p. 171.
$^{\Psi}$ Bishop Adalbert only paid 500 Veronese pounds on July 23, 1185. The rest of the amount remained as debt owed to the Count of Eppan, who retained rights over Romeno in accordance with the pledge agreement confirmed by Bishop Adalbert.

Fig. 5.2 Money payments made by bishops of Trent, in Veronese denarii, A.D. 1160–1218

exchange for cereals, in a regional division of labor that sustained agrarian profits and rents. Overall, striking and minting silver currency deepened the integration of Trent to wider mint markets of the region, especially Brescia, Como, Domodossola, Ivrea, Novasta, Piacenza, Cremona, Mantova, Aquilea, Gorizla, and Trieste.[6] Even when the Counts of Tyrol established mint in Merano in A.D. 1272, absorbing silver from metallic mines of the region, the mint of Trent played a considerable role in the money market of the city. It came second in longevity only to the mints of Venice, Verona, Milan, and Pavia.[7]

Third, mineral revenues added value to agrarian lands and wealth of this episcopal city. The mass of taxable wealth that labor made possible increased in this period. The one-tenth parishes including seignorial parishes administered by laymen paid progressively became a one-tenth of annual incomes of all ecclesiastical institutions subordinated to the Church

[6] Travaini, 'Mint organization in Italy between the twelfth and fourteenth century,' p. 41.
[7] For description of coins minted at Merano, see Gremes and Zanoni, 'Le monete rinvenute a Castel Corno,' p. 125, 129.

of Trent.[8] The *taxatio* also reflected changes in valuation of ecclesiastical lands. It was based upon the sum of annuities paid by institutions subordinated to the Church of Trent. Drawing upon a *taxatio* for the year A.D. 1309, parishes in Bolzano, Caldaro, Saint Michele, Arco, and Maia paid the highest amount of taxes. Fiscal institutions continued to evolve, so that later the one-tenth became a semi-annual payment equivalent to a one-hundredth of the total sum of annuities of institutions.

Finally, mining revenues allowed Bishop Wanga to strengthen public authority and political power. A lordly rebellion that erupted immediately after his election proved propitious for a radical reterritorialization of power. Although details of the rebellion are scanty, it is clear that the Arco and Beseno lords took the lead. These 'conspirators,' as citizens remembered them, were intent upon expanding jurisdictions of rents in Garda region which they acquired under Bishop Conrad. Conspirators included local lords and canons who had supported Bishop Conrad.[9] The rebellion possibly erupted as a violent conflict that led to the destruction of a watermill in the Sarca River. The conflict involved the *barcaioli* from the village of Mori. They held fluvial trade rights, and their rafts connected Bolzano to the Torbole Pass in the Garda Lake. Wanga put down the rebellion by relying upon his allies, in particular the Count of Tyrol. He secured a *laudamenta regio* against the Arco and Beseno lords, granted by King Otto VI sometime between A.D. 1209 and 1210 (when Otto was still the favorite for the imperial crown). The *laudamenta* included a severe curtailment of the jurisdiction of rents of Odolrich of Arco. Most likely, Wanga and the Count of Tyrol advanced the legal reasoning that the previous donation made by Conrad had been in detriment of the Imperial Church.

Armed with the privilege of *laudamenta regio*, and supported by his aristocratic allies, Wanga issued a ban against the dissident lords. A resentful lord of Beseno went into exile, accepting the ban imposed by Wanga. Count Odolrich of Arco, however, refused to leave Garda but knew that the royal ban put him in a precarious position. He had no choice but to submit to the conditions imposed by Wanga, if he wanted the curia to lift the ban. The bishop was merciless. He forced the Arco lords to accept 'humiliating conditions of vassalage,' in the words of Curzel, when appealing to the Garda *curtis* for the criminal inquiry against Oldorich of Beseno.

[8] Curzel, *Le pievi trentine*, p. 57. The rest of the paragraph comes from this work, unless otherwise noted.

[9] Castagnetti, *Governo vescovile, feudalità, 'communitas' cittadina*, pp. 178–179.

Beseno turned from ally of the lords of Arco to vassals responding to the *curtis* of the Garda district over criminal matters pertaining to the rebellion against Wanga. The Beseno lord admitted responsibility in the insurrection against Wanga, and accepted the punishment imposed by the bishop. The Arco lords also had to pass judgment over other names of citizens of Garda who had assisted in the rebellion. The rebel lords accepted the conditions for peace imposed by Wanga and ended their quarrels with the Count of Tyrol and other allies of the bishop.[10]

These political events marked the beginnings of hegemonic power of Bishop Wanga. His donations of rights effectively strengthened the basis of political authority of the Imperial Church of Trent. In A.D. 1209, the bishop granted monopoly rights of trade in timber and charcoal pitch to *sindici* and *procuratores* of Trent. In exchange for these rights, they owed half of the *lucrum* to the Church of Trent. The *sindici* swore loyalty to the bishop and the ecclesiastical principality. Wanga also solved a pressing rent battle between the Campo lords and the Verona bishop. The parties contested Breguzzo pasture rights, which kin the end, four judges of the imperial court decided that jurisdiction belonged to the bishop of Verona.[11] The turmoil of the southern lands, however, gave way to a short but significant period of political stability. The bishop imposed upon his military vassals the obligation of maintaining castles, in exchange for certain administrative rights. Wanga also exploited the legal privileges of a *laudamenta regio* that confirmed various feudal and fiscal rights in the title of Prince-Bishop. Many rights were a direct threat against any attempt to harm the incomes of the bishop that could arise from ministerials (among whom there were allies of dissident lords). The *laudamenta* prohibited the alienation of patrimonial and feudal assets of the Bishop. The rationale was the need to shield the Church from falling into a state of 'grave poverty.'[12]

Above all, Wanga relied upon feudal courts to erode lordly competition for rents. Just as he did in the case of the Arco lords, Wanga made the most of the feudal *curtis* of his vassals. He relied upon this instrument of competing feudal powers to enact 20 *laudamenta* during his years as Prince-Bishop of Trent.[13] The bishop also exploited the contradictions of

[10] Curzel, *Il capitolo della cattedrale di Trento*, p. 497.

[11] Ball, *The Central Alps*, p. 484; Varanini and Demo, 'Allevamento, transumanza, lanificio,' p. 272.

[12] Curzel, *Il capitolo della cattedrale di Trento*, pp. 495–498.

[13] Ibidem.

overlapping jurisdictions when settling rent controversies using his curia. The curia intervened in a controversy over Ossenigo on the right side of Garda Lake. Held by a Veronese lord, the village was one of the many assets that Bishop Adelpret had given away to allies from Verona. The curia compiled testimony from Briano of Castelbarco, who set the record straight about feudal customs in the region. Circumscribed to its own jurisdictional limits, the curia overwhelmed the lord of Castelbarco with its questions about legitimacy of feudal investitures in the region. It proved useful for Wanga to justify taking over the fief of Ossenigo. Castelbarco confirmed that renewals of rights required that a vassal asked for confirmation of investitures. He added that vassals had to make the request exactly one year and one day after the initial investiture was granted by the lord. If a vassal failed to ask for conformation of rights, the investiture returned back to the lord, according to his testimony. It is possible that this interpretation of feudal law was meant to please Wanga. The bishop had been elected exactly a year and a half before the inquiry took place. The curia gained legitimate reasons for taking over fiefs in Garda region, expanding rent rights of the city. In the inquiry over Ossenigo, the curia also discussed questions about the meaning of *fidelitas* or loyalty between lords and vassals. It defined feudal bond of loyalty in a manner that reinforced the rising hegemony of Wanga over the whole district. It proclaimed that a vassal that conspired against his lord by making alliances with other lords relinquished his rights to his fiefs given that alliances with other lords presupposed failure to fulfill the foundational principle of vassalage. The curia defended the oath of *fidelitas* as the original ground for society, legitimizing the history of expansion of feudal powers in the lands of the district.

Underlying political developments sustained by mineral wealth, a slow but enduring evolution of feudal property rights was in the making. Monte Calisio joined the mosaic of improved lands, imposing its own contractual demands on a society in transformation. Legal understanding of *fodere*, *fodinae*, *fief*, and *feudum* changed in tandem with success of private mining and drainage works.[14] The more mineral incomes strengthened political power, the stronger the 'feudal attitudes'[15] on the utility of the *fictum*. While emanating from feudal law, the mineral *fictum* represented economic organization of a subterranean space that emphasized functionality

[14] Albertoni, *Vassalli, feudi, feudalismo*, p. 52.

[15] For the concept of feudal attitudes, see Heers, 'The "feudal" economy and capitalism: words, ideas and reality.'

of mine drainage works. A 'triumphalist vision' of the role of capital in mine drainage was on ascent. This vision shaped the political culture of this ecclesiastical principality and its neighbors.[16] It reflected a common interest that tied lords together but one that could be expressed only through hegemonic competition.[17] Indeed, mining rights were the outcome of earlier hegemonic clashes. After the emperor suffered an attack on his men by Italian forces, he declared that silver mines were governed by imperial regalian rights. This proclamation made in the Diet of Roncaglia had considerable consequences for the rise of mining rights. The legal formula that summarized the new territorial dominion of imperial power was cum *omnis argentifodina ad jura pertineat imperii et inter regalia nostra.*[18] Mines of silver were 'his by right' or so the emperor ordered his Bolognese lawyers to draft in a decree published in November of the same year.[19] Imperial diplomas granted to bishops and secular lords recognized the presence of valuable metals and minerals in the subsoil.[20] However, these were understood as substances that required capital and labor, as suggested in the legal formula *in rectum feudum conceffimus, omne genus metalli tam in auro & argento.*[21]

Mineral usufruct rights emerged as precondition for the consolidation of imperial hegemony.[22] But the real, historical creation of mining rights

[16] Boureau, 'How law came to the monks,' p. 31.

[17] Hilton, 'A crisis of feudalism,' p. 5.

[18] Kink, *Fontes Rerum Austriacarum*, p. 430, foonote 2.

[19] Pacaut, *Frederick Barbarossa*, p. 85.

[20] Hübner, *A history of Germanic private law*, pp. 292–294.

[21] The text comes from a grant by Emperor Frederick II in A.D. 1229 to Ludovico, Duke of Bavaria. The second formula comes from an imperial donation of mines to the King of Bohemia in A.D. 1232. Haiminsfeldi, *Collectio Constitutionum Imperialium*, pp. 298–299.

[22] For a general history of medieval iron mining, see Angel, *Mines et fondaries au XVIe siècle*; Braunstein (ed.), *La sidérurgie dans les Alpes italiennes*; Cortese, 'Opifici idraulici per la lavorazione del ferro nel comprensorio del Monte Amiata'; by the same author see *L'acqua, il grano, il ferro*; La Salvia, *Iron making during the migration period: the case of the Lombards*; Vázquez De Prada, 'La coyuntura de la minería y de la metalurgia europeas'; Williams, 'A note on liquid iron in medieval Europe.' For pearl fishing, see Narasimha Rao, 'Industry in medieval Āndhradeśa'; for soapstone, see Santi, Antonelli, and Renzulli, 'Provenance of medieval *pietra ollare*, artefacts found in archaeological sites of central-eastern Italy'; Storemyr and Heldal, 'Soapstone production through Norwegian history.' Also, Bailly-Maitrê and Benoît, 'Les mines d'argent de la France médiévale'; Franzini and Lezzerini, 'The stones of medieval buildings in Pisa and Lucca provinces'; Morel, Bodart, Boulvain et al., 'Les calcaires de Lorraine dans l'architecture et la sculpture gothiques de la région mosane'; Palme, 'Alpine salt mining in the Middle Ages'; Rippon, Claughton, and Smart, *Mining in a*

was in the hands of bishops and secular lords. Bishops like Wanga were on their own when they confronted the problem of flooded mines. They acted upon the need to improve ore-yielding lands almost impulsively, as part of their battles for territoriality of power. Certainly, imperial lawyers codified the *iura regalia*, pushing 'feudalization of mining rights' forward, but only in relation to the real challenges and opportunities lords confronted in the exercise of these rights.[23] Bishops invoked the *iura regalia* principle when competing lords threatened rent rights and privileges, as seen before in the legal controversy between Bishop Adelpert and the Counts of Eppan over the Tassullo mine. In the exercise of territorialization of mineral rights, Wanga widened the political horizon of this feudal right. He forced this right to adapt to a mining economy that demanded the rise of capital through mine drainage works. Expanding the political horizon of *iura regalia* allowed Bishop Wanga to enjoy bullion produced from the mines of Trent. However, the same process of mine improvement triggered contradictory forces, as seen in the discussion about incomes owed to the bishop and the need for agreement with *silbrarii*. This contradiction suggests that feudalization of mining rights was not only a top-down process, but involved overlapping layers of horizontal jurisdictions of lordly power. Only at the conjuncture point of these vertical and horizontal layers of power, competition nested the rise of one of the most spectacular mining mountains of the medieval world.

The advantages of Bishop Wanga never fully eliminated lordly clashes for jurisdictions of rent rights and privileges. Lordly struggles continued throughout the thirteenth century, fueling ongoing processes of class differentiation. Competitive dynamics from below also mattered. The class of non-free vassals that supplied the mass of value-producing labor endured important changes. A segment of this class left serfdom behind in the thirteenth century, pushed upward by changes in rent rights. This group joined the lower rural nobility. Its members gained administrative roles in the courts of bishops and secular lords. In time, its upward mobility created new hereditary political offices, hastening political change of the rural society. Some members of this new 'class' occupied relatively high ranks in castles, including the position of chamber officer.[24] This lower nobility class included vassals who originated in the *homines ecclesiae* or serfs owned by

medieval landscape; Verna, 'Innovations et metallurgies en Méditerranée Occidentale'; Veseloský, 'History of discovery and study of new primary minerals at Jáchymov.'

[23] Maioni, 'La politica dell'argento e del ferro nella Lombardia medieval,' pp. 437–439.

[24] Mor and Schmidinger, *I poteri temporali dei vescovi in Italia*, p. 201.

the Church of Trent.[25] It had its own competition, especially from the mid-thirteenth century onward, when it had to accommodate free men migrants from Italian and Germanic lands.[26] How this dynamic class built functions relevant to mining works is an intriguing question. It is possible that members of this class performed roles and functions that gained a certain marketability. Assistants to scribes, bookkeepers, and notaries with experience in the business of mining are a case in point. Within the lower nobility class, nobles of serf origins or *gentilis macinata* also experienced major change. Bishop Wanga had *gentilis macinata sancti Vigilii*, which joined a group of low-ranked knights under the jurisdiction of the Church and directly subordinated to the bishop.[27] This group of knights of serf origins enjoyed economic privileges, in particular exemption of taxes in the district of Trent. Some members of this class earned enfeoffments of public taxes, in a process accelerated by changes in fiscal institutions described earlier.

Aristocratic lords also created their own knights of serf origins, as part of the need to legitimize dominion of patrimonial lands. In many cases, this class included serfs who received knighthood privileges after they served in the aristocratic *milites* of lords. Local lords also granted low-rank knighthood privileges to members of their militias or *arimanni*, as the Castelbarco lords did in A.D. 1246.[28] Members of the class of low-ranked knights possibly played a role in the development of mines, too, as knights could nominally gain mining rights from bishops. Generally, the rise of 'noble hierarchies'[29] slowly changed relations among bishops, the Tyrolean aristocracy, and rent-paying villages. However, the hostility of the aristocracy toward this class prevailed for centuries, if the words of Bishop Hinderbach about the lower nobility in A.D. 1467 are to be taken seriously: '[P]easants no more no less than the others, and like them, they spread manure in the fields.'[30]

The economic forces that led to the rise of mineral incomes conspired to keep the mass of value-producing labor at the bottom of the social hierarchy. *Macinatae* men and women remained attached to the *mansus*.[31]

[25] Voltelini, *Giurisdizione signorile*, pp. 109–110.

[26] *Idem*, p. 106.

[27] Curzel, *Il capitolo della Cattedrale di Trento*, p. 46; Voltelini, *Giurisdizione signorile*, p. 119.

[28] Voltelini, *Giurisdizione signorile*, p. 112.

[29] Bettotti, 'Famiglie signorili delle valli di Non e di Sole,' p. 49.

[30] Ibidem.

[31] Voltelini, *Giurisdizione signorile*, p. 107.

They remained most vulnerable to lordly power, squeezed by the violence of territorialization of feudal power. War, pestilence, and diseases took a heavy toll in this class, especially in women, who 'fared much worse than men'[32] in the medieval economy. As mentioned earlier, bishops sold, bought, and donated *servus de macinatae* and *femina de macinatae*.[33] However, the conditions from which this class emerged were in retreat by the thirteenth century, incompatible as they were with the rise of agrarian wealth.[34] Even though contradictions built in lordly competition opened a door for resistance and change, class struggles 'from below' did not play a major role in processes of economic change discussed in this book.[35] Continual territorialization of power restricted the impact of these struggles by shifting the spatial basis of resistance. The increasing presence of the Counts of Tyrol in local affairs of the Church cannot be overlooked either. This aristocracy, among the most powerful of the entire Carolingian empire, gained the upper hand in Trent when Count Adalbert III obtained hereditary rights for incomes from the Church of San Vigil sometime after A.D. 1233. The Count gained possession of Mezzo Castle in San Pietro in Mezzolombardo, on the left side of the Adige River, in A.D. 1271. His family prevailed in the hereditary controversy that emerged after the death

[32] Carlo Cipolla in Cipolla (ed.), *The Fontana economic history of Europe*, p. 44.

[33] Voltelini, *Giurisdizione signorile*, pp. 119.

[34] Curzel and Franceschini, 'L'agricoltura trentina nel tardo medioevo,' pp. 26–27; Mor and Schmidinger, *I poteri temporali dei vescovi in Italia*, p. 201.

[35] For the Marxist debate, see: Aston and Philpin (eds.), *The Brenner debate: agrarian class structure and economic development*; Brenner, 'The rises and declines of serfdom in medieval and early modern Europe'; Bryer, 'The roots of modern capitalism: a Marxist accounting history'; Byres, 'Differentiation of the peasantry under feudalism'; 'Modes of production and non-European pre-colonial societies'; Dimmock, *The origin of capitalism in England*; Graça, 'Feudal dynamics and Runciman's competitive selection practices in late medieval Castile'; Hilton, 'A crisis of feudalism'; Kriedte, *Feudalismo tardío y capital mercantil*; Le Roy Ladurie, 'L'historie immobile'; Le Roy Ladurie, *The peasants of Languedoc*; Mielantis, 'Perspectives on the origins of merchant capitalism in Europe'; Miller and Hatcher, *Medieval England, towns, commerce and crafts, 1086–1348*; Moore, 'Nature and the transition from feudalism to capitalism'; Postan and Hatcher, 'Agrarian class structure and economic development in pre-industrial Europe'; Wickham, 'Productive forces and the economic logic of the feudal mode of production'; Wood, *The origins of capitalism: a longer view*. For a discussion of climate and epidemics, see: Bavel, 'Land, lease and agriculture: the transition of the rural economy in the Dutch river area'; Campbell, 'National incomes and economic growth in pre-industrial Europe'; 'Panzootics, pandemics and climatic anomalies in the fourteenth century'; 'Physical shocks, biological hazards, and human impacts'; Cavaciocchi (cur.), *Le interazioni fra economia e ambiente biologico nell'Europa preindustriale*.

of the Counts of Eppan, enlarging his domains as to include the Monreale or Königsberg Castle in Faedo. An imperial decree dated A.D. 1276 confirmed its rights to the castle.

Another factor that explains the limited role of anti-lord resistance was the strong 'lord-capital' nexus fostered by mining production. Monte Calisio had none of the rebellions that the mines of Harz and Kutná Horá experienced between the tenth and thirteenth centuries.[36] Bishop Wanga enjoyed the mineral incomes, while groups of *silbrarii* rapidly spread beyond Trent. The latter reached other Alpine cities, exploiting 'differentiated advantages' as members of a mining entrepreneurial class.[37] Private mine-drainage works spread from Monte Calisio to Terlano, Nalles, Villandro, Vitipeno, Gossensass, Fleres, Hall, and Schwaz, in Tyrol. In Styria, groups of private miners took over the works of the *fodinae* in the lands of the Benedictine Admont Abbey in A.D. 1185, in the same year as they arrived in Trent. They also appeared in Styria, where lords confirmed that *fodinam illam nostrum super Zezzen, quam illuvies aquarum superducens inutilem reddidit.*[38] In A.D. 1185, *socii* appeared in connection to *fodinam* [...] *quam dicunt aquaticam*. Mining lands in Ardesio, Vercelli, and Milan also saw the rise of various *consilium.*[39] *Silbrarii* found in the Alps societies engulfed by violent processes of territorialization of power and lords eager to score victories against members of their class. This condition opened the door for these entrepreneurs to secure mining monopolies and privileges that guaranteed the reproduction of their class.

The Premium Placed on Water Control: The Scars on a 'Hydraulic-Made Mountain'

Monopoly of landed property, Marx wrote, was a historical premise of capital, and remained the basis of production of value.[40] But what Marx overlooked was that this monopoly imposed the demand to conquer hydrogeological conditions. Water was not 'an accessory to the soil,' as

[36] For a general description of events involving mining disturbances and 'strikes,' see Blanchard, *Mining, metallurgy and minting in the Middle Ages, vol. 3 Continuing Afro-European supremacy*; Boyce, *The mines of the Upper Harz from 1514 to 1589*.

[37] Dobb, 'The entrepreneur myth,' p. 74.

[38] Paulinyi and Teil, 'Die Auflösung des grundherrschaftlichen Grudenbetriebes in den Zezzener Gruben,' p. 265, footnote 5.

[39] Mainoni, 'La politica dell'argento e del ferro nella Lombardia medieval,' pp. 441–442.

[40] Marx, *Capital, vol. 3 The process of capitalist production as a whole*, p. 723.

Marx wrongly said.[41] Hydrological conditions were never external to the rise of capitalist landed property, but integral to its historical possibilities. The development of these possibilities in the Adige Valley placed a premium on water control. The relations that ascertained the economic value that water control added to monopolies of land rights emerged early in villages and communities that specialized in riverine trade and transport. 'The first statutes which established rules for water transportation in this part of Italy are those of the Adige River rafters, written in 1260,' according to Agnoletti.[42] This was only possible because economic life depended upon fluvial trade routes. Farmers, shepherds, and miners relied for their sustenance upon imported grains and cereals, as well as fish, timber, and many other commodities coming from other districts.[43]

Since river driving was a specialized economy before mining took off, it transfer unto mining and all other extractive economies the value of water control as prerequisite of production as well as a gain of production. River driving enlarged the market catchment area of Trent. Raft owners or *barcaioli* dominated this economy and controlled riverine trade. They built competitive advantages in opportunities they found in territorialization of lordly power in the region. Their contribution to the premium on water control cannot be underestimated.[44] *Barcaioli* built their own rafts and dealt directly with timber dealers. They moved considerable quantities of low-value commodities. Made of fir, spruce, and larch, their rafts were approximately 28 meters long, 5 meters wide in the front part but reaching 6 meters, and had a one-meter draft.[45] Growth of their enterprises forced bishops to grant rights and intervene to settle disputes concerning privileged use of routes, lake ports, and tolls. In A.D. 1188, shippers from Mori obtained navigation privileges in a section of the river running from Lagarina and Bolzano. Wanga confirmed their rights, and granted additional shipping privileges over a larger tract of the river, where waters connected the Church of Ravazzone and Neuhaus near Terlano. In A.D. 1216,

[41] *Idem*, p. 722.

[42] Agnoletti, 'From the Dolomites to Venice: rafts and river driving along the Piave River,' p. 16.

[43] Appuhn, *A forest on the sea: environmental expertise in Renaissance Venice*, p. 113, 142.

[44] Agnoletti, 'From the Dolomites to Venice: rafts and river driving along the Piave River,' p. 17.

[45] Bonoldi, 'La risorsa mutevole, l'Adige nell'economia della regione trentino-tirolese,' p. 227, footnote 32.

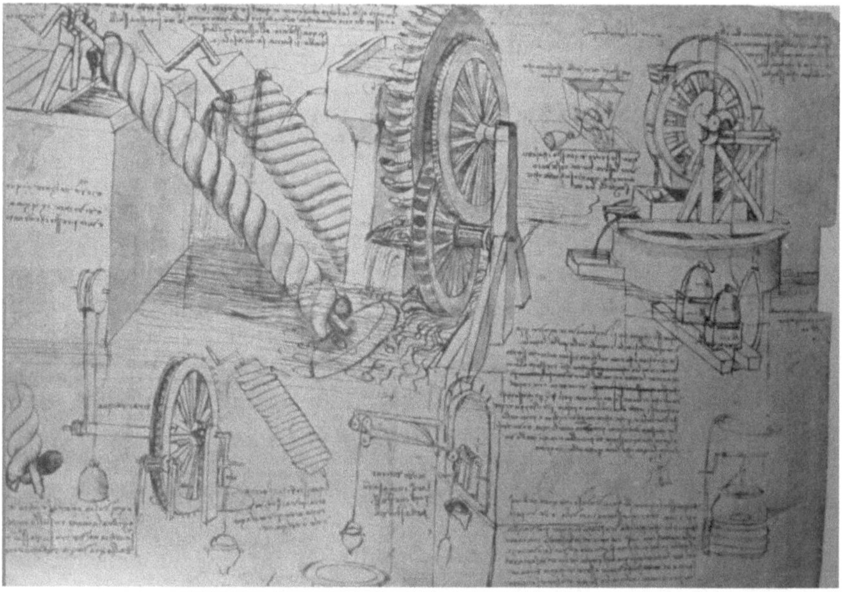

Fig. 5.3 Various designs of watermills and screws, in *Codex Atlanticus* by Leonardo Da Vinci. Hydraulic-machine designs illustrate the interest of medieval society in harnessing water for energy production and the dynamics of 'patrimonialization' of water resources. Biblioteca Ambrosiana, Milan, Italy/Art Resource, N.Y.

a riverine tax emerged for those shipping merchandise against the direction of the run of the river. The tax amounted to two *staia* of Trent for each raft[46] (Fig. 5.3).

The premium on water control embedded in Alpine commodity trade was an extension of the value added to fluvial trade. *Vectuarii* monopolized the business of moving goods, people, and money over long

[46]The *staia* was a unit of measurement of solids and liquids. Twenty-four *staia* or *staria* generally equaled one *modium*, but regional variations prevailed in the case of oil. Schneller, *Quellen und forschungen zur geschichte*, p. 151; Zupko, *Italian weights and measures from the Middle Ages to the nineteenth century*, pp. 269–274.

distances.[47] They were inland trade carriers that specialized in crossing Alpine passes. *Vectuarii* functioned in ways analogous to the *barcaioli*. They moved 'profit producing merchandise' on behalf of capitalists from Flanders in the north and Genoa to the south, crossing the Alps in every direction.[48] They also provided security to travelers and commodities, at a price. Their activities increased the cost of trade. Operating at the smallest trade circuit of the medieval economy, they reinforced the pattern of monopoly prices imposed by sea leagues that controlled continental trade such as the Hanseatic League and Genoese merchant houses. Their monopolies of maritime trade and shipping transferred the cost of trade to each and all local economies they attracted into their orbit. Their influence was felt in increasing costs of travel across Danube routes.[49]

Shipping and trade monopolies increased prices of luxury commodities, spreading unto society the premium on water control. The patrimonial aristocracy and the nobility of the district naturally adapted and responded to this force. Consumption of imported luxury goods distinguished the aristocratic class from the rest of the upper class.[50] It endowed this class with a sense of lifestyle and high status, a condition that sustained the premium on water control. Water was to this class a symbol of glittering ships and vessels, an element that roused vassals from 'natural indolence,' and the cause of agricultural progress. Treatises on hydraulic machines circulated among members of the aristocracy. Some aristocrats collected the medieval best sellers on the subject of hydraulic machines.[51] *De redus bellicis*, that accompanied the *Notitia dignitatum*, was a compilation of images of hydraulic machines used in Carolingian times. The Florentine Niccolò Ridolfi, nephew of the Medici, owned an eleventh-century copy of this work. Alfonso X of Castile, nicknamed 'The Wise,' sponsored the

[47] Moore, 'Nature and the transition from feudalism to capitalism,' p. 101.

[48] Reynolds, 'Merchants of Arras and the overland trade with Genoa,' p. 502.

[49] Edson, *The world map 1300–1492, the persistence of tradition and transformation*, p. 90; Spufford, *Power and profit: the merchant in medieval Europe*, p. 317.

[50] Packard, *12th century Europe. an interpretative essay*, p. 64.

[51] Allen, *The Industrial Revolution: a very short introduction*, p. 49; Assadourian, 'La bomba de fuego de Newcomen y otros artificios de desagüe'; Ceccarelli, 'Renaissance machines in Italy: from Brunelleschi to Galileo,' pp. 1532–1533 for drawings by Mariano di Jacopo; García Tapia, *Patentes de invención españolas en el siglo de oro*; 'Ingenios para desagüar las minas a principios del siglo XVII'; 'La máquina de vapor inventada y patentada en 1606 por Jerónimo De Ayanz'; Grau Fernández (cur.), *Ars Mechanicae ingeniería medieval en España*; Lambton, 'The qānāts of Yazd'; Multhauf, 'Mine pumping in Agricola's time and later'; Rossi, 'The precursors of Leonardo Da Vinci's studies.'

translation of the ninth-century work entitled *Kitāb al-Ḥiyal* (translated as *El libro de los instrumentos maravillosos*). This richly illuminated treatise was an Arabic compilation of ancient Greek works on the subject of hydraulic machines done by 'Banū (sons of) Mūsà.'[52] Treatises by figures of the Islamic Golden Age period, including Ismail Al-Jazari (A.H. 548–630/A.D. 1136–1206) from Persia and Alī ibn Riḍwān (d. A.H. 460/A.D. 1067–8) from Syria, were part of the private library of Emperor Frederick II.[53]

Aristocratic obsession with water was a historical imposition of inter-continental economic change. Population and income expansion forced European societies to battle against 'chaotic hydrologies,' for such battle determined the possibilities of profits in Afro-Eurasian trade. As mentioned earlier, the Islamic State and the Mongol Empire endured a reorganization of power that had consequences for world silver trade.[54] The reorganization of 'the thirteenth-century world system'[55] created conditions for mining districts to look inward and mobilize the entire society in a collective but uneven battle against waters. Production and trade possibilities of mining lands reinforced the premium on water control. The upper class soon received rewards in emerging profit and rent horizons including profits from the trade of silver currencies[56] (Fig. 5.4).

Climate influenced the premium society placed on water control. The second half of the eleventh century was a time of regular winters, short duration of snow cover, and no freezing of major rivers. Leaving the notable exception of the winter of A.D. 1076/1077 aside, sources of the period studied by Pfister and his colleagues highlighted the 'snowiness' of winters.[57] The medieval warm period had started well. The cold winter of A.D. 1099–1100 had no adverse impacts in rivers either, at least none observed by contemporaries. The severe winter of A.D. 1149–1150 that froze the Rhine and Thames rivers, allowing horses to use the rivers as ice roads,

[52] Hill (trans.), *The Book of Ingenious Devices (Kitāb al-Ḥiyal)*, p. 3.

[53] Gille, *Les ingénieurs de la Renaissance*, p. 18, pp. 72–76.

[54] Petech, 'Les marchands italiens dans l'empire mongol'; Tilly, *Coercion, capital and European states.*

[55] Gunder Frank, 'The thirteenth-century world system: a review history';

[56] Saccocci, 'La monetazione del *Regnum Italiae* e l'evoluzione complessiva del sistema monetario Europea,' p. 1037.

[57] Pfister, Luterbacher, Schwarz-Zanetti et al., 'Winter air temperature variations in western Europe,' p. 542.

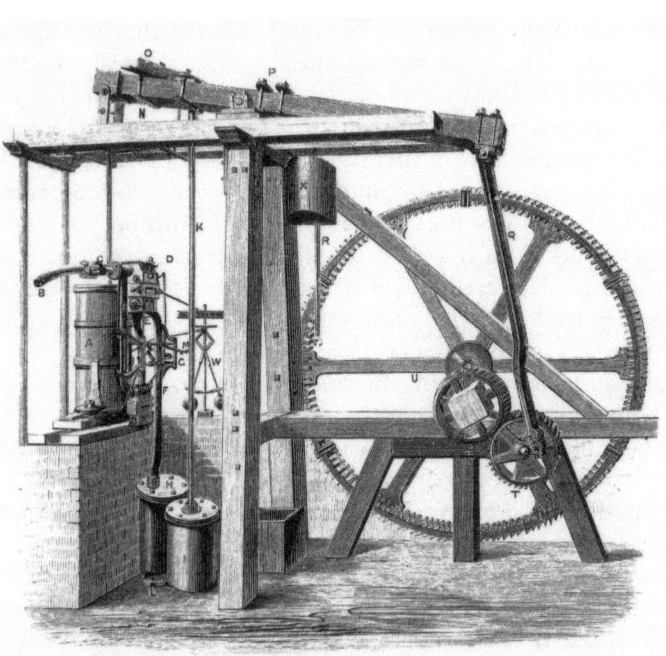

Fig. 5.4 A prototype of the steam engine by James Watt, in *Lives of Boulton and Watt* (London, 1865). The invention of the steam engine was according to Marx the 'prime mover' of the modern capitalist production because it put coal and water 'entirely under man's control.' The machine was 'an improvement upon steam or fire engines for raising water, and other mechanical purposes,' according to James Watt in his *Letter Patent* of A.D. 1782. Today, experts agree that the true origins of the machine are to be found in the hydraulic revolution that took place in medieval landscapes of Italy and the Mediterranean. Art Resource, N.Y.

produced nothing of that sort in the Adige Valley.[58] The cold wave affecting northern Europe, in particular the severe winter of A.D. 1204–1205, failed to extend to north Italy or did not affect north Italy in the same way it affected the northern plains. With the exception of the winter of A.D. 1233–1234, a calamitous season that brought 'continuous frosts' and frozen rivers everywhere in the Alps, Trent and its valleys truly enjoyed the best of the medieval warm period.[59]

[58] *Idem*, pp. 543–544.
[59] Comiti, 'How natural are Alpine valleys?' p. 695.

Miners seized the premium on water control that emerged in this rural economy. They conquered the hydrogeological conditions of Monte Calisio, but did so while creating water-management contradictions that society passed unto its future generations. Contradictions were not independent from their geographic setting. Here, the benevolent hand of Nature, as Adam Smith referred to good geography, transformed the Alps into the 'water tower of Europe.'[60] This feature exempted miners from the need to adapt hydraulic techniques to water conservation and recycling. While arid Mediterranean geographies imposed the need for scrupulous management of water waste, Alpine settings instilled upon miners different views about waste.[61] Waste that accumulated in the womb of the mountain represented value of mining works. Thus, waste symbolized the freedom to exploit the subterranean wealth of the mountain. Such powerful drive was the outcome of a whole economy that encouraged rapid depletion of mineral resources. The mining method of *silbrarii* was to exhaust the mineralization body by increasing extraction rates. It meant digging continuously so as to extract as much matter as possible. As noted earlier, to avoid expenses of hauling and transporting unwanted material, miners buried mine waste inside the mountain. The decision enhanced production possibilities of Monte Calisio, sustaining the structures of lordly competition that organized this medieval society.[62]

However, discarding mine waste in water basins led to the classical problem of 'marginal lands' inside the mining mountain. This problem had long-term impacts on mineral profits and rents. Outside the mining mountain, pollution created by smelting operations, with boles sending fumes and pollutants into the air and nearby streams and rivers, triggered ecological problems that exacerbated clashes over rents.[63] Tuberculosis, 'the great white plague,'[64] was possibly more devastating in mining villages. People got the disease in early childhood and became

[60] Margit Schwikowski and Anja Eichler in Bundi (ed.), *Alpine waters*, p. 149.

[61] For general comparisons, see Ashtor and Kedar, *Technology, industry and trade: the Levant* versus *Europe*; Canto García and Cressier (comp.), *Minas y metalurgia en al-Andalus y Magreb occidental*; Vryonis, 'The question of Byzantine mines.'

[62] Martin Straßburger, 'About Monte Calisio' Zoom video-meeting and emails to Jeannette Graulau, September 9–10, 2024.

[63] Moore, 'Nature and the transition from feudalism to capitalism,' p. 99.

[64] Carlo Cipolla, in Cipolla (ed.), *The Fontana economic history of Europe*, p. 52.

definitely ill in early manhood. No account of the impacts of diseases and plagues in mines are available for this period, but the following sixteenth-century account describes in detail the effects of *mala metallicorum* on miners:

> Where water in shafts is abundant and very cold, it frequently injures the limbs, for cold is harmful to the sinews. To meet this, miners should make themselves sufficiently high boots of rawhide, which protect their legs from the cold water; the man who does not follow this advice will suffer much ill-health, especially when he reaches old age. On the other hand, some mines are so dry that they are entirely devoid of water, and this dryness causes the workmen even greater harm, for the dust which is stirred and beaten up by digging penetrates into the windpipe and lungs, and produces difficulty in breathing. ... If the dust has corrosive qualities, it eats away the lungs, and implants consumption in the body; hence in the mines of the Carpathian mountains women are found who have married seven husbands, all of whom this terrible consumption has carried off to a premature death. At Altenberg in Meissen there is found in the mines black *pompholyx*, which eats wounds and ulcers to the bone; this also corrodes iron, for which reason the keys of their sheds are made of wood. Further, there is a certain kind of *cadmia* which eats away the feet of the workmen when they have become wet, and similarly their hands, and injures their lungs and eyes.[65]

There is no doubt that the burden of water control was never uniformly spread in society. The premium on water control, however, set a uniform level of the average rate of profits and rents as the thirteenth century progressed. It heavily influenced the rise of mining hydraulic works, which in turn led to development of smelting, assaying, and diverse uses of metals.[66] As the primordial source of strength of mining profits and rents, drainage works possibly dissolved serfdom in the mines, increasing the premium on water control. Drainage works scarred Monte Calisio. They created a 'hydraulic-made mountain' bearing the cost of the premium on water control[67] (Fig. 5.5).

[65] Hoover and Hoover (trans.), *De re metallica*, pp. 214–215.

[66] Ashtor and Kedar, *Technology, industry and trade: Levant v. Europe*; Bork, Montgomery, Neumann de Vegvar et al. (eds.), *De re metallica: the uses of metal in the Middle Ages.*

[67] Stovall, 'Queer mountains made by placer miners,' p. 695.

Fig. 5.5 Watermill in the mountains and a draftsman, by Albrecht Dürer (A.D. 1471–1528). Dürer was known for his rapid sketching technique. His 'training as a goldsmith had taught him precision of stroke and accuracy of eye,' and in all possibility, the watermill of the drawing was very close to how he saw it somewhere in the Alps. bpk Bildagentur/Kupferstichkabinett, Staatliche Museen zu Berlin, Germany. Photo: Jörg P. Anders. Art Resource, N.Y.

Mining and Hegemonic Power Beyond Trent

Mineral wealth allowed Wanga to temporarily contain the explosive internal divisions and politics of the Church of Trent. Monte Calisio remained a valuable mining mountain for some time after the death of Wanga. From obscurity in Carolingian times, it emerged in the thirteenth century as testament to the pursuit of feudal power. Medieval writers and artists associated mountains with 'attributes of royal power, privileged legal spaces embodied in montane statutes, and residence of God.'[68] *Mons arçentarie* embodied these ideas and more. It stood as symbol of feudal power and vibrant mining times. Territorialization of power continued to shift jurisdictions of rent rights and privileges. Confirmation of rights *ad rectum feudum* by the Counts of Tyrol allowed the small nobility to withstand forces of economic change. The lords of Campo enlarged their possessions until the mid-fourteenth century. They owned numerous *homines et persone sive vassalli* scattered in the Giudicarie, acquired with the rise of Tyrolean hegemony. Their patrimonial rights extended into the Laghi Valley, Ranzo, Toblino, Vezzano, and Bleggio and Banale. However, they lost feudal rights over the Campo Castle, giving away their most strategic asset situated between Duron Pass and Trent. The Lodron lords also increased possessions of agrarian lands in the Giudicarie. Faithful only to their class interests, both noble families forged alliances with local lords, trying to resist the territorial expansion of the Tyrolean aristocracy. Reconciling old quarrels became a survival prerequisite for this class.

Exploiting opportunities after the death of Wanga, the Arco lords deepened their claims for rents in Garda. They confirmed charters of rights to villages located in different valleys, issuing over 40 *postae*, *ordinamenta*, and *statute* in agrarian villages surrounding Trent. Granting fiscal autonomy to villages exempted the Arco lords from spending their resources in putting together *milites* to confront the bishops. They entered the fourteenth century as local lords of considerable political weight. In A.D. 1277, the lord of Arco enjoyed the right to impose castle-guard labor obligations and other labor services to communities of the Giudicarie.[69] The spatial dispersion of assets minimized their dependency upon one single niche of agrarian production. It shielded the agrarian wealth of the family from short-term crises associated to hydrological and environmental factors. In the long run, however, the Arco lords suffered significant losses, although they retained rights over strategic castles in the contested Giudicarie area. They survived the Tyrolean expansion after securing politico-military alliances with Brescia and Lombardian communes, before aligning with the nobility of Venice in the fifteenth century.

[68] Thomasset and James-Raoul (eds.), *La montagne dans le texte medieval, entre mythe et réalité*, pp. 126–127.

[69] Franceschini, 'Castelli e campagnie in area trentine,' pp. 210–211.

The forces of economic change that carried on land exploitation had already chosen the winners. The Count of Tyrol rapidly enlarged his jurisdiction of rights and privileges in the Adige Valley.[70] The death of Emperor Frederick II in A.D. 1250 added pressures onto the upper class for reterritorialization of power. A successor of Bishop Wanga appointed Count Meinhard II to lead a territorial reorganization of the Giudicarie on behalf of the city. A political change that seemed quite irrelevant opened the door to a series of small but meaningful legal changes. The power of feudal law in the hands of an expansionist nobility soon had effects. What followed were a series of transfers of rent-yielding lands by the local nobility to Count Meinhard II, who used the law to erode the basis of power of his competitors. The Tyrolean count confirmed rent rights to Nicolò, son of the late Silvestro of Lodron in A.D. 1284, in exchange for loyalty.[71] The investiture included lands previously granted to the Counts of Eppan and Ultimo. Years later, the son of Nicolò swore loyalty to the Count of Tyrol, the Duke of Carinthia, and the Church of Trent in A.D. 1302. Armed with the power of feudal law, the Counts of Tyrol removed local rural lords from the House of Canons of the Chapter of the Church of Trent, replacing them with his own noble allies from the Tyrolean nobility. The latter were to become faithful *milites* of Count Meinhard II.[72]

Ongoing conflicts among aristocratic families north and south of the Alps, and internal strife in Trent, forced Emperor Rudolf I (r. A.D. 1273–1291) to intervene in the city. Economic and military allies in northern Italy came in handy to the first emperor of a rising Habsburg dynasty.[73] The emperor granted the seat of the bishopric to Filippo Bonacolsi of Mantua (r. A.D. 1289–1303). But soon Bishop Bonacolsi discovered the legal and economic power the Tyrolean aristocracy exercised in the district. His title was only a semblance of political authority. He could not even live in the city, choosing instead a safer place outside the

[70] Dematté, 'Immagini di dame e cavalieri: affreschi cavallereschi,' pp. 14–16.

[71] Olschki, 'Il ruolo di vescovi e conti nello sviluppo urbano del Tirolo'; Stenico, 'Signorie rurali e risorse economiche.'

[72] Bettotti and Landi, 'Signorie rurali, coscienza nobiliare e autorappresentazione,' pp. 300–303.

[73] Dematté, 'Immagini di dame e cavalieri: affreschi cavallereschi,' p. 16.

gaze of Count Meinhard II. Forced to build alliances, Bonacolsi granted the Garda and Tenno castles to sons of the Count. The bishop sealed his fate. Bonacolsi never regained the territories that once belonged to Bishop Wanga, and eventually gave up the title of Prince-Bishop. The Tirolean aristocrats occupied the grand Arco Castle and expanded jurisdictional rights into the Giudicarie region. A new imperial hegemony was on the rise, and one that would transform Trent into a 'client state' of the Habsburg dynasty (Figs. 5.6 and 5.7).

The crisis announced the ascent of new hegemonic clashes that paved the way for a mining renaissance in the region. Monte Calisio ceded the center stage to Pergine, Terlano, Nalle, Villandro, Vipiteno, Gossensass, Flères, Hall, and Schwaz.[74] Silver and copper mining works flourished in these places, in the hands of German capitalists. German capital unleashed the productive forces of European mining, rehearsing competitive advantages that in time proved crucial to the Spanish Empire.[75] They introduced considerable mine improvements, such as the two-wheel wagon and the wooden track found at the Faedo mine. Faedo became a mining factory. Inside the mine, the scene was dark but noisy, while outside 'no friendly trees and beasts and clouds greet the eye.'[76] As Monte Calisio miners had experienced centuries earlier, Faedo miners incessantly faced the 'predominant power of nature.'[77] They responded to sudden tearing of wood beams, loud noises beneath a shaft floor, and unexpected 'cracks of rocks,' advancing further conditions that sustained mining profits and rents.[78]

The subterranean wealth of the region attracted Venetian capitalists. War between Venice and the Habsburg emperor gave these capitalists compelling reasons to dig wealth in rural lands north of the city.[79] Venetian

[74] Coativy, 'La montagne est-elle une frontière?,' p. 46; Földváry, *Geology of the Carpathian region*, p. 11.

[75] On the subject, see Friede, 'La introducción de mineros alemanes en América por la compañía Welser de Ausgburg'; García Tapia, 'Ingenios para desagüar las minas a principios del siglo XVII'; Graulau, 'Finance, industry and globalization: the example of the House of the Fugger.'

[76] Mumford, *Technics and civilization*, p. 69.

[77] Paul, *Mining lore*, p. 510.

[78] *Idem*, p. 511.

[79] Stenico, 'Signorie rurali e risorse economiche.'

Fig. 5.6 St. Barbara, detail from stained glass window in Parish Church of St. Stephen in Villanders, South Tyrol (A.D. 1520). After Virgin Mary, St. Barbara was the 'most generated female saint of the Middle Ages,' states historian Derolez. According to legend, her father locked her in a tower, where she converted to Christianity against his will. Furious about her conversion, the man turned her to a Roan judge for sentencing. Then, a rock opened herself to the young virgin, where she hid until betrayed by a shepherd. The father found her and beheaded her, but he was 'punished on the spot by being struck by lightning.' She became patroness of miners, masons, architects, and gunners. Institute for Material Culture, University of Salzburg

mercatores purchased large quantities of silver mined in Trent, Tyrol, and Styria, which they sent to the mint of Venice. In a letter to the bishop of Trent, Venetian merchant Pietro Luna politely requested that the government of the city built a new mint, for him and silver traders, *mercato res*

Fig. 5.7 St. Daniel, detail from stained glass window in Parish Church of St. Stephen, Villanders, South Tyrol (A.D. 1520). To Alpine miners, the image of Prophet Daniel meant 'triumph over suffering' because he was cast into the lion's den. It symbolized the wrestling of man with nature. Daniel is portrayed holding a rock, in allusion to his words, 'I have forenamed you a spiritual mountain, whence a stone was cut out, Oh, spotless Virgin Mother!' Institute for Material Culture, University of Salzburg

minerarum, to sell ores exploited in nearby Tyrolean mines. He offered his services to the bishop, as *expertissimus in hac arte*.[80] The Habsburg

[80] Graulau, 'Finance, industry and globalization: the example of the House of the Fugger'; Irsigler, 'Rheinisches kapital in Mitteleuropäischen montanunternehmen des 15. und 16. Jahrhunderts'; Jeannin, 'Le cuivre, les Fugger et la Hanse'; Kellenbenz, 'Le miniere di

dynasty under Maximilan I (emperor during A.D. 1486–1519; archduke of Austria during A.D. 1493–1519) exploited this bonanza. It implemented stringent technical and regulatory policies that aimed at monopolizing mine revenues. It placed governing functions in a tribunal of mines established at Pergine in Valsugana in A.D. 1489. Surplus produced by miners in Pergine in Fersina Valley found its way to Innsbruck, where Emperor Maximilian I impatiently waited. Pergine had thus become the mining frontier of Innsbruck (Fig. 5.8).

The rural landscape also changed. Many families of the nobility progressively abandoned feudal castles for newly built palaces in the city. Some families embellished and reconstructed castles that were once symbol of lordly power. Some new families took stock of available rural patrimony and claimed noble ancestors, giving birth to fifteenth-century ennobled lineages.[81] Heraldic seals and coat of arms, social forms of feudal power, flourished in Trent from the fifteenth century onward. Certainly, hegemonic competition created conditions for clinging to nobility titles. A European world shaped by Habsburg geopolitical interests opened spaces for the cultural survival of the old nobility.[82] Members of this class joined the Order of the Golden Fleece, particularly the lords of Arco, Caldes, Castelbarco, Firmiano, and Thun.[83]

Renewed 'vestiges of feudalism,' however, lacked economic conditions to reach stature. The mining renaissance of 'the long sixteenth century' (A.D. 1450–1650) was not enough to build material development on a wider scale.[84] Neither German nor Venetian capitalists were to blame for the disappointment. Rather, the force of change came from across the Atlantic. Discovery of rich silver mines of Zacatecas, Guanajuato, and especially Potosí, the richest silver mine in the orbit of Habsburg power,

Primiero e le relazioni dei Fugger con Venezia nel quatrocento'; 'Firmenarchive und ihre bedeutung für die Europäische wirtschafts -un sozialgeschichte'; Kellenbenz, (ed.), *Precious metals in the age of expansion*; Stromer, 'Nuremberg in the international economics of the middle ages.'

[81] Bettotti and Landi, 'Signorie rurali, coscienza nobiliare e autorappresentazione,' pp. 304–307.

[82] Benecke, 'Maximilian I and his subjects.'

[83] Bettotti and Landi, 'Signorie rurali, coscienza nobiliare e autorappresentazione,' pp. 320–321.

[84] Stenico, 'Signorie rurali e risorse economiche: forme di prelievo e di gestione,' pp. 238–239.

Fig. 5.8 Stages of mining, in *Magnalia Dei in locis subterraneis* by Franz Ernst Brückmann (A.D. 1697–1753). Physician Franz Brückmann, following the example set by Agricola two centuries earlier, captured vividly the mining world he saw in Jáchymov. His book, titled The Greatness of God in Subterranean Sites, contains handsome plates depicting mining and smelting sites in this town. The drawing shows all stages of mining but prospection. In the lower left side, three miners dig the rockwall of a shaft while a fourth workman blows fresh air by using a ventilation machine. An overshot wheel is mounted on another shaft. Five miners work in the smelting factory, while other miners transport crude ores from neighboring shafts to the factory. This is how mining works at Pergine must have looked like a few centuries after the death of Bishop Wanga. ETH-Bibliothek Zürich, E-Rara

reoriented mining activity to the Atlantic world.[85] With the exception of small iron mines and quarries in Monte Baldo, the glory of the medieval Alpine industry was long gone by.[86]

[85] For global silver production and trade in this period, see: Bakewell, *Miners of the Red Mountain; Indian labor in Potosí*; Bazant, 'Minería medieval de la plata y el cobre en Europa Central'; Brading, 'Las minas de plata en el Perú y México'; Flynn and Giráldez, *China and the birth of globalization in the 16th century*; Kellenbenz (ed.), *Precious metals in the age of expansion*.

[86] Marco Stenico offers evidence of decline of mining works, based upon accounting books of the mining judge of Pergine. The books included details about tax collected during the

Back in the thirteenth century, Wanga put in place a mode of mining governance that emphasized the supremacy of the notarized contract. His was a political world dominated by *instrumentum notarile*. Law was central to the exercise of public authority and *publica fides* in the district.[87] The *carta ficto* discussed earlier not only legitimized the ascent of private drainage works, but endowed mining with a foundational legal structure unto which *silbrarii* built advantages and gains. Lawyers came from mountain cities rather than urban communes. Imperial strategies against the expansion of the Lombardian culture of dissent placed them in a privileged position. As mentioned earlier, notaries had the benefit of immersion in feudal and Lombardian law. Exempted from military service, they joined *gastaldia* and ministerials of bishops.[88] From *Malwarnitus*, the first notary of Trent in A.D. 1165, to *Ercetus*, imperial notary of Wanga, they confirmed political authority of bishops over Trent.[89] Their craft and offices changed, too, in response to lordly competition. Wanga was one the last bishops who used *avvocatia* to share power with patrimonial families. *Avvocatia* was a bundle of civil and criminal-justice powers entrusted to noble families in exchange for loyalty. In time, it became a de facto transfer of rent rights to patrimonial families. After Wanga, the institution

period A.D. 1605–1616. The Viarago mines, also in Fersina Valley, officially had no revenues from the *fron* or decimal tax on raw minerals during the years A.D. 1607–1610 and 1613–1615. They had *wegerlon* incomes for the years A.D. 1608–1613. The latter was a tax on the weighing of copper. Consequently, the number of officers at the Pergine mining office decreased, and so did annual salary of the chief judge. The latter decreased from 100 florins in A.D. 1508, to 75 florins in the mid-sixteenth century, and 40 florins in the mid-seventeenth century. Stenico, 'Signorie rurali e risorse economiche: forme di prelievo e di gestione,' p. 244; Tasser and Westermann (eds.), *Der Tiroler bergbau und die depression der europäischen montanwirtschaft*.

[87] Only Count Albert III of Tyrol, Count Ulrich II of Eppan-Ulten, and the noblemen Alberone II, Beraldo, and Frederick II of Wanga had heraldic seals, used exclusively when confirming rent donations to ecclesiastical institutions in German lands including Bressanone. Marco Bettotti and Walter Landi found only one heraldic seal in Trent, which belonged to a man who came from the *macinatae* of the counts of Eppan-Ulten. His name was Ulrich II of Greinsberg in Eppan. The seal was used in A.D. 1224 to confirm the authenticity of a donation in favor of the monastery of St. Georgenberg, where Bishop Conrad enjoyed his retirement. Bettotti and Landi, 'Signorie rurali, coscienza nobiliare e autorappresentazione,' pp. 308–309; Curzel and Varanini, *La documentazione dei vescovi di Trento*, pp. 11–14.

[88] Leicht, *Studi sulla proprietà fondiaria nel medio evo*, p. 88.

[89] Curzel and Varanini, *La documentazione dei vescovi di Trento*, pp. 61–62, footnote 101.

evolved into a seat opened for competition among aristocratic families who sought the office as a way of gaining rights from bishops.[90]

Due to his boldness and commitment to imperial politics, Wanga succeeded in the exercise of lordly power. He took the principality into a brief but enduring period of splendor. His zealot views on Christianity and the Carolingian Church served the empire and the Papacy well. After a decade ruling Trent, Wanga joined the call by Pope Honorius III to the Fifth Crusade.[91] The troubled relation that King John of Jerusalem had with Emperor Frederick II most likely influenced his desire to join the crusading army. Earlier, many aristocratic *milites* from eastern Alpine lands had joined Emperor Henry VI in the Fourth Crusade (A.D. 1197–1198). The group included some names well known in the city of Trent: Count Meinhard II; Count Ulrich II of Eppan; Count Otto II of Ortenburg in Carinthia; 'and most likely also Ulrich II of Spanheim, Duke of Carinthia.'[92] Wanga most likely reached Acre by October 1217, where Duke Leopold of Austria mustered the crusading army. It is possible that two years earlier, the bishop witnessed the coronation of Emperor Frederick II as King of the Romans in Aachen. For it was in Aachen, the city of Roman baths, that Charlemagne had so much cherished, where German princes made the bow to 'take the cross' to Jerusalem.[93] Wanga died in Acre, far away from his treasured city, on November 6, 1218.

The name of the bishop and his legacy were to stay in Roncolo Castle built by the Wanga family. Locals refer to this castle as *Schloss Runkelstein*.[94] This 'massive structure,' imposed on top of Tondo Mountain in Bolzano, offers unrivaled views of the road leading toward Trent.[95] Overlooking a fertile vineyard, the castle stood above hardships of peasants who populated the foot of the valley. Far away from the nearest city of Toggenburg, it afforded protection and security from urban riots. It displayed 'the growing prosperity' of the Wangas. But even here, vicious lordly competition followed the Wangas; the castle was wrecked in A.D. 1277, in one of

[90] Castagnetti, *Governo vescovile, feudalità, 'communitas' cittadina*, p. 39; Curzel and Varanini, *La documentazione dei vescovi di Trento*, p. 70.

[91] Bird, Peters, and Powell (eds.), *Crusade and Christendom*, p. 103; for a history, see also Cahen, 'Notes sur l'histoire des croisades et de l'Orient Latin'; Phillips, *The Crusades*; Rasmo, *L'èta cavalleresca in Val d'Adige*.

[92] Kosi, 'The Fifth Crusade and its aftermath,' p. 93.

[93] *Idem*, p. 95.

[94] Rasmo, *Cultura atesina*, pp. 6–9.

[95] *Idem*, p. 2.

the last episodes of violent clashes between patrimonial families. Soon after, the Wanga family disappeared, and the city of Trent claimed jurisdiction of the castle. A lawyer and relative of Duke Leopold III of Austria made the castle his residence, after major remodeling and construction works in the fourteenth century. A century later, Emperor Maximilian transformed the castle into 'a pleasant residence' embellished with fifteenth-century frescoes. General Giorgio di Frundsberg, after distinguishing himself in the sack of Rome headed by Emperor Charles V in A.D. 1527, lived in the old Wanga residence. The castle changed hands again, and again, until the city of Bolzano added the castle to its urban patrimony in the last years of the nineteenth century. The city remodeled the castle over the years and made it a tourist attraction. Today, visitors admire the well-preserved frescoes, along with magnificent vistas of vineyards that surround the castle grounds. Even when parts of the original walls were lost to wars and feuds, the castle stands, surrounded by green hills that quietly evoke the *inquietante essenzialità* of Bishop Wanga.

Bibliography

Abballe, Michele, and Marco Cavalazzi. 2022. Flood risk and socio-ecological resilience in a late antique and medieval countryside: Managing a post-Roman alluvial landscape in the Ravenna hinterland. In *Juvenes: The Middle Ages seen by young researchers, vol. 2, Space(s)*, ed. André F. Oliveira da Silva, André Madruga Coelho, José Simões, et al., 1–22. Évora.

Aberth, John. 2013. *An environmental history of the Middle Ages, the crucible of nature*. New York.

Abulafia, David. 1988. *Frederick II: A medieval emperor*. Oxford.

Abulafia, David. 1993. *Commerce and conquest in the Mediterranean 1100–1500*. Hampshire.

Abulafia, David, ed. 1999. *The new Cambridge medieval history, vol. 5, c.1198–1300*. Cambridge.

Abu-Lughod, Janet. 1991. *Before European hegemony: The world system A.D. 1250–1350*. Cambridge.

Adams, Jonathan. 2013. *A maritime archaeology of ships Innovation and social change in medieval and early modern Europe*. Oxford and Oakville.

Adams, Norma. The judicial conflict over tithes. *The English Historical Review* 52 (205): 1–22.

Agnew, John A. 2013. Editorial. Territory, politics, governance. *Territory, Politics, Governance* 1:1–4.

Agnoletti, Mauro. 1995. From the Dolomites to Venice: Rafts and river driving along the Paive river in Italy (13th to 20th centuries). *The Journal of the Society for Industrial Archeology* 21:15–32.

J. Graulau, *Medieval Mining and Power in Thirteenth-Century Europe*, https://doi.org/10.1007/978-3-031-99239-1

Alberti, Francesco F. 1860. *Annali del principato ecclesiastico di Trento dal 1022 al 1540*, reint. T. Gar. Trento.

Albertoni, Giuseppe. 2010. Law and the peasant: Rural society and justice in Carolingian Italy. *Early Medieval Europe* 18:417–445.

Albertoni, Giuseppe. 2015. *Vassalli, feudi, feudalesimo*. Roma.

Albertoni, Giuseppe, and Luigi Provero. 2003. *Il feudalismo in Italia*. Roma.

Allen, Martin. 2011. Silver production and the money supply in England and Wales, 1086–c.1500. *The Economic History Review* 64:114–131.

Allen, Robert C. 2017. *The Industrial Revolution: A very short introduction*. Oxford.

Ambrosi, Francesco. 1881. *Trento e il suo circondario, descritti al viaggiatore*. Trento.

Anderolli, Bruno. 1999. *Contadini su terre di signori: Studi sulla contrattualistica agraria dell'Italia medievale*. Bologna.

Andersen, Thomas B., Peter S. Jensen, and Christian Volmar Skovsgaard. 2016. The heavy plow and the agricultural revolution in medieval Europe. *Journal of Development Economics* 118:133–149.

Angel, Michael. 1989. *Mines et fondaries au XVIe siècle*. Paris.

Angelakis, Andreas N., Giovanni De Feo, Pietro Laureano, et al. 2013. Minoan and Etruscan hydro-technologies. *Water* 5:972–987.

Appuhn, Karl. 2009. *A forest on the sea, environmental expertise in renaissance Venice*. Maryland.

Archetti, Gabriele. 2011. "Fecerunt malgas in casina" Alevamento transhumante e alpeggi nella Lombardia medieval. In *La pastorizia mediterranea storia e diritto (secoli XI-XX)*, ed. A. Mattone and P. F. Simbula, 486–509. Roma.

Arhin, Kwame. 1978. Gold-mining and trading among the Ashanti of Ghana. *Journal des Africanistes* 48:89–100.

Arnold, Benjamin. 1989. German bishops and their military retinues in the medieval empire. *The German History Society* 7:161–183.

Arnold, Ellen F. 2013. *Negotiating the landscape: Environment and monastic identity in the medieval Ardennes*. Philadelphia.

Arrighi, Giovanni. 2010. *The long twentieth century. Money, power and the origins of our times*. London and New York.

Ashtor, Eliyahu, and Benjamin Z. Kedar. 1992. *Technology, industry and trade: The Levant versus Europe, 1250–1500*. London and New York.

Assadourian, Carlos S. 2001. La bomba de fuego de Newcomen y otros artificios de desagüe: Un intento de transferencia de tecnología inglesa a la minería novohispana, 1726–1731. *Historia Mexicana* 1:385–457.

Aston, Trevor H., and Charles H. E. Philpin, eds. 1985. *The Brenner debate: Agrarian class structure and economic development in pre-industrial Europe*. New York.

Ault, Warren O. 1965. Open-field husbandry and the village community: A study of agrarian by-laws in medieval England. *Transactions of the American Philosophical Society* 55:1–102.

Baedeker, Karl. 1871. *Southern Germany and Austria, including the eastern Alps, handbook for travelers.* Koblenz.

Baillie-Grohman, William A. 1907. *The land in the mountains, being an account of the past & present of Tyrol.* London.

Bailly-Maître, Marie C., and Paul Benoît. 1997. Les mines d'argent de la France médiévale. In *Actes des congrès de la Société des Historiens Médiévistes de l'Enseignement Supérieur Public, 28ᵉ congrès, L'argent au Moyen Âge*, ed. Claude Gauvard, 17–45. Clermont-Ferrand.

Bakewell, Peter. 1984. *Miners of the Red Mountain: Indian labor in Potosí, 1545–1650.* Albuquerque.

Baldwin, Joseph W. 1959. The medieval theories of the just price: Romanists, Canonists, and theologians in the twelfth and thirteenth centuries. In *Pre-capitalist thought: Three modern interpretations, Series The evolution of capitalism*, ed. Leonard S. Silk, 5–92. Philadelphia.

Ball, John. 1873. *The Central Alps, including the Bernese Oberland.* London.

Barbiera, Irene, and Gianpiero Dalla-Zuana. 2024. Demographic systems of medieval Italy (6th–15th centuries AD). *Population and Development Review* 50:541–570.

Barthélemy, Dominique, and Stephen D. White. 1996. Debate, the feudal revolution. *Past & Present* 152:196–223.

Bassetti, Michele, and Andrea Borsato. 2005. Evoluzione geomorfologica della Bassa Valle dell'Adige dall'Ultimo Massimo Glaciale: Sintesi delle conoscenze e riferimenti ad aree limitrofe. *Studi Trentini di Scienze Naturali Acta Geologica* 82:31–42.

Bath, Slicher. 1963. *The agrarian history of Western Europe, A.D. 500-1850.* London.

Battista Pellegrini, Giovan. 1991. *La genesi del retoromanzo (o ladino).* Tübingen.

Bautier, Robert-H. 1991. L'or et l'argent en Occident de la fin du XIIIᵉ siècle au début du XIVᵉ siècle. *Comptes rendus des séances de l'Académie des Inscriptions et Belles-Lettres* 95:169–174.

Bavel, Bas J. P. 2001. Land, lease and agriculture: The transition of the rural economy in the Dutch river area from the fourteenth to the sixteenth century. *Past & Present* 172:3–43.

Bazant, Jan. 1953. Minería medieval de la plata y el cobre en Europa Central. *El Trimestre Económico* 20:676–690.

Bell, Adrian R., Chris Brooks, and Tony K. Moore. 2017. *Cambium non est mutuum*: Exchange and interest rates in medieval Europe. *The Economic History Review* 70:373–396.

Bellabarba, Marco. 2012. The feudal principalities: The east (Trent, Bressanone/Brixen, Aquilea, Tyrol and Gorizia). In *The Italian Renaissance State*, ed. Andrea Gamberini and Isabella Lazzarini, 197–219. Cambridge.

Bellabarba, Marco, Hannes Obermair, and Hitomi Sato, eds. 2015. *Communities and conflicts in the Alps*. Translated by Joy Avery, Garin Taylor, and Kayoko Yukimura. Bologna and Berlin.

Bellero, Marisa. 1985. I cistercensi e il paesaggio rurale: L'abbazia di S. Maria di Lucedio fra il XII e il XV secolo. *Studi Storici* 26:337–351.

Belluzzo, Giuseppe. 1927. *La politica mineraria della Repubblica Veneta*. Roma.

Benecke, Gerhard. 1979. Maximilian I and his subjects: Aspects of town, court and countryside in Renaissance Austria, circa 1500. *Histoire Sociale—Social History* 12:36.

Bennett, Henry S. 1937. *Life on the English manor: A study of peasant conditions, 1150–1400*. Cambridge.

Bernhardt, John W. 2002. *Itinerant kingship and royal monasteries in early medieval Germany, c. 936–1075*. Cambridge.

Bertoldi, Daniela, Tomas Roman, Roberto Larcher, et al. 2013. Arsenic present in the soil-wine-vine chain in vineyards situated in an old mining area in Trentino, Italy. *Environmental Toxicology and Chemistry* 32:773–779.

Bettotti, Marco. 2023. Famiglie signorili delle valli di Non e di Sole. In *La signoria rurale nell'Italia del tardo medioevo. 6 Le signorie trentine*, ed. Marco Bettoti and Gian Maria Varanini, 35–59. Firenze.

Bettotti, Marco, and Walter Landi. 2023. Signorie rurali, coscienza nobiliare e autorappresentazione. In *La signoria rurale nell'Italia del tardo medioevo. 6 Le signorie trentine*, ed. Marco Bettoti and Gian Maria Varanini, 297–329. Firenze.

Bianchini, Gianluca, Claudio Natali, Paolo Ferretti, et al. 2019. Trace-element distribution on sulfide mineralization in Trento Province, NE Italy. *Minerals* 9:736.

Bird, Jesalyn, Edward Peters, and James M. Powell, eds. 2013. *Crusade and Christendom: Annotated documents in translation from Innocent III to the fall of Acre, 1187–1291*. Philadelphia.

Bisson, Thomas N. 1994. The feudal revolution. *Past & Present* 42:6–42.

Blanchard, Ian. 2005. *Mining, metallurgy and minting in the Middle Ages, vol. 3 Continuing Afro-European supremacy*. Stuttgart.

Bloch, Marc. 1935. Avènement et conquêtes du moulin à eau. *Annales d'histoire economique et sociale* 7:538–563.

Bodmer, Ueli, and Werner Aegerter. 1983. Ber Bergbau im Val Minor, Bernina. *Verein der Freunde des Bergbaues in Graubünden* 25:2–7.

Böhmer, J. F. 1971. *Regesta Imperii V, Jüngere Staufer 1198-1272, Die Regesten des Kaiserreichs unter Philipp, Otto IV, Friedrich II, Heinrich (VII), Conrad IV, Heinrich Raspe, Wilhelm und Richard. 1198–1272, Bd. 1–3*. Hildesheim.

http://monasterium.net/mom/RIViI/1209-01-13_1_0_5_1_1_559_254/charter. Accessed 13 July 2017.
Bonoldi, Andrea. 2013. La risorsa mutevole, l'Adige nell'economia della regione trentino-tirolese. In *Il fiume, le terre, l'immaginario, L'Adige come fenomeno storiografico complesso*, ed. Vito Rovigo, 219–250. Trento.
Borgo, Michaela. 2001. Le corporazioni di Mestiere Veneziane e le attività economico-comerciali delle *Nation Foreste*: Ebrei, turchi, tedeschi, greci e armeni. *Mediterranean World* 16:184–195.
Bork, Robert, Scott Montgomery, Carol Neumann de Vegvar, et al., eds. 2005. *De re metallica: The uses of metal in the Middle Ages*. Aldershot.
Boureau, Alain. 2000. How law came to the monks: The use of law in English society at the beginning of the thirteenth century. *Past & Present* 167:29–74.
Boutoulle, Frédéric. 2000. La vigne et le négoce du vin en Bordelais et Bazadais (fin XIe-début XIIIe siécle). *Annales du Midi: Revue archéologique, historique et philologique de la France méridionale* 112:275–298.
Boyce, Hellen. 1920. *The mines of the Upper Harz from 1514 to 1589*. Wisconsin.
Bradbury, Jim. 1992. *The medieval siege*. Suffolk.
Brătianu, George I. 1927. *Actes des notaires génois de Péra et de Caffa de la fin du treizième siècle*. Bucarest.
Braudel, Fernand 1992. *Civilization and capitalism, 15th–18th century, vol. 2, The wheels of commerce*. Translated by Siân Reynold. Berkeley.
Braudel, Fernand, and Frank C. Spooner. 1967. Prices in Europe from 1450 to 1750. In *The Cambridge economic history of Europe, IV, The economy of expanding Europe in the 16th and 17th centuries*, ed. Edwin E. Rich and Charles H. Wilson, 374–486. Cambridge.
Braunstein, Philippe. 1965. Les enterprises minières en Vénétie au XVe siècle. *Mélanges d'archéologie et d'histoire de l'Ecole française de Rome* 77:529–607.
Braunstein, Philippe, ed. 1982. *La sidérurgie dans les Alpes italiennes, XIIIe-XVIe siècle*. Roma.
Brázdil, Rudolf, Rüdiger Glaser, Christian Pfister, et al. 1999. Flood events of selected European rivers in the sixteenth century. *Climatic Change* 43:239–285.
Brenner, Robert. 1976. Agrarian class structure and economic development in pre-industrial Europe. *Past and Present* 70:30–75.
Brenner, Robert. 1982. The agrarian roots of European capitalism. *Past and Present* 97:16–103.
Brenner, Robert. 1996. The rises and declines of serfdom in medieval and early modern Europe. In *Serfdom & slavery, studies in legal bondage*, ed. Michael L. Bush, 247–276. Edinburgh.
Bromehead, C. E. N. 1940. The evidence for ancient mining. *The Geographical Journal* 96:101–118.

Brooks, George. 2006. The "Vitruvial Mill" in Roman and medieval Europe. In *Wind & water in the Middle Ages: Fluid technologies from antiquity to the Renaissance*, ed. Steven A. Walton, 1–38. Arizona.

Bruce, Scott G. 2010. *Ecologies and economies in medieval and early modern Europe: Studies in environmental history for Richard C. Hoff.* Leiden.

Brugnoli, Andrea, and Gian M. Varanini, eds. 2005. *Olivi e olio nel medioevo italiano.* Bologna.

Bryer, Anthony. 1986. Byzantine agricultural implements: The evidence of medieval illustrations of Hesiod's "Work and Days". *The Annual of the British School at Athens* 81:45–80.

Bryer, Rob. 2004. The roots of modern capitalism: A Marxist accounting history of the origins and consequences of capitalist landlords in England. *Accounting Historians Journal* 31:1–56.

Bundi, Ulrich, ed. 2010. *Alpine waters.* Dübendorf.

Burton, Janet E. 1999. *The Monastic order in Yorkshire, 1069–1215.* Cambridge.

Burton, Janet E. 2011. *The Cistercians in the Middle Ages.* Suffolk.

Butler, William F. T. 1906. *The Lombard communes, a history of the republics of North Italy.* London.

Butlin, Robin A. 1993. Proto-industrial regions of Europe, with a brief European contextual perspective. In *The early-modern world-system in geographical perspective*, ed. Hans J. Nitez, 136–150. Stuttgart.

Byres, Terrence J. 1999. Modes of production and non-European pre-colonial societies: The nature and significance of the debate. In *The feudalism debate*, ed. Harbans Mukhia, 13–33. New Delhi.

Byres, Terence J. 2006. Differentiation of the peasantry under feudalism and the transition to capitalism: In defense of Rodney Hilton. *Journal of Agrarian Change* 6:17–68.

Byres, Terence J. 2016. In pursuit of capitalist agrarian transition. *Journal of Agrarian Change* 16:432–451.

Cagol, Franco. 2023. Le Giudicarie e la val Vestino: I Lodron e i da Campo. In *La signoria rurale nell'Italia del tardo medioevo. 6 Le signorie trentine*, ed. Marco Bettotti and Gian Maria Varanini, 113–140. Firenze.

Cahen, Claude. 1951. Notes sur l'histoire des croisades et de l'Orient Latin. *Bulletin de la Faculté des Lettres de Strasbourg* 8:328–345.

Cameron, Rondo. 1967. *Banking in the early stages of industrialization: A study in comparative economic history.* New York.

Campbell, Bruce M. S. 2010. Physical shocks, biological hazards, and human impacts: The crisis of the fourteenth century revisited. In *Le interazioni fra economia e ambiente biologico nell'Europa preindustriale secc. XIII-XVIII*, ed. Simonetta Cavaciocchi, 13–32. Firenze.

Campbell, Bruce M. S. 2011. Panzootics, pandemics, and climatic anomalies in the fourteenth century. In *Beiträge zum Göttinger Umwelthistorischen Kolloquium 2010–2011*, ed. Bernd Herrmann, 177–215. Göttingen.

Campbell, Bruce M. S. 2013. National incomes and economic growth in pre-industrial Europe: Insights from recent research. *Quaestiones Medii Aevi Novae* 167–196.

Campopiano, Michele. 2013. Rural communities, land clearance and water management in the Po Valley in the central and late Middle Ages. *Journal of Medieval History* 39:377–393.

Camuffo, Dario, and Silvia Enzi. 1990. Locust invasions and climatic factors from the Middle Ages to 1800. *Theoretical & Applied Climatology* 43:43–73.

Cannan, Edwin. 1894. *A history of the theories of production and distribution in English political economy from 1776 to 1848.* London.

Cannan, Edwin, and Max Lerner, eds. 1937. *The wealth of nations: An inquiry into the nature and causes of the wealth of nations.* New York.

Canto García, Alberto, and Patrice Cressier, comp. 2007. *Minas y metalurgia en al-Andalus y Magreb occidental. Explotación y poblamiento.* Madrid.

Cantù, Cesare. 1859. *Illustrazione del Tirolo italiano e della Svizzera italiana.* Milano.

Carandi, Andrea. 1989. L'economia italica fra tarda Reppublica e medio Imperio considerata dal punto di vista di una mercé: Il vino. *Publications de l'École française de Rome* 114:505–521.

Carpentieri, Nicola. 2024. Love poetry as social practice: On the function of medieval Sicilian love lyric in Arabic and Italian. *Postmedieval: A Journal of Medieval Cultural Studies* 15:763–782.

Carpintero Benítez, Francisco. 2004. *Justicia y ley natural: Tomás de Aquino y otros escolásticos.* Madrid.

Carrer, Francesco, and Diego E. Angelucci. 2018. Continuity and discontinuity in the history of upland pastoral landscapes: The case study of Val Molinac and Val Poré (Val di Sole, Trentino, Eastern Italian Alps). *Landscape Research* 43:862–877.

Carrer, Francesco, and Viola Gheller, eds. 2015. *Invisible cultures: Historical and archaeological perspectives.* Newcastle-upon-Tyne.

Casagranda, M., Lara Casagrande, F. Dell'Amore, et al. 2018. Updates from the Mons Argentarius. Paper delivered at *Echoes of a mining past, 13th International symposium on archaeological mining history, Kelmis, May 10–13, 2018.* Kelmis. https://www.academia.edu/37357879/Updates_from_the_Mons_Argentarius_a_summary_of_five_years_of_fieldwork. Accessed 22 July 2024.

Casagrande, Lara. 2013. Paesaggi minerari del Trentino. In *Apsat 2. Paesaggi d'altura del Trentino, evoluzione naturale e aspetti culturale*, ed. Diego E. Angelucci, Lara Casagrande, Annalisa Colecchia, et al., 177–306. Mantova.

Casagrande Mazzoli, Maria A., Lorena Dal Poz, Donatella Frioli, et al., eds. 1996. *I manoscritti datati della provincia di Trento*. Firenze.

Casagrande, Lara, Bernd Päffgen, and Martin Straßburger. 2014. Mining archeological research of medieval silver ore mining at Trent. *IES Yearbook*1 87–195.

Casaretto, Pier F. 1928. *La moneta genovese in confronto con le altre valute mediterránee nei secoli XII e XIII*. Genova.

Cascio, Elio, and Paolo Malanima. 2008. Mechanical energy and water power in Europe: A long stability? In *Vers une gestion intégrée de l'eau dans l'Empire Romain, actes du Colloque International Université Laval, 2006*, ed. Ella Hermon, 201–208. Roma.

Castagnetti, Andrea. 1982. *Uomini e civiltà agraria in territorio veronese*. Verona.

Castagnetti, Andrea. 1983. *La comunità rurali dalla soggezione signorile alla giurisdizione del comune cittadino*. Verona.

Castagnetti, Andrea. 1988. *Arimanni in "Romania" fra conti e signori*. Verona.

Castagnetti, Andrea. 2001. *Governo vescovile, feudalità, 'communitas' cittadina e qualifica capitaneale a Trento fra XII e XIII secolo*. Verona.

Castelnuovo, Guido. 2000. Centri urbani, organizzazione del territorio e vie di traffico nell'area alpina occidentale: Chambéry, Torino e loro montagne (X-XV secolo). *Histoire des Alpes* V:109–123.

Castiglione, Elisabetta, and Mauro Rottoli. 2010. Il *sorgo* (sorghum bicolor) nel medioevo in Italia settentrionale. *Archeologia Medievale* XXXVII:485–495.

Cavaciocchi, Simonetta. 2003. *Il mercato della terra secc. XIII-XVIII*. Prato.

Cavaciocchi, Simonetta, ed. 2010. *Le interazioni fra economia e ambiente biologico nell'Europa preindustriale, secc. XIII-XVIII*. Firenze.

Cavada, Enrico, and Tullio Pasquali. 1982. Aspetti di cultura materiale medioevale a Castel Bosco presso Civezzano (Trento). *Studi trentini di scienze storiche. Sezione seconda* 61:139–150.

Ceccarelli, Marco. 2008. Renaissance machines in Italy: From Brunelleschi to Galileo through Francesco di Giorgio and Leonardo. *Mechanism and Machine Theory* 43:1530–1542.

Centofanti, Mario, Stefano Brusaporci, and Vittorio Lucchese. 2015. Historical watermills, architectural, mechanical, and hydraulic heritage. In *Essays on the history of mechanical engineering*, ed. Francesco Sorge and Giuseppe Genchi, 81–98. New York.

Chaudhuri, Kirti N. 2005. *Trade and civilization in the Indian Ocean, an economic history from the rise of Islam to 1750*. Cambridge.

Chayanov, Aleksander V. 1986. *Theory of peasant economy*, introd., ed. Theodor Shahin. Madison, WI.

Chetwode, Philip, Cecil H. Desch, Hugh Scott, et al. 1940. The evidence for ancient mining: Discussion. *The Geographical Journal* 96:118–120.

Chiogna, Gabriele, Bruno Majone, Karina Cano Paoli, et al. 2016. A review of hydrological and chemical stressors in the Adige catchment and its ecological status. *Science of the Total Environment* 540:429–443.

Christie, Neil. 2006. *From Constantine to Charlemagne: An archeology of Italy, A.D. 300–800.* Ashgate.

Cipolla, Carlo M. 1907. Un fiorentino a Trento nel sec. XIV. *Archivio Trentino* XXII:193–195.

Cipolla, Carlo M. 1914. *Publicazzioni sulla storia medioevale italiana.* Venezia.

Cipolla, Carlo M. 1976a. *Before the Industrial Revolution: European society and economy, 1000–1700.* New York.

Cipolla, Carlo M., ed. 1976b. *The Fontana economic history of Europe, Vol. 1, The Middle Ages.* New York.

Clark, Gregory. 2010. *The consumer revolution: A turning point in human history or statistical artifact?* Paper Department of Economics, University of California, Davis, July 4, 2010.

Classen, Albrecht. 2017. *Water in medieval literature, an ecocritical reading.* Maryland.

Coativy, Yves. 2003. La montagne est-elle une frontière? Le témoignage de la circulation monétaire d'après les trésors alpins. In *Actes des congrès de la Société des Historiens Médiévistes de l'Enseignement Supérieur Public, 34e congrès, Montagnes médiévales*, ed. Patrick Boucheron and Elisabeth Mornet, 41–62. Chambéry.

Coia, Valentina, Ilaria Boschi, Federica Trombetta, et al. 2012. Evidence of high genetic variation among linguistically diverse populations on a micro-geographic scale: A case study of the Italian Alps. *Journal of Human Genetics* 57:254–260.

Collatera, Marco, and Domenica Primerano. 2012. *Un vescovo, la sua cattedrale, il suo tesoro: La committenza artistica di Federico Vanga (1207–1218).* Trento.

Coltorti, Mauro, and Lorenzo Dal Ri. 1985. The human impact on the landscape: Some examples from the Adige Valley. In *Papers in Italian Archaeology IV: The Cambridge Conference, part 1, The human landscape*, ed. Caroline Malone and Simon Stoddart, 105–134. Oxford.

Comiti, Francesco. 2012. How natural are Alpine valleys? Evidence from the Italian Alps. *Earth Surface Processes and Landforms* 37:693–707.

Conlin, Michael V., and Lee Jolliffee, eds. 2011. *Mining heritage and tourism: A global synthesis.* London.

Constable, Giles. 1964. *Monastic tithes: From their origins to the twelfth century.* Massachusetts.

Coolidge, W. A. B. 1980. *The Alps in nature and history.* New York.

Corniani Degli Algarotti, C. Marco A. 1823. *Dello stabilimento delle miniere relative fabbriche nel distretto di Agordo: Trattato storico, mineralogico, disciplinare.* Venezia.

Corona, Christophe, Joel Guiot, Jean-Louis Edouard, et al. 2010. Millennium-long summer temperature variations in the European Alps as reconstructed from tree rings. *Climate Past* 6:379–400.

Corritore, Renzo P. 2008. Verona e Mantova nell'età comunale: *Mercatum fori*, granai privati e istituzioni annonarie nell'area medio transpadana nel Duecento. *Mélanges de l'école française de Rome* 120–121:55–72.

Cortese, Maria E. 1997. *L'acqua, il grano, il ferro: Opifici idraulici medievali nel bacio Farma-Merse*. Firenze.

Cortese, Maria E. 2000. Opifici idraulici per la lavorazione del ferro nel comprensorio del Monte Amiata (secc. XIII-XIV). In *I mulini nell'Europa medieval*, ed. Paola Galetti and Pierre Racine, 329–350. Siena.

Cortese, Maria E. 2017. L'Imperio e la Toscana durante il regno di Federico Barbarossa. *Reti Medievali Rivista* 18:49–88.

Cosgel, Metin M. 1990. Scattering and contracts in medieval agriculture: Challenges ahead. *The Journal of Economic History* 50:663–668.

Crabbe, Philippe J. 1985. Turgot's Brief on mines and quarries: An early economic analysis of mineral land tenure. *Natural Resource Journal* 25:267–273.

Cracco, Giorgio, Jacques Le Goff, Hagen Keller, et al. 2006. *Europa in costruzione: La forza delle identità, la ricerca di unità: Secoli IX-XIII*. Bologna.

Craddock, Paul T. 1995. *Early metal mining and production*. Edinburgh.

Crowley, Thomas J., and Thomas S. Lowery. 2000. How warm was the Medieval Warm Period? *AMBIO: A Journal of the Human Environment* 29:51–54.

Cucini, Costanza. 1989. Uno strumento da minatore nel territorio di Scarlino (GR). *Archeologia Medievale* XVI:729–736.

Curtis, Daniel R., and Michele Campopiano. 2014. Medieval land reclamation and the creation of new societies: Comparing Holland and the Po Valley, c. 800–c. 1500. *Journal of Historical Geography* 44:93–108.

Curzel, Emanuele. 1999. *Le pievi trentine, trasformazioni e continuità nell'organizzazione teritoriale della cura d'anima dalle origini al XIII secolo (studio introduttivo e schede)*. Bologna.

Curzel, Emanuele. 2007. *Il Codice Vanga: Un principe vescovo e il suo governo, Tomo II*. Trento.

Curzel, Emanuele. 2015. *Il capitolo della cattedrale di Trento dal XII secolo al 1348*. Bologna.

Curzel, Emanuele, and Italo Franceschini. 2022. L'agricoltura trentina nel tardo medioevo. *Rivista di Storia dell Agricoltura* LXII:23–30.

Curzel, Emanuele, and Gian M. Varanini. 2007. *Codex Wangianus, i cartulari della Chiesa trentina (secoli XIII-XIV), Tomo I*. Bologna.

Curzel, Emanuele, and Gian M. Varanini. 2011. *La documentazione dei vescovi di Trento (XI secolo-1218)*. Bologna.

Cusin, Fabio. 1938a. *I primi due secoli del principato ecclesiastico di Trento*. Urbino.

Cusin, Fabio. 1938b. *I primi due secoli del Principato Ecclesiastico*. Urbino.

Czaja, Stanisław. 2001. Mining and hydrological transformations in Upper Silesia from fifteenth to nineteenth centuries. *The Geographical Journal* 167:57–71.

D'Achiardi, Giovanni. 1920. La miniera del Bottino nelle Alpi Apuane. *Memoria Soc. Lunig. "G. Cappellini" Storia Nat. Reg.* 1:132–140.

D'Amato, Raffaele. 2017. Armi e strumenti di lavoro da Iasos. *Bolletino dell'Associazione Iasos Di Caria* 23:2–13.

Dai Prà, Elena. 2010. La cartografia storica come interfaccia dialettica tra discipline e competenze territoriali, progetti ed esperienze in Trentino, In *Atti 14ª Conferenza Nazionale ASITA*, ed. Federazione italiana delle Associazioni Scientifiche per le Informazioni Territoriali e Ambientali, 713–718. Brescia.

Dai Prá, Elena, and Davide Allegri. 2016. Il fiume tra scienza e percezione: l'Adige nella cartografia storica. In *Il fiume, le terre, l'immaginario: l'Adige come fenomeno storiografico complesso, atti del convegno Rovereto, 21–22 febbraio 2013*, ed. Vito Rovigo, 45–68. Rovereto.

Day, William R., Jr. 2010. Fiorentini e altri italiani appaltatori di zecche straniere (1200–1600): Un progetto di ricerca. *Annali di Storia di Firenze* V:9–29.

de Borchgrave, Émile. 1865. Histoire des colonies belges qui s'établirent en Allemagne pendant le XIIe et le XIIIe siècle. *Mémoires de l'Académie royale de Belgique* 32:1–376.

de Huesca, Ramón. n.d. *Teatro histórico de las Iglesias del reyno de Aragón Ms. 69–74*. https://bibliotecavirtual.aragon.es/es/consulta/registro.do?id=1178.

De Roover, Raymond. 1938. Characteristics of bookkeeping before Pacioli. *The Accounting Review* 13:144–149.

De Roover, Raymond. 1948. *Money, banking and credit in medieval Bruges, Italian merchant bankers, Lombard and money-changers, a study in the origins of banking*. Cambridge, MA.

De Roover, Raymond. 1951. Monopoly theory prior to Adam Smith: A revision. *Quarterly Journal of Economics* 65:492–524.

De Roover, Raymond. 1955. Scholastic economics: Survival and lasting influence from the sixteenth century to Adam Smith. *Quarterly Journal of Economics* 69:161–190.

De Roover, Raymond. 1958. The concept of the just price: Theory and economic policy. *The Journal of Economic History* 18:418–434.

Debelmas, Jacques, Arthur Escher, and Rudolf Trümpy. 1983. Profiles through the Western Alps. In *Profiles of orogenic belts*, ed. Nicholas Rast and Frances M. Delany, 83–96. Washington, DC.

Decker, Michael. 2017. Animal and zoonotic diseases in the ancient and late antique Mediterranean: Three case studies. In *Discipuli dona ferentes: Glimpses of Byzantium in honour of Marlia Mundell Mango*, ed. Tassos Papacostas and Maria Parani, 99–118. Belgium.

Demattè, Claudia. Immagini di dame e cavalieri: Affreschi cavallereschi ed arturiani in Trentino Alto Adige (presentazione di un progetto internazionale). In *Il mondo cavalleresco tra immagine e testo Atti di convegno Sc. Antic. Filol. Lett. e Storico-Artistiche, 20–22 novembre 2008.* Università di Trento. https://iris.unitn.it/handle/11572/85565?mode=full. Accessed 19 April 2023.

Denecke, Dietrich. 1993. Mining regions and metal trade in early modern Europe. In *The early-modern world-system in geographical perspective*, ed. Hans J. Nitez, 162–171. Stuttgart.

Denemark, Robert A., and Kenneth P. Thomas. 1988. The Brenner-Wallerstein debate. *International Studies Quarterly* 32:47–65.

Derolez, Albert. 1991. A devotee of Saint Barbara in a Belgian beguinage (Marston MS 287). *The Yale University Library Gazette* 66:197–218.

Destro Bisol, Giovanni, Paolo Anagnostou, Chiara Batini, et al. 2008. Italian isolates today: Geographic and linguistic factors shaping human biodiversity. *Journal of Anthropological Sciences* 86:179–188.

Dickinson, Robert E. 1942. The development and distribution of the medieval German town: I. The West German lands. *Geography* 27:9–21.

Didron, Adolphe N. 1886. *Christian iconography, vol. II.* Translated by Margaret Stokes. London.

Dimmock, Spencer. 2014. *The origin of capitalism in England, 1400–1600.* Leiden and Boston.

Dobb, Maurice H. 1924. The entrepreneur myth. *Economica* 10:66–81.

Dolomieu, Deódat. 1801. *Sur la philosophie minéralogique, et sur l'espèce minéralogique.* Paris.

Domandi, Mario, transl. 1970. *Francesco Guicciardini Maxims and reflections of a Renaissance statesman (Ricordi).* Gloucester, MA.

Drew, Katherine F. 1962. The immunity in Carolingian Italy. *Speculum* 37:182–197.

Drew, Katherine F. 1964. The Carolingian military frontier in Italy. *Traditio* 20:437–447.

Duby, Georges. 1954. La révolution agricole médiévale. *Revue de géographie de Lyon* 29:361–366.

Duby, Georges. 1982. *The three orders: Feudal society imagined.* Chicago.

Dumas, Françoise, and Jean-Nöel Barrandon. 1995. Sur les traces de l'argent de Melle à l'époque carolingienne. *Bulletin de la Société Nationale des Antiquaires de France* 28:187–189.

Dunlop, Douglas M. 1957. Sources of gold and silver in Islam according to al-Hamdānī (10th century). *Studia Islamica* 8:9–59.

Dyer, Christopher. 2002. *Making a living in the middle ages, the people of Britain, 850–1520.* New Haven, CT.

Dygo, Marian. 2003. Land prices and crises: Central Europe from the 15th to the 17th centuries. In *Il mercato della terra secc. XIII-XVIII, Atii della "Trentacinquesima Settimana di Studi" 5–9 maggio 2003*, ed. Simonetta Cavaciocchi, 547–567. Prato.

EAB [European Academy of Bozen/Bolzano]. 2013. Effects of migrations: 'Closed holdings' on DNA of Alpine peoples. *Science Daily*, 12 December 2013. www.sciencedaily.com/releases/2013/12/131212095822.htm. Accessed 3 August 2019.

Eck, Alexander. 1983. *Les liens de vassalité et les immunities*. Paris.

Edbury, Peter. 1999. Warfare in the Latin East. In *Medieval warfare a history*, ed. Maurice Keen, 89–112. Oxford.

Editore. 2016. L'Adige rompe gli argini: 50 anni fa l'alluvione che sconvolse Trento. *I Dolomitici*, 4 Novembre 2016. https://www.ildolomiti.it/societa/ladige-rompe-gli-argini-50-anni-fa-lalluvione-che-sconvolse-trento-e-stato-il-panico-cera. Accessed 6 April 2023.

Edson, Evelyn. 2007. *The world map 1300–1492, the persistence of tradition and transformation*. Baltimore, MD.

Einaudi, Luigi. 1900. *La rendita mineraria: Origini e basi*. Torino.

Ellenblum, Ronnie. 2012. *The collapse of the eastern Mediterranean: Climate change and the decline of the East, 950–1072*. New York.

Engels, Frederick. 1892. *The condition of the working class in England in 1844*. Translated by F. Kelley Wischnewetzky. London.

Ertl, Thomas. 2017. Small landlords: Land transactions in and around Bozen (South Tirol) in the mid-thirteenth century. *Vierteljahrschrift für sozial -und Wirtschaftsgeschichte* 104:7–28.

Evans, Allans, ed. 1936. *Francesco Balducci Pegolotti: La pratica della mercatura*. Cambridge, MA.

Ewbank, Thomas. 1857. *A descriptive and historical account of hydraulic and other machines ancient and modern with observations on various subjects connected with the mechanic arts*. New York.

Face, Richard D. 1957. *The caravan merchants and the fairs of Champagne: A study in the techniques of medieval commerce*. The University of Wisconsin-Madison ProQuest Dissertations & Theses.

Farinelli, Roberto. 1996. Le risorse minerarie amiatine e il loro sfruttamento (secoli IX-XVI). In *Carta archeologica della provincia di Siena vol. II, Il Monte Amiata (Abbadia San Salvatore)*, ed. Franco Cambi, 38–55. Siena.

Fasoli, Gina. 1980. Città e feudalitá. *Publications de l'École française de Rome* 44:365–385.

Feller, Laurent. 2014. Measuring value in the Middle Ages. *Economic Sociology—The European Economic Newsletter* 15:30–340.

Ferrandi, Mario. 1955. *L'alto Agige nella storia*. Bolzano.

Ferretti, Paolo. 2011. Storia e geologia della "miniera d'oro" di Val Gerlano presso Speccheri (Vallarsa, Trentino-Alto Adige). *Studi Trentini di Scienze Naturali* 88:191–202.

Feugère, Michel, Georges Depeyrot, and Max Martin. 1996. Balances monétaires à tare fixe: Typologie, métrologie, interpretation. *Gallia* 53:345–362.

Fiore, Alessio. 2023. Luoghi sacri, pellegrinaggi e scambi tra i due versanti delle Alpi occidentali (X-XII secolo). In *Spazi sacri, luoghi di culto, santuari in area alpina: Persistenze e sviluppi dall'antichità all'età contemporanea*, ed. Paolo Cozzo, 83–94. Roma.

Flatscher, Elias. 2021. (Self-) Supply in a medieval castle. The archaeological perspective based on the excavations in the economy tract of Castle Tyrol. *Château Gaillard* 29:115–131.

Fleming, Robin. 1998. *Domesday Book and the Law: Society and legal custom in medieval England*. Cambridge.

Flynn, Dennis O. 2018. Six monetary functions over millennia. In *Money, currency and crisis In search of trust, 2000 BC to AD 20000*, ed. R. J. Van Der Spek and Bas van Leeuwen, 13–36. London and New York.

Flynn, Dennis O., and Arturo Giráldez, eds. 1997. *Metals and moneis in an emerging global economy*. London.

Flynn, Dennis O., and Arturo Giráldez. 2010. *China and the birth of globalization in the 16th*. London.

Földváry, Géza Z. 1988. *Geology of the Carpathian region*. New Jersey.

Fontana, Alessandro, Livio Ronchi, and Paolo Mozzi. 2019. The diluvium aquarum: Geologic evidence and geoarchaeological constrains of extreme floods in northern Italy during early Middle Ages. Paper presented at *Workshop Ex-aqua 2019 "Palaeohydrological extreme events: Evidence and archives," September 26-29, 2019*. Zagreb.

Forbes, Robert J. 1950. *Metallurgy in Antiquity: A notebook for archaeologists and technologists*. Leiden.

Fors, Hjalmar. 2015. *The limits of matter: Chemistry, mining & enlightenment*. Chicago.

Franceschini, Italo. 2016. Le paludi dell'Adige, diritti di sfrutamento e tentativi di bonifica tra XIII e XIV secolo. In *Scorci di un fiume: l'Adige come problema storiografico complesso, Atti del convegno, Rovereto, 21–22 febbraio 2013*, ed. Vito Rovigo, 251–272. Rovereto.

Franceschini, Italo. 2023a. Castelli e campagne in area trentina. I rapport tra i signori e le comunità rurali. In *La signoria rurale nell'Italia del tardo medioevo. 6 Le signorie trentine*, ed. Marco Bettotti and Gian Maria Varanini, 197–220. Firenze.

Franceschini, Italo. 2023b. Signorie in un'area di strada. La Valsugana nel XIV secolo. In *La signoria rurale nell'Italia del tardo medioevo. 6 Le signorie trentine*, ed. Marco Bettotti and Gian Maria Varanini, 85–112. Firenze.

Franzini, Marco, and Marco Lezzerini. 2003. The stones of medieval buildings in Pisa and Lucca provinces (western Tuscany, Italy). 1-The Monte Pisano marble. *European Journal of Mineralogy* 15:217–224.

Fraser, Rob. 1993. On the neutrality of the resource rent tax. *Economic Record* 69:56–60.

Frechette, Darren L. 1991. Scarcity rents and the returns to mining. *Resources Policy* 25:39–49.
Freed, John B. 1986. Reflections on the medieval German nobility. *The American Historical Review* 91:553–575.
Freschi, Louis. 2004. L'axe du Brenner. *Collection EDYTEM—Cahiers de géographie* 2:43–52.
Frey, Karl A., and Henri Rouger. 1988. Un axe transalpin méconnu et inutilisé: Le Septimer (Canton des Grisons, Suisse). *Revue de géographie alpine* 76:287–299.
Friede, Juan. 1961. La introducción de mineros alemanes en América por la compañía Welser de Ausgburg. *Revista de Historia de América* 51:99–104.
Fumagalli, Vito. 1979. Il potere civile dei vescovi italiani al tempo di Ottone I. In *I poteri temporali dei Vescovi in Italia e in Germania nel medioevo*, ed. Carlo Guido Mor and Heinrich Schmidinger, 77–86. Bologna: Società editrice il Mulino.
Fumagalli, Alberto. 1997. *Vie dell'anno Mille nella Lombardia orientale*. Milano.
Gade, John A. 1951. *The Hanseatic control of Norwegian commerce during the late Middle Ages*. Leiden.
Gallard, J. 1915. European mining finance. *Transactions of the International Engineering Congress*, Paper No. 160: 253–267.
Gallo, Agostino. 1572. *Le vinti giornate dell'agricoltura et de' piaceri della villa*. Venezia.
Gandilhon, René. 1987. Henri IV et el vin. *Bibliothèque de l'école des chartes* 45:383–406.
García Tapia, Nicolás. 1987. La máquina de vapor inventada y patentada en 1606 por Jerónimo De Ayanz. *Técnica Industrial* 186:3–11.
García Tapia, Nicolás. 1988. Ingenios para desagüar las minas a principios del siglo XVII. In *Seminario de Antiguas Obras Hidráulicas Hispanoamericanas*. México, DF.
García Tapia, Nicolás. 1994. *Patentes de invención españolas en el siglo de oro*. Madrid.
Garçon, Marion, Catherine Chauvel, Emmanuel Chapron, et al. 2012. Silver and lead in high-altitude lake sediments: Proxies for climate changes and human activities. *Applied Geochemistry* 27:760–773.
Gardien, Guy. 2001. *Deodat Gratet de Dolomieu Un Dolomois au Siècle des Lumières*. Paris.
Garegnani, Pierangelo. 1984. Value and distribution in the classical economists and Marx. *Oxford Economic Papers* 36:291–325.
Garipzanov, Ildar H. 1999. The image of authority in Carolingian coinage: The image of a ruler and Roman imperial tradition. *Early Medieval Europe* 8:197–218.
Garlandini, Alberto, Bruna Micheletti, and Pier Paolo Poggio, eds. 1991. *Il patrimonio storico industriale della Lombardia: Censimento regionale*. Brescia.

Gazzoletti, Antonio. 1858. *Della Zecca di Trento*. Trento.

George, Hereford B. 1907. *The relations of geography & history*. Oxford.

Gille, Bertrand. 1964. *Les ingéniers de la Renaissance*. Paris.

Giovanelli, Benedetto. 1812. *Intorno all'antica zecca Trentina e a due monumenti Reti: Lettere tre*. Trent.

Giovanni, P., and R. Parenti. 2008. Torre Vanga a Trento. Aspetti metodologici e operativi dell'analisi stratigrafica finalizzata al cantiere di restauro. In *Archeologia dell'architettura. L'analisi stratigrafica dell'elevato: Contributi alla conoscenza delle architetture fortificate e al progetto di restauro*, ed. Alessandra Quendolo, 69–86. Florence.

Giulio, Tecini. 1845. Sull' insalubrità della Valle dell'Adige da Trent a Merano e come vi si potrebbe rimediare. *Giornale Agrario dei distretti trentini e roveretani* 29:115–118.

Glaser, Rüdiger, Dirk Riemann, Johannes Schönbein, et al. 2010. The variability of European floods since AD 1500. *Climatic Change* 101:235–256.

Gógan, Liam S. 1930. A perforated stone pickaxe form North East Louth: Its position in Irish archaeology. *Journal of the County Louth Archaeological Society* 7:153–167.

Górecki, Piotr. 1993. *Parishes, tithes, and society in earlier medieval Poland c. 1100–c. 1250*. Philadelphia.

Gorini, Giovanni. 1986. Aspetti della documentazione numismatica medievale nel Trentino-Alto Adige. *Atti del V Accademia Roveretana degli Agiati* 236:237–241.

Graça, Laura. 2003. Feudal dynamics and Runciman's competitive selection practices in late medieval Castile: An essay on differing processes of social differentiation in a pre-capitalist context. *Journal of Agrarian Change* 3:333–366.

Grandis, Claudio. 1994–1995. I mulini ad acqua del Padovano. *Università poppolare, Rassegna* XCIII:22–23.

Gras, Michel. 1983. Vin et société à Rome et dans le Latium à l'époque archaïque. *Publications de l'École française de Rome* 67:1067–1075.

Grass, N. S. B. 1939. *Business and capitalism: An introduction to business history*. New York.

Grasso, Ana M. n.d. *La viticoltura come indicatore paleoeconomico, paleoambientale e paleoclimatico applicato allo studio dei contesti archeologici medievali*, 1–26. Università Degli Studi di Siena, Sculoa Dottorado di Ricerca "Riccardo Francovich." Projeto di ricerca.

Grau Fernández, Marta, ed. 2008. *Ars Mechanicae, ingeniería medieval en España*. Madrid.

Graulau, Jeannette. 2008. Finance, industry and globalization: The example of the House of the Fugger. *Rivista Di Studi Politici Internazionali* 4:554–598.

Graulau, Jeannette. 2019a. Capitalist miners in feudal Europe: A commentary on Marxist agrarian history. *Journal of Agrarian Change* 19:596–613.

Graulau, Jeannette. 2019b. *The underground wealth of nations: On the capitalist origins of silver mining,* A.D. *1150–1450.* New Haven.

Gremes, Alessandro, and Liliana Zanoni. 1988. Le monete rinvenute a Castel Corno. *Annuario Museo Civico Rovereto* 4:123–135.

Grierson, Philip, and Lucia Travaini. 1999. *Medieval European coinage, Vol. 14 Italy (III) (South Italy, Sicily, Sardinia).* Cambridge.

Guckelsberger, Kurt, and Klaus Geus. 2022. Two great maps of Italy—A comparison. In *Walking through Italy An interdisciplinary approach to Flavio Bondo's spaces in the "Italia Illustrata"*, ed. Tanja Michalsky and Martin Thiering, 35–52. Berlin.

Gumiero, Bruna, Bruno Maiolini, Francesco Comiti, et al. 2009. The Italian rivers. In *Rivers of Europe*, ed. Klement Tockner, Christiane Zarfl, and Christopher T. Robinson, 467–497. London.

Gunder Frank, André. 1990. The thirteenth-century world system: A review essay. *Journal of World History* 1:249–256.

Gunder Frank, André. 1998. *ReOrient: Global economy in the Asian age*. Berkeley.

Gunder Frank, André, and Barry Gills, eds. 1993. *The world system: Five hundred or five thousand?* London and New York.

Haiminsfeldi, Melchior G. 1743. *Collectio Constitutionum Imperialium, Tomo I.* Frankfurt.

Harding, Alan. 2002. *Medieval law and the foundations of the State.* Oxford.

Harding, Julia. 2015. *The Oxford companion to wine.* Oxford.

Harris, Marvin. 1959. The economy has no surplus. *American Anthropologist* 61:185–199.

Haskins, Charles H. 1955. *The Renaissance in the twelfth century.* Cambridge, MA.

Hatinguais, Catherine. 2019. Catching the flood: River navigation from the Adige to the Po in Shakespeare's Italy. *The Oxfordian* 21:95–142.

Heers, Jacques. 2008. The "feudal" economy and capitalism: Words, ideas and reality. In *Internal colonization in medieval Europe*, ed. Felipe Fernández-Armesto and James Muldoon, vol. 2, 45–89. London and New York.

Heiss, Andreas G., Werner Kofler, and Klauss Oeggel. 2005. The Ulten Valley in South Tyrol, Italy: Vegetation and settlement history of the area, and macrofossil record from the Iron Age cult site of St. Walburg. *Palyno-Bulletin* 1:63–73.

Hemker, Christiane, and Ivonne Burghardt. 2015. Medieval mining in Saxony—Selected results from excavations of high medieval silver mines in Dippoldiswalde and Niederpöbel. *Mining History* 19:52–60.

Henning, Joachim. 2009. Revolution of relapse? Technology, agriculture, and early medieval archaeology in Germanic Central Europe. In *The Langobards before the Frankish conquest, an ethnographic perspective*, ed. Giorgio Ausenda, Paolo Delogu, and Chris Wickham, 149–164. Suffolk.

Herlihy, David. 1960. The Carolingian *mansus. The Economic History Review* 13:79–89.

Hernández Esteve, Esteban, ed. 2000. *Moneda y monedas en la Europa medieval, siglos XII-XV*. Pamplona.

Higounet, Charles. 1958. Une carte agricole de l'Albigeois vers 1260. *Annales du Midi: Revue archéologique, historique et philologique de la France méridionale* 70:65–71.

Hilferding, Rudolf. 1981. *Finance capital a study of the latest phase of capitalist development*. London.

Hill, Donald R., transl. 1979. *The Book of Ingenious Devices (Kitāb al-Ḥiyal) by the Banū (sons of) Mūsà bin Shākir*. Dordrecht.

Hill, Donald R. 1998. *Studies in medieval Islamic technology: From Philo to al-Jazarī, from Alexandria to Diyār Bakr*.

Hilton, Rodney H. 1978. A crisis of feudalism. *Past & Present* 80:3–19.

Hirt, Alfred M. 2010. *Imperial mines and quarries in the Roman world: Organizational aspects 27 BC–AD 235*. Oxford.

Hodkin, Thomas, transl. 1886. *The letters of Cassiodorus, being a condensed translation of the variae epistolae of Magnus Aurelius Cassiodorus Senator*. London.

Hoffman, J. Wesley. 1923. The commerce of the German Alpine passes during the early middle ages. *The Journal of Political Economy* 31:826–839.

Hoover, Herbert C., and Lou H. Hoover, transl. 1950. *Georgius Agricola De Re Metallica*. New York.

Hoppenbrouwers, Peter, and Jan Luiten van Zanden, eds., Peasants into farmers? The transformation of the rural economy and society in the Low Countries (Middle Ages—19th century) in light of the Brenner debate (2001).

Housley, Norman. 1999. European warfare c.1200–1320. In *Medieval warfare: A history*, ed. Maurice Keen, 113–135. Oxford.

Hübner, Rudolph. 1918. *A history of Germanic private law*. Translated by Francis S. Philbrick. Boston.

Hunt, B. G. 2006. The Medieval Warm Period, the Little Ice Age and simulated climatic variability. *Climate Dynamics* 27:677–694.

Hunt, Edwin S., and James M. Murray. 1999. *A history of business in medieval Europe 1200–1550*. Cambridge.

Irsigler, Franz. 1976. Rheinisches kapital in Mitteleuropäischen montanunternehmen des 15. und 16. Jahrhunderts. *Zeitschrift für Historische Forschung* 3:145–164.

Jackson, Lowis. 1882. *Modern metrology*. London.

Jannon, Roberto, and Federica Trento. 2011. *Manufatti e fabbricati legati all'antico uso dell'acqua nel territorio del GAL Prealpi e Dolomiti, Studio/Ricerca no. 4*. Comunità Montana Feltrina.

Jansen, Katherine, Joanna Drell, and Frances Andrews, eds., The Middle Ages series: Medieval Italy, texts in translation (2011).

Jeanne-Rose, Olivier. 1996. Trouvailles isolées de monnaies carolingiennes en Poitou: Inventaire provisoire. *Revue Numismatique* 151:241–283.

Jeannin, Pierre. 1955. Le cuivre, les Fugger et la Hanse. *Annales. Économies, Sociétés, Civilisations* 10:229–236.

Johnson, Edgar A. J. 1965. *Predecessors of Adam Smith The growth of British economic thought.* New York.

Jones, Eric L. 1968. Agricultural origins of industry. *Past & Present* 40:58–71.

Jones, Michael J. 2018. Domesday Book: An early fiscal, accounting narrative? *The British Accounting Review* 50:275–290.

Jordan, Karl. 1963. *Goslar und das Reich im 12. Jahrhundert.* Hildesheim.

Judson, Sheldon, and Anne Kahane. 1963. Underground drainageways in southern Etruria and northern Latium. *Papers of the British School at Rome* 31:74–99.

Kaláb, Zdenkě, and Markéta Lednická. 2008. Mine water movement in shallow medieval Mine Jeroným (Czech Republic). In *Mine water and the environment, proceedings of 10th International Mine Water Association Congress*, ed. Karlovy Vary, 19–22. Ostrava.

Kaplan, Jed O., Kristen M. Krumhardt, and Niklaus Zimmermann. 2009. The prehistoric and preindustrial deforestation of Europe. *Quaternary Science Reviews* 28:3016–3034.

Kelleher, Richard. 2018. From the Commercial Revolution to the Black Death (c.1150–1350). In *Money and coinage in the Middle Ages*, ed. Rory Naismith, 122–150. Leiden.

Kellenbenz, Hermann. 1969. Firmenarchive und ihre bedeutung für die Europäische wirtschafts -un sozialgeschichte. *Tradition: Zetschrift für Firmengeschichte und Unternehmerbiographie* 14:1–20.

Kellenbenz, Hermann, ed. 1981. *Precious metals in the age of expansion: Papers of the XIV International Congress on Historical Sciences.* Stuttgart.

Kellenbenz, Hermann. 1990. Le miniere di Primiero e le relazioni dei Fugger con Venezia nel quattrocento. *Atti della Accademia roveretana degli Agiati* 28:365–385.

Keller, Hagen. 1995. *Signori e vassalli nell'Italia delle città (secoli IX-XII).* Translated by A. Piazza. Turin.

Kink, Rudolf. 1852. *Fontes Rerum Austriacarum: Oesterreichische Geschichts-Quellen, Diplomataria et Acta, V Band, Codex Wangianus.* Wien.

Kinkade, Richard P. 1994. Money in the Poema De Mio Cid: A reassessment. *Anuario Medieval* 6:103–126.

Kirhner, Julius, ed. 1974. *Business, banking and economic thought in late medieval and early modern Europe.* Chicago.

Kirnbauer, Franz. 1958. Die Bergordnung von Trient aus dem Jahre 1208 und ihre Beziehung zur Bergbautechnik. *Blätter für Technikgeschichte* 20:1–24.

Knorn, Henry H. 1680. *Dissertation historica de metallifodinarum Hartzicarum prima origine et progressu.* Helmstadt.

Kosi, Miha. 2018. The Fifth Crusade and its aftermath: Crusading in the Southeast of the Holy Roman Empire in the first decades of the thirteenth century. *Crusades* 17:91–113.

Kovačević-Kojić, Desanka. 1960. Les mines d'or et d'argent en Serbie et Bosnie. *Annales, Économies, Sociétés, Civilisations* 15:248–258.

Kriedte, Peter 1994. *Feudalismo tardío y capital mercantil.* Translated by J. Luis Vermal. Barcelona.

Kula, Witold. 2014. *Measures and men*. Princeton.

La Salvia, Vasco. 2007. *Iron making during the migration period: The case of the Lombards.* Oxford.

Lachmann, Richard. 1989. Origins of capitalism in Western Europe: Economic and political aspects. *Annual Review of Sociology* 15:47–72.

Lackman, Conway L. 1976. The classical base of modern rent theory. *The American Journal of Economics and Sociology* 35:287–300.

Lambton, Ann Katherine S. 1992. The qānāts of Yazd. *Journal of the Royal Asiatic Society* 2:21–35.

Lanconelli, Angela. 1992. *Terra, acque e lavoro nella Viterbo medievale*. Roma.

Landi, Walter. 2015. L'incastellamento di fronte al diritto feudale: Il caso dell'episcopato di Trento fra XII e XIII secolo. In *Geschichte und Region/Storia e regione, Ländliche Ökonomien/Economie rurali*, ed. Hannes Obermair, 97–156. Innsbruck, Wien and Bozen.

Laubenheimer, Fanette, and Jean-Claude Notet. 1986. Les amphores produites à Gueugnon (S. et L.) et les débuts du vignoble bourguignon. *Dialogues d'histories ancienne* 12:431–453.

Le Jan, Régine. 2003. Avant-propos. In *Actes des congrès de la Société des Historiens Médiévistes de l'Enseignement Supérieur Public, 34e congrès, Montagnes médiévales*, ed. Patrick Boucheron and Elisabeth Mornet, 7–8. Chambéry.

Le Roy Ladurie, Emmanuel. 1974. L'historie immobile. *Annales* XXIX:680–686.

Le Roy Ladurie, Emmanuel. 1976. *The peasants of Languedoc*. Illinois.

Leicht, Pier S. 1903. *Studi sulla proprietà fondiaria nel medioevo, Parte I.* Verona.

Leighton, Albert C. 1972. *Transport and communication in early medieval Europe.* New York.

Lemoine, Marcel, ed. 1978. *Geological atlas of Alpine Europe and adjoining areas.* Leiden.

Leonardi, Andrea, and Andrea Bonoldi. 1999. L'economia della montagna interna Italiana: Un approccio storiografico. In *Seminario permanente sulla storia dell'economia e dell'imprenditorialità nelle Alpi, Atti della sessione tenutasi a Trento il 5 dicembre 1997.* Trento. http://eprints.biblio.unitn.it/14/.

Lombard, Maurice. 1947. Les bases monétaires d'une suprématie économique: L'or musulman du VIIe au XIe siècle. *Annales* 2:143–160.

Lopez, Robert S. 1967. *The birth of Europe*. New York.

Lopez, Robert S. 2005. *The commercial revolution of the Middle Ages, 950–1350*. Cambridge.

Lopez, Robert S., and Irving W. Raymond, transl. 2001. *Medieval trade in the Mediterranean world, illustrative documents*. New York.

Loudon, John C. 1835. *An encyclopedia of agriculture*. London.

Lucas, Adam. 2016. *Ecclesiastical lordship, seigneurial power and the commercialization of milling in medieval England*. London.

Luetscher, Marc. 2013. Alpine permafrost thawing during the medieval warm period identified from cryogenic cave carbonates. *The Cryosphere* 7:1073–1081.

Lupi, Mario. 1805. *Giuseppe Ronchetti Memorie istoriche della città e chiesa di Bergamo, Tomo I*. Bergamo.

Lutz, Stephanie, Stefano Mallucci, Elena Diamantini, et al. 2016. Hydroclimatic and water quality trends across three Mediterranean river basins. *Science of the Total Environment* 571:1392–1406.

Lynch, Katherine A. 2003. *Individuals, families, and communities in Europe, 1200–1800 The urban foundations of Western society*. Cambridge.

Macini, Paolo, and Ezio Mesini. 2004. Hydraulic pumps of Agricola's *De re metallica* (1556). *Journal of Hydraulic Engineering* 1051–1054.

Magnusson, Roberta. 2001. *Water technology in the Middle Ages: Cities, monasteries, and waterworks after the Roman Empire*. Baltimore.

Magnusson, Roberta, and Paolo Squatriti. 2000. The technologies of water in medieval Italy. In *Working with water in medieval Europe*, ed. Paolo Squatriti, 217–266. Leiden.

Maier, Christoph T. 1994. *Preaching the crusades: Mendicant friars and the cross in the thirteenth century*. Cambridge.

Mainoni, Patrizia. 1999. Fiscalidad directa e indirecta en la Italia medieval del centro y del norte. Algunas orientaciones historiográficas recientes. *Edad Media: Revista de historia* 2:151–166.

Mainoni, Patrizia. 2001. La politica dell'argento e del ferro nella Lombardia medievale. In *La sidérurgie alpine en Italie (XIIe–XVIIe siècle)*, ed. Philippe Braunstein, 417–453. Rome.

Maissen, Thomas. 2024. Libertà fra tardo medioevo e prima età moderna: Il mondo germanofono. In *Libertas e libertates nel tardo medioevo realtà italiane nel contesto europeo*, ed. Andrea Zorzi, 245–264. Firenze.

Majer, Jirf. 1994. Ore mining and the town of St. Joachimsthal/Jáchymov at the time of Georgius Agricola. *Geojournal* 32:91–99.

Malfatti, Bartolomeo. 1878. *Degli idiomi parlati anticamente nel Trentino e dei dialetti odierni*. Livorno.

Malfatti, Bartolomeo. 1883. I confini dei Principato de Trento. In *Archivio Storico per Trieste, L'Istria e il Trentino, Vol. Sec.*, dir. Salomone Morpurgo and Albino Zenatti, pp. 1–32. Roma.

Malthus, Thomas R. 1969. *An inquiry into the nature and progress of rent and the principles by which it is regulated, 1815.* 1st ed. New York.

Mandel, Ernest. 1973. *An introduction to Marxist economic theory.* New York.

Marchéville, Marcel. 1890. Le rapport entre l'argent et l'or au temps de St Louis. *Annuaire de la Societè française de numismatique et d'archéologie* 1–174.

Marcone, Paola. 2022. I vigneti terrazzati della Valle di Cembra: Paesaggio e identità di un territorio. *ViniPlus di Lombardia*, 02 agosto 2022. https://www.aislombardia.it/viniplus/territori-lombardi/i-vigneti-terrazzati-della-valle-di-cembra-paesaggio-e-identita-di-un-territorio.htm. Accessed 2 February 2024.

Martin, René. 1990. "Vinum dulce, gloriosum…" Le thème du vin dans la poésie latine médiévale. *Bulletin de l'Association Guillaume Budé* 49:356–370.

Martínez Salvador, Carmen 1995. La moneda del califato andalusí: Algunos aspectos de su organización. In *V Semana de Estudios Medievales*, ed. Instituto de Estudios Riojanos, pp. 227–231. La Rioja.

Martini, Angelo. 1883. *Manuale di metrologia ossia misure, pesi e monete.* Torino.

Martini, I. Peter, Giovanni Sarti, and Pasquino Pallechhi. 2011. Landscape influences on the development of the medieval-early Renaissance city-States of Pisa, Florence, and Siena, Italy. In *Landscapes and societies: Selected cases*, ed. I. Peter Martini and Ward Chesworth, 203–221. Berlin.

Martiñón-Torres, Marcos, Nicolas Thomas, Thilo Rehren, et al. 2008. Some problems and potentials of the study of cupellation remains: The case of post-medieval Montbéliard, France. *ArcheoSciences* 1:59–70.

Marx, Karl. 1906–1909. In *Capital, a critique of political economy, vol. 1 The process of production of capital*, ed. Frederick Engels. Chicago.

Marx, Karl. 1913. In *Capital, a critique of political economy, vol. 3 The process of capitalist production as a whole*, ed. Frederick Engels. Chicago.

Massimo, Fabio. 1914. *Corografia d'Italia, Vol. Primo.* Milano.

Matthews, John A., and Keith R. Briffa. 2005. The 'Little Ice Age': Re-evaluation of an evolving concept. *Geografiska Annaler Series A, Physical Geography* 87:17–36.

Matthies, Andrea L. 1992. Medieval treadwheels: Artists' views of building construction. *Technology and Culture* 33:510–547.

McClellan, George B. 1904. *The oligarchy of Venice.* Boston.

McCrackan, William D. 1914. *The spell of Tyrol, 1905.* 1st ed. Boston.

Melve, Leidulf. 2006. The revolt of the medievalists': Directions in recent research on the twelfth-century renaissance. *Journal of Medieval History* 32:231–252.

Micheletto, Paolo. 2024. Ricostruire tre anni dopo la tempesta: Dai vivai provinciali più di 350mila piante. *l'Adige* sabato, 26 ottobre 2024. https://www.ladige.it/cronaca/2021/10/28/ricostruire-tre-anni-dopo-la-tempesta-dai-vivai-provinciali-piu-di-350mila-piante-1.3039448. Accessed 13 April 2023.

Mielantis, Eric. 2000. Perspectives on the origins of merchant capitalism in Europe. *Review Fernand Braudel Center* 23:229–292.

Miller, Maureen C. 1993. *The formation of a medieval Church: Ecclesiastical change in Verona, 950–1150.* Ithaca.

Miller, Edward, and John Hatcher. 1995. *Medieval England, towns, commerce and crafts, 1086–1348.* New York.

Mills, George. 1994. Early accounting in northern Italy: The role of commercial development and the printing press in the expansion of double-entry from Genoa, Florence and Venice. *The Accounting Historians Journal* 21:1–16. https://egrove.olemiss.edu/aah_journal/vol21/iss1/4/.

Molenda, Danuta. 1976. Mining towns in Central-Eastern Europe in feudal times problems outline. *Acta Poloniae Historica* 34:165–188.

Molenda, Danuta. 1988. Technological innovation in Central Europe between the XIVth and the XVIIth centuries. *Journal of European Economic History* 17:63–84.

Monsalbatje y Fossas, Francisco. 1899. *Monasterio de S. Martín de Canigó, Tomo IX.* Madrid.

Monsalve, Fabio. 2010. Scholastic just price and current market price: Is it merely a matter of labeling? *Working Paper Series Economics, finance and mathematics from a high standpoint.* Castilla-La Mancha.

Montanari, Massimo. 1979. *L'alimentazione contadina nell'alto medioevo.* Napoli.

Moore, Jason W. 2003. Nature and the transition from feudalism to capitalism. *A Journal of the Fernand Braudel Center* 26:97–172.

Mor, Carlo G., and Heinrich Schmidinger. 1979. *I poteri temporali dei vescovi in Italia e in Germania nel Medioevo.* Bologna.

Morel, David, Emmanuel Bodart, Frédéric Boulvain, et al. 2012. Les calcaires de Lorraine dans l'architecture et la sculpture gothiques de la région mosane. Origine, utilisation et diffusion d'un matériau au Moyen Âge. *Bulletin du centre d'études médiévales d'Auxerre* 16:1–9.

Mouthon, Faubrice. 2003. Les communautés alpines et l'État (milieu XIIIe-début XVIe siècle). In *Actes des congrès de la Société des Historiens Médiévistes de l'Enseignement Supérieur public, 34e congrès, Montagnes médiévales*, ed. Patrick Boucheron and Elisabeth Mornet, 151–178. Chambéry.

Muendel, John. 1995. Friction and lubrication in medieval Europe: The emergence of olive oil as a superior agent. *Isis* 86:373–393.

Multhauf, Robert P. 1959. Mine pumping in Agricola's time and later. *United States National Museum Bulletin* 218:113–120.

Mumford, Lewis. 1963. *Technics and civilization, 1934.* 1st ed. New York.

Munro, John H. 1992. *Bullion flows and monetary policies in England and the Low Countries, 1350–1500.* Hampshire.

Munro, John H. 2002. *Industrial energy from water mills in the European economy, 5th to 18th centuries: The limitations of power.* MPRA Paper no. 11027: 1–57.

Munro, John H. n.d. *The West European woollen industries and their struggles for international markets, c.1000–1500*, 1–170. Working Paper No. 4, Department of Economics and Institute for Policy Analysis University of Toronto. https://core.ac.uk/download/pdf/9307075.pdf.

Murray, John. 1905. *Handbook for Switzerland and the adjacent regions*. London.

Murray, Robin. 1977. Value and theory of rent, part one. *Capital & Class* 3:100–122.

Naismith, Rory. 2014. The social significance of monetization in the early Middle Ages. *Past & Present* 223:3–39.

Narasimha Rao, R. 1967. Industry in medieval Āndhradeśa. *Proceedings of the Indian History Congress* 29:286–294.

Newfield, Timothy P. 2015. Human-bovine plagues in the early Middle Ages. *Journal of Interdisciplinary History* XLVI:1–38.

Nicholas, David. 1978. Structures du peuplement, fonctions urbaines et formation du capital dans la Flandre médiévale. *Annales Histoire, Sciences Sociales* 33:501–527.

Nickel, Helmut. 1991. Arms & armors: From the permanent collection. *The Metropolitan Museum of Art Bulletin* 49:1–64.

Nissen-Jaubert, Anne. 2006. Le haut Moyen Âge. In *Histoire de l'agriculture en Gaule 500 av. J.-C.–1000 apr. J.-C.*, ed. Alain Ferdière, Véronique Matterne, Patrice Méniel, et al., 141–197. France.

Nnate Nwoke, Chibuzo. 1984. World mining rent: An extension of Marx's theories. *Review Fernand Braudel Center* 8:29–89.

Noonan, Thomas S. 1988. The start of the silver crisis in Islam: A comparative study of Central Asia and the Iberian peninsula. In *Problems of medieval coinage in the Iberian area, Vol. III*, ed. Mario Gomes Marques and D. Michael Metcalf, 119–144. Santarém.

O'Callaghan, Joseph F. 2003. *Reconquest and crusade in medieval Spain*. Philadelphia.

Oberländer-Târnoveanu, Ernest. 2004. The coinage of the Genoese settlements of the Western Black Sea shore and on the Danube. *Peuce Serie Nouă* II:285–296.

Olschki, Leo S. 2004. Il ruolo di vescovi e conti nello sviluppo urbano del Tirolo meridionale in età medievale (secoli XI-XIII). In *Semifonte in Val d'Elsa e i centri di nuova fondazione dell'Italia medievale: Atti del Convegno Nazionale organizzato dal Comune di Barberino Val d'Elsa, Barberino Val d'Elsa, 12–13 ottobre 2002*, ed. Paolo Pirillo, 1000–1025. Firenze.

Orlando, Ermanno. 2016. Venezia, L'Adige e la viabilità nel Basso Medioevo. In *L'Adige come fenomeno storiografico complesso, Atti del Convegno, Rovereto, 21–22 febbraio 2013*, ed. Vito Rovigo, 99–122. Rovereto.

Orsi, Paolo. 1885a. *Saggio di toponomastica trentina, ossia contributo alla etnografia e topografia antica del Trentino*. Trentino.

Orsi, Paolo. 1885b. Saggio di toponomastica tridentina, P. II. *Archivio Trentino* IV:3–19.

Overton, Mark. 1996. *Agricultural revolution in England: The transformation of the agrarian economy, 1500–1850.* Cambridge.

Pacaut, Marcel. 1970. *Frederick Barbarossa.* Translated by Arnold J. Pomerans. New York.

Packard, Sydney R. 1973. *12th century Europe: An interpretative essay.* Amherst, MA.

Paladin, Alice, Negahnaz Moghaddam, Agnieszka E. Stawinoga, et al. 2020. Early medieval Italian Alps: Reconstructing diet and mobility in the valleys. *Archaeological and Anthropological Sciences* 12:1–20.

Pallares, María C., and Ermelindo Portela. 2014. El complejo minero-metalúrgico de la granja cisterciense de Constantín. Bases para el desarrollo de una investigación en arqueología medieval. *Arqueología y Territorio Medieval* 7:81–91.

Palme, Rudolf. 1990. Alpine salt mining in the Middle Ages. *Journal of European Economic History* 19:117–136.

Panella, Clementina, and André Tchernia. 1992. Produits agricoles transportés en amphores: L'huile et surtout le vin. *Publications de l'École française de Rome* 198:145–165.

Papadopoulou, Pagona. 2013. Betwixt Greeks, Saracens and Crusaders. Lusignan coinage and its place in the Eastern Mediterranean (1192–1324). *Cahiers du Centre d'Etudes Chypriotes* 43:473–492.

Parker, George. 2014. *Sovereign City: The city-state through history.* London.

Patterson, Clair C. 1972. Silver stocks and losses in ancient and medieval times. *The Economic History Review* 25:205–235.

Paul, Wolfgang. 1970. *Mining lore, an illustrated composition and documentary compilation with emphasis on the spirit and history of mining.* Portland.

Paulinyi, O., and I. Teil. 1966. Die anfänglichen Formen des Unternehmens im Edelerzbergbau zur Zeit des Feudalismus, II Teil. *Acta Historica Academiae Scientiarum Hungaricae* 12:261–318.

Peattie, Roderick. 1936. *Mountain geography: A critique and field study.* Cambridge, MA.

Pereira de Souza, Marcos A. 1994. Les Barbares et le vin. *Annales littéraires de l'Université de Besançon* 145–162.

Perini, Agostino. 1834. *Il castelli del Tirolo colla storia delle relative antiche potenti famiglie, vols. 1–3.* Milano.

Perini, Agostino. 1845. Appendice: La miniera d'oro di Tassullo. *Giornale agrario dei distretti trentino e roveretani* 35:142.

Perini, Agostino. 1856. *Dizionario geografico, statistico del Trentino.* Trentino.

Perini, Carlo, and Carlo Lurati. 1859. *Illustrazione del Tirolo italiano e della Svizzera italiana.* Milano.

Petech, Luciano. 1962. Les marchands italiens dans l'empire mongol. *Journal Asiatique* 250:549–574.

Pfister, Christian, Jürg Luterbacher, Gabriela Schwarz-Zanetti, et al. 1998. Winter air temperature variations in Western Europe during the early and high Middle Ages (AD 750–1300). *The Holocene* 8:535–552.

Phillips, Jonathan. 2014. *The Crusades.* New York and London.

Pinamonti, Gioseffo. 1845. La miniere d' oro di Tassullo. *Giornale agrario dei distretti Trentini e Roveretani* VI:142.

Pini, Antonio I. 1989. *Vite e vino del medioevo*, pref. Vito Fumagalli. Bologna.

Pirenne, Henry. 1936. *Economic and social history of medieval Europe.* Translated by Ivy E. Clegg. London.

Pivano, Silvio. 1904. *I contratti agrari in Italia nell'Alto Medio-evo.* Torino.

Poggi, Enrico. 1861. *Discorsi economici, storici e giuridici.* Firenze.

Polanyi, Karl. 1947. On belief in economic determinism. *The Sociological Review* 39:96–102.

Pollard, Sydney. 1997. *Marginal Europe: The contribution of marginal lands since the Middle Ages.* Oxford.

Porteous, John. 1969. *Coins in history.* New York.

Postan, Michael M. 1959. Money, population and economic change in late medieval Europe: Note. *The Economic History Review* 12:77–82.

Postan, Michael M., ed. 1966. *The Cambridge economic history of Europe from the decline of the Roman Empire, vol. 1, Agrarian life of the Middle Ages.* Cambridge.

Postan, Michael M. 1973. *The medieval economy and society: An economic history of Britain, 1100–1500.* Berkeley.

Postan, Michael M., and John Hatcher. 1978. Agrarian class structure and economic development in pre-industrial Europe: Population and class relations in feudal society. *Past & Present* 78:24–37.

Pounds, Norman J. G. 1973. *An historical geography of Europe: 450 B.C.–A.D.1330.* Cambridge.

Precopi Lombardo, Annamaria. 2006. Artigianato ebraico dei metalli preziosi nella Sicilia medievale. *Sicilia archeologica: XXXIX* 104:55–84.

Prestwich, Joseph. 1886. *Geology: Chemical, physical, and stratigraphical.* London.

Racine, Pierre. 1986. Poteri medievali e percorsi fluviali nell'Italia Padana. *Quaderni storici* 21:9–32.

Raju, Alison. 2011. *Via Francigena, pilgrim trail Canterbury to Rome, Part I, Canterbury to the Great St. Bernard Pass.* Singapore.

Rasmo, Nicolò. 1964. *Cultura atesina/Kultur des Etschlandes.* Bolzano.

Rasmo, Nicolò. 1980. *L'èta cavalleresca in Val d'Adige.* Venezia.

Razi, Zvi. 2003. The peasant land market and family in England, c. 1250–c. 1450. In *Il mercato della terra secc.XIII-XVIII, Atii della "Trentacinquesima Settimana di Studi" 5–9 maggio 2003*, ed. Simonetta Cavaciocchi, 559–567. Prato.

Rehren, Thilo, Christoph Bartels, and Jens Schneider. 1999. Medieval lead-silver smelting in the Siegerland, West Germany. *Historical Metallurgy* 33:73–84.

Reich, Desiderio. 1891. Toponomastica storica di Mezocorona. *Archivio Trentino* X:67–149.

Reich, Desiderio. 1903. Documenti di Mezocorona. *Archivio Trentino* XVIII:5–27.

Reich, Desiderio. 1905. I diplomi dell'istituzione del Principato vescovile di Trento. *Archivio Trentino* 24:95–106.

Rende, Pino. 2013. La vigna e la vite nella Valle del Tacina. Alcune caratteristiche e particolarità. Archivio storico Crotone. www.archiviostoricocrotone.it. Accessed 7 November 2019.

Reti, Ladislao. 1967. On the efficiency of early horizontal waterwheels. *Technology and Culture* 8:388–394.

Reuter, Timothy, ed. 1999. *The new Cambridge medieval history, Volume 3, c.900–c.1024.* Cambridge.

Rey Pastor, Julio. 1957. *Técnica en la historia de la humanidad.* Buenos Aires.

Reynolds, Robert L. 1930. Merchants of Arras and the overland trade with Genoa twelfth century. *Revue belge de philologie et d'histoire* 9:495–533.

Reynolds, Robert L. 1952. Origins of modern business enterprise: Medieval Italy. *The Journal of Economic History* 12:350–365.

Reynolds, Terry S. 1983. *Stronger than a hundred men: A history of the vertical water wheel.* Baltimore.

Reynolds, Terry S. 1984. Medieval roots of the Industrial Revolution. *Scientific American* 251:122–131.

Reynolds, Susan. 2001. *Fiefs and vassals: The medieval evidence reinterpreted.* Oxford.

Rippon, Stephen, Peter F. Claughton, and Chris Smart. 2009. *Mining in a medieval landscape, the royal silver mines of the Tamar Valley.* Exeter.

Robertson, C. J. 1938. Agricultural regions of the North Italian Plain. *Geographical Review* 28:573–596.

Rodríguez García, José M. 2014. *Ideología cruzada en el siglo XIII.* Sevilla.

Rogers, J. Michael. 1990. To and from, aspects of Mediterranean trade and consumption in the 15th and 16th centuries. *Revue du monde musulman et de la Méditerranée* 55–56:57–74.

Rohr, Christian. 2003. Man and natural disaster in the late Middle Ages: The earthquake in Carinthia and northern Italy on 25 January 1348 and its perception. *Environment and History* 9:127–149.

Romani, Marina. 2019. Denaro, monete-merce e merci-moneta: Una storia economica e sociale. *Cheiron: Materiali e strumenti di aggiornamento storiografico* 1 (2): 167–190.

Rosen, William. 2014. *The Third Horseman: Climate change and the Great Famine of the 14th century.* New York.

Rosenwein, Barbara H. 1999. *Negotiating space: Power, restraint and privileges of immunity in early medieval lands.* Ithaca, New York.

Rossi, Cesare. 2015. *The precursors of Leonardo Da Vinci's studies*, 1–10. Paper delivered at the 14th International Federation for the Promotion of Mechanism and Machine Science World Congress, Taipei, Taiwan. October 25–30, 2015. https://doi.org/10.6567/IFToMM.14TH.WC.OS7.005.

Rossini, Egidio. 1986. La Via dell'Adige e il commercio del legname nel Basso Medio Evo. *Academia Roveretana degli Agiati di Scienze, Lettere ed Arti* XXVI:243–256.

Rostow, Walter W. 1991. *The stages of economic growth: A non-communist manifesto*. New York and Cambridge.

Roux, Simone. 1999. À Paris, au bord de l'eau. *Médiévales* 36:63–70.

Rusu, Adrian A. 2013. On a possible abbatial crosier from Bizere Monastery (Frumuşeni), Arad County. *European Journal of Science and Technology* 9:211–219.

Saccocci, Andrea. 2005. La monetazione del *Regnum Italiae* e l'evoluzione complessiva del sistema monetario Europea. In *XIII Congreso Internacional de Numismática*, ed. Carmen Alfaro Asins, Carmen Marcos, Paloma Otero, et al., 1037–1049. Madrid.

Saccocci, Andrea. 2010. L'introduzione dei grossi agli inizi del XIII secolo e la massicia esportazione di argento dall'Europa Occidentale ai territory islamici: Una semplice coincidenza? In *The 2nd Simone Assemani symposium on Islamic coins*, ed. Bruno Callegher and Arianna D'Ottone, 127–156. Trieste.

Salvioli, Giuseppe. 1888. *Storia delle immunità delle signorie e giustizie delle chiesa in Italia*. Modena.

Salvioli, Giuseppe. 1889. *Il diritto monetario italiano dalla caduta dell'imperio romano ai nostri giorni*. Milano.

Sandars, Thomas C., transl. 1917. *The Institutes of Justinian with English introduction, translation and notes*, 14th ed. London.

Santi, Patrizia, Fabrizio Antonelli, and Alberto Renzulli. 2005. Provenance of medieval *pietra ollare* artefacts found in archeological sites of central-eastern Italy: Insights into the Alpine soapstone trade. *Archaeometry* 47:253–264.

Sapori, Armando. 1947. *Studi di storia economica medievale*. Florence.

Sarti, Nicoletta. 2012. Tra mestiere e scienze giuridica. La difficile professionalità dell'avvocato medieval. *Historia et ius: Rivista di storia giuridica dell'età medieval e moderna* 1:1–7.

Savery, Thomas. 1910. *The Miner's Friend, or an engine to raise water by fire, described, and the manner of fixing it*. London.

Say, Jean Baptiste. 1816. *Catechism of political economy; or, familiar conversations on the manner in which wealth is produced, distributed, and consumed in society*. Translated by John Richter. London.

Schaer, Jean-Paul, and J. Michael Rodgers, eds. 1987. *The anatomy of mountain ranges*. Princeton.

Schneider, Hans J., ed. 2012. *Mineral deposits of the Alps and of the Alpine epoch in Europe, proceedings of the IV ISMIDA 1981*. Berlin.

Schneller, Christian. 1893. *Beiträge zur Ortsnamenkunde Tirols*. Innsbruck.

Schneller, Christian. 1898. *Quellen und forschungen zur geschichte, litteratur und sprache Osterreichs und seiner Kronländer, IV, Tridentinische Urbare aus dem dreizehnten Jahrhundert mit einer urkunde aus judicarien von 1244–1247*. Innsburck.

Schofield, Roger S. 1965. The geographical distribution of wealth in England, 1334–1649. *The Economic History Review* 18:483–510.

Schreg, Rainer. 2019. Late medieval deserted settlements in Southern Germany as a consequence of long-term landscape transformations. In *Settlement change across medieval Europe: Old paradigms and new vistas*, ed. Nial Brady and Claudia Theune, 161–170. Leiden.

Schröcke, Helmut. 1994. Mining and German settlement in Slovakia, an historical summary. *Geojournal* 32:127–135.

Schumpeter, Joseph A. 1955. In *History of economic analysis*, ed. Elizabeth B. Schumpeter. London.

Segarizzi, Arnoldo. 1906–1907. I Trentini nel fondaco dei tedeschi in Venezia. *Archivio Trentino* XXI–XXII:1–35.

Segers-Glocke, Christiane, Harald Witthöft, and Friedrich Balck, eds. 2000. *Aspects of mining and smelting in the Upper Harz Mountains (up to the 13th/14th century)-in the early times of a developing European economy*. St. Katharinen.

Semirurali, Museo delle, ed. 2013. *Semirurali e dintorni*. Bolzano.

Sereni, Emilio. 1997. *History of the Italian agricultural landscape*. Trans. and introd. by R. Burr Litchfield. Princeton.

Sforza, I. Cesarini. 1907. Italiani non Trentini nel Trentino. *Archivio Trentino* XXII:66–76.

Shelby, Lon R. 1975. Mariano Taccola and his books on engines and machines. *Technology and Culture* 16:466–475.

Simmons, Ian G. 2003. *The Moors of England and Wales: An environmental history 8000 BC to AD 2000*. Edinburgh.

Simonin, Louis. 1869. *Underground life, or mines and miners*. New York.

Sinclair, Tom. 2012. Some conclusions on the use of coins on the Ayas-Tabriz route (late 13th and first half of 14th century A.D.). *Publications de l'Institut Français d'Études Anatoliennes* 25:87–103.

Smith, John M. 1969. The silver currency of Mongol Iran. *Journal of the Economic and Social History of the Orient* 12:16–41.

Smith, Elizabeth B., and Michael Wolfe. 1997. *Technology and resource use in medieval Europe: Cathedrals, mills, and mines*. Hampshire.

Snooks, Graeme D. 1996. *The dynamic society Exploring the sources of global change*. New York and London.

Sombart, Werner. 1929. Economic theory and economic history. *The Economic History Review* 2:1–19.

Sombart, Werner. 1967. *The quintessence of capitalism, a study of the history and psychology of the modern business man*. Translated by M. Epstein. New York.

Spengler, Joseph J., and William R. Allen. 1960. *Essays in economic thought: Aristotle to Marshall*. Chicago.

Spicciani, Amleto. 1996. *Benefici livelli feudi. Intreccio di rapporti tra chierici e laici nella Tuscia medioevale: La creazione di una società politica*. Pisa.

Spufford, Peter. 1988. *Money and its use in medieval Europe*. Cambridge.

Spufford, Peter. 2002. *Power and profit: The merchant in medieval Europe*. London.

Squatriti, Paolo. 1998. *Water and society in early medieval Italy*. Cambridge.

Squatriti, Paolo. 2002. Digging ditches in early medieval Europe. *Past & Present* 176:11–65.

Squatriti, Paolo. 2013. *Landscape and change in early medieval Italy, chestnut, economy and culture*. Cambridge.

Stadel, Christoph. 1993. The Brenner Freeway (Austria-Italy): Mountain highway & controversy. *Mountain Research & Development* 13:1–17.

Stanly, Cyril. 1980. *The Hoover Collection of mining and metallurgy*. Los Angeles.

Stark, Werner. 1972. The contained economy: An interpretation of medieval economic thought. In *Pre-capitalist thought: Three modern interpretations, Series The evolution of capitalism*, ed. Leonard S. Silk, 3–22. New York.

Stenico, Remo. 1979. Dazio al passo del Tonale: 6 agosto 1460–13 ottobre 1461. *Studi trentini di scienze storiche* 58:15–77.

Stenico, Marco. 2023. Signorie rurali e risorse economiche: Forme di prelievo e di gestione. In *La signoria rurale nell'Italia del tardo medioevo. 6 Le signorie trentine*, ed. Marco Bettotti and Gian Maria Varanini, 221–252. Firenze.

Steuer, Heiko. 2011. Settlements in the southern Black Forest: Castles and mining (dominance through commerce). *Ruralia* 9:123–138.

Stiebel, Guy D. 2003. Arms from the large Byzantine structure in Area XV. In *The Temple Mount excavations in Jerusalem 1968–1978 directed by Benjamin Mazar, final reports*, ed. Eilat Mazar, vol. II, 153–158. Jerusalem.

Štih, Peter. 2010. *The Middle Ages between the eastern Alps and the northern Adriatic*. Leiden.

Stöllner, Thomas. 2003. Mining and economy a discussion of spatial organisations and structures of early raw material exploitation. In *Man and mining. Studies in honour of Gerd Weisgerber*, ed. Thomas Stöllner, Gabriela Körlin, Gero Steffens, et al., 415–446. Bochum.

Stöllner, Thomas. 2008. Montan-archaeology and research on old mining: Just a contribution to economic history? In *Anatolian Metal, IV Der Anschnitt, Beiheft 21*, ed. Ünsal Yalçin, 1–13. Bochum.

Stolz, Otto. 1910. Zur geschichte der organisation des transportwesens in Tirol im Mittelalter. *Vierteljahrschrift für Sozial- und Wirtschaftsgeschichte* 8:196–267.

Storemyr, Per, and Tom Heldal. 2002. Soapstone production through Norwegian history: Geology, properties, quarrying and use. *Asmosia* 5:359–369.

Stovall, Dennis E. 1909. Queer Mountains made by placer miners. *The Mining World*, October, p. 695.

Stroll, Mary. 1997. *The medieval abbey of Farfa: Target of papal and imperial ambitions.* Leiden.

Suárez, Fernández Luis. 1986. *Historia de España antigua y media, 3 vols.* Madrid.

Tabacco, Giovanni. 1989. *The struggle for power in medieval Italy, structures of political rule.* Translated by R. Brown. Cambridge.

Tasser, Rudolf, and Ekkehard Westermann, eds. 2004. *Der Tiroler bergbau und die depression der europäischen montanwirtschaft im 14. und 15. Jahrhundert: Akten der internationalen bergbaugeschichtlichen Tagung Steinhaus.* Innsbruck.

Taylor, Griffith. 1940. Trent to the Reschen Pass, a cultural traverse of the Adige corridor. *Geographical Review* 30:215–237.

Tchernia, André. 1986. *Le vin de l'Italie romaine: Essai d'histoire économique d'après les amphores.* Rome.

Téreygeol, Florian, and Claude Dubois. 2003. Mines et métallurgie carolingienne à Melle (Deux-Sèvres): L'apport des charbons de bois archéologiques. *Archéologie médiévale* 33:91–102.

Thomasset, Claude, and Danièle James-Raoul, eds. 2000. *La montagne dans le texte medieval, entre mythe et réalité.* Paris.

Tilly, Charles. 1992. *Coercion, capital and European states, A.D. 990–1992.* Cambridge, MA.

Titow, John Z. 1961. Some evidence of the thirteenth century population increase. *The Economic History Review* 14:218–224.

Titow, John Z. 2018. *English rural society, 1200–1350, 1969.* 1st ed. New York.

Tizzoni, Costanza C. 1985. Le scorie della riduzione di minerale argentifero dal Monte Calisio. In *Il Monte Calisio e l'argento nelle Alpi dall'antichità al XVIII secolo*, ed. Luciano Brigo and Marco Tizzoni, 281–296. Trent.

Toch, Michael. 2008. Lords and peasants: A reappraisal of medieval economic relations. In *The expansion of Latin Europe, 1000–1500*, ed. Felipe Fernández-Armesto and James Muldoon, vol. 2, 281–300. Farnham.

Tognana, Francesco. 2017. La costruzione del sistema economico integrato nella pianura Veneto-Atesina e il mercato di Este nel medioevo. *Turismo e Pscicologia* 10:12–17.

Tognon, Alisia, Nicola Martellozzo, and Alessandro Gretter. 2023. Collective properties of Trentino: From traditional competences to modern solution providers. *Land* 12:1–20.

Tomedi, Andrea. 2017. Giuramenti di fedeltà e investiture nel comitatus Tridentinus (XII-XIII secolo): Le forme locali della "fides" e della concessione di beni. *Storia e Regione* 26:111–128.

Tomedi, Andrea. 2023. Tra nord e sud. Le signorie rurali in valle dell'Adige, nella piana Rotaliana e in valle di Cembra. In *La signoria rurale nell'Italia del tardo medioevo. 6 Le signorie trentine*, ed. Marco Bettotti and Gian Maria Varanini, 61–84. Firenze.

Toubert, Pierre. 1980. Discours inaugural: Les féodalités méditerranéennes: Un problème d'histoire comparée. In *Structures féodales et féodalisme dans l'Occident méditerranéen (Xe-XIIIe siècles), Bilan et perspectives de recherches, Actes du Colloque de Rome, 10–13 octobre 1978*, comp. École Française de Rome, pp. 1–14. Rome.

Trabut-Cussac, Jean-Paul. 1950. Les costumes ou droits de douanes perçus à Bordeaux sur les vins et les marchandises par l'administration anglaise de 1252 à 1307. *Annales du Midi: Revue archéologique, historique et philologique de la France méridionale* 62:135–150.

Travaini, Lucia. 1988. Mint organisation in Italy between the twelfth and fourteenth centuries: A survey. In *Late medieval mints: Organisation, administration and techniques*, ed. Nicholas J. Mayhew and Peter Spufford, 39–60. Oxford.

Turner, Michael. 2003. Comparative land prices in Europe, 1500–1800. In *Il mercato della terra secc.XIII-XVIII, Atii della "Trentacinquesima Settimana di Studi" 5–9 maggio 2003*, ed. Simonetta Cavaciocchi, 521–545. Prato.

Turri, Eugenio, and Sandro Ruffo, eds. 1997. *L'Adige: Il fiume, gli uomini, la storia*. Verona.

Umlauft, Friedrich. 1889. *The Alps*. London.

Vaj, S. Giorgio. 1903. *Notizie storiche della Valle di Fiemme*. Trent.

Vallone, Giancarlo. 2012. La costituzione medievale delle terre e le giurisdizioni di Federico II. *Studi storici* 53:781–816.

Valone, Carolyn. 2001. Matrons and motives: Why women built in early modern Romen. In *Beyond Isabella secular women patrons of art in Renaissance Italy*, ed. Sheryl E. Reiss and David G. Wilkins, 317–336. Philadelphia.

Varanini, Gian M. 1996. Itinerari commerciali secondari nel Trentino bassomedioevale. In *Die Erschließung des Alpenraums für den Verkehr im Mittelalter und in der frühen Neuzeit*, ed. Erwin Riedenauer, 101–128. Bozen.

Varanini, Gian M. 2000. Le relazioni istituzionali ed economiche fra città e montagna sul versante meridionale delle Alpi orientali nel tardo medioevo: Alcuni esempi. *Histoire des Alpes* 5:125–138.

Varanini, Gian M., and Edoardo Demo. 2012. Allevamento, transumanza, lanificio: Tracce dall'alto e dal pieno Medioevo veneto. In *La lana nella Cisalpina romana. Economia e Società. Studi in onore di Stefania Pesavento Mattioli*, ed. Maria Stella Busana and Patrizia Basso, 269–287. Padova.

Vauchez, André, Barrie Dobson, and Michael Lapidge, eds. 2000. *Encyclopedia of the Middle Ages*. Cambridge.

Vázquez De Prada, Valentín. 1988. La coyuntura de la minería y de la metalurgia europeas (siglos XIII-XVIII). *Revista de Historia Económica* VI:257–273.

Vergani, Raffaello. 1979. Lessico minerario e metllurgico dell'Italia nord-orientale. *Quaderni Storici* 14:54–79.

Verhagen, H. L. E. 2013. The evolution of *pignus* in classical Roman law, *Ius honorarium* and '*ius novum*'. *The Legal History Review* 81:51–79.

Verna, Catherine. 2011. Innovations et métallurgies en Méditerranée Occidentale (XIIIe-XVe siècles). *Anuario de Estudios Medievales* 41:623–644.

Veselovský, František, et al. 2003. History of discovery and study of new primary minerals at Jáchymov. *Journal of the Czech Geological Society* 48:207–208.

Villani, Giovanni. 1857–1858. *Croniche di Giovanni, Matteo e Filippo Villani: Secondo le migliori stampe e corredate di note filologiche e storiche: Testo di lingua, vol. 1, Cronica di Giovanni Villani*. Trieste.

Violante, Cinzio, ed. 1993. *Nobiltà e chiese nel Medioevo e altri saggi: Scritti in onore di Gerd G. Tellenbach*. Roma.

Violante, Cinzio. 1994. Un beneficio vassallatico instaurato con una carta di livello, Cremona, 8 novembre 1036. In *Cristianità ed Europe. Miscellanea di studi in onore di Luigi Prosdocini, T. I*, ed. Cinzio Violante and Amletto Spicciani, 191–200. Roma.

Voltelini, Hans. 1907. *Immunität, grund- und leibherrliche gerichtsbarkeit in Südtirol*. Vienna.

Voltelini, Hans. 1981. *Giurisdizione signorile su terre e persone nel trentino medievale*. Translated by Vigilio Mattevi. Trent.

von Stromer, Wolfgang. 1970. Nuremberg in the international economics of the middle ages. *The Business History Review* 44:210–225.

Vryonis, Speros. 1962. The question of Byzantine mines. *Speculum* 37:1–17.

Waddell, Peter J. A. 1986. The pump and pump well of a sixteenth century galleon. *International Journal of Nautical Archeology* 15:137–148.

Wallerstein, Immanuel. 1974. *The modern world-system Vol. I, Capitalist agriculture and the origins of the European world-economy in the sixteenth century*. New York.

Wallerstein, Immanuel. 1980. *The modern world-system, Vol. II, Mercantilism and the consolidation of the European world-economy, 1600–1750*. New York.

Watson, Andrew M. 1967. Back to gold -and silver. *The Economic History Review* 20:1–34.

Weber, Max. 2003. *General economic history*, 1st ed. 1927. New York.

Weisgerber, Gerd, and Lynn Willies. 2000. The use of fire in prehistoric and ancient mining: Firesetting. *Paléorient* 26:131–149.

West-Harling, Veronica. 2019. Female monasticism in Italy in the early Middle Ages: New questions, new debates. *Reti Medievali Rivista* 20:329–347.

Wickham, Chris. 1985. The uniqueness of the East. In *Feudalism and non-European societies*, ed. Terence J. Byres and Harbans Mukhia, 166–196. New Jersey.

Wickham, Chris. 2008. Productive forces and the economic logic of the feudal mode of production. *Historical Materialism* 16:3–22.

Wickham, Chris. 2009. *The inheritance of Rome, a history of Europe from 400 to 1000.* New York.

Wickham, Chris. 2010. Historical transitions: A comparative approach. *Medieval History Journal* 13:1–21.

Wickham, Chris. 2015. *Medieval Europe.* New Jersey.

Wickham, Chris. 2021. How did the feudal economy work? The economic logic of medieval societies. *Past & Present* 251:3–40.

Wiener, Leo. 1915. *Commentary to the Germanic Laws and medieval documents.* Cambridge, MA.

Williams, Alan. 2009. A note on liquid iron in medieval Europe. *Ambix* 56:68–75.

Wilson, Andrew. 2002. Machines, power and the ancient economy. *The Journal of Roman Studies* 92:1–32.

Wolff, Philippe. 1982. Monnaie et développement économique dans l'Europe médiévale. *Histoire, économie & société* 1–4:491–510.

Wolff, Philippe. 2015. The significance of the "feudal period" in the monetary history of Europe. In *Order and innovation in the Middle Ages: Essays in honor of Joseph R. Strayer*, ed. William C. Jordan, Bruce McNab, and Teófilo F. Ruiz, 77–85. Princeton.

Woods, Andrew R. 2018. From Charlemagne to the Commercial Revolution (c.800–1150). In *Money and coinage in the Middle Ages*, ed. Rory Naismith, 93–121. Leiden.

Yamey, Basil S. 1978. *Essays on the history of accounting: The development of contemporary accounting thought.* New York.

Yelling, James A. 1977. *Common field and enclosure in England 1450–1850.* London.

Zadoks, Jan C. 2013. *Crop protection in medieval agriculture: Studies in pre-modern organic agriculture.* Leiden.

Zammatteo, Paolo. 2016. L'arte mineraria sulle Alpi centrali e la diffusione delle idee nei secoli XII-XIV. *La Ricerca Folklorica* 71:37–51.

Zulberti, Marco. 2018. Il Castello di Arco nell'iconografia del Dürer. *Judicaria* 1–7.

Zupko, Ronald E. 1981. *Italian weights and measures from then Middle Ages to the nineteenth century.* Philadelphia.

General Terms for Index, Medieval Mining and Power[1]

[1] Note: Page numbers followed by 'n' refer to notes.

J. Graulau, *Medieval Mining and Power in Thirteenth-Century Europe*, https://doi.org/10.1007/978-3-031-99239-1

C

D

N

O

Geographic Terms[1]

[1] Note: Page numbers followed by 'n' refer to notes.

J. Graulau, *Medieval Mining and Power in Thirteenth-Century Europe*, https://doi.org/10.1007/978-3-031-99239-1

Names of Peoples[1]

[1] Note: Page numbers followed by 'n' refer to notes.

J. Graulau, *Medieval Mining and Power in Thirteenth-Century Europe*, https://doi.org/10.1007/978-3-031-99239-1

FSC
www.fsc.org
MIX
Papier | Fördert
gute Waldnutzung
FSC® C083411

Kolibri 360 GmbH
Ferdinand-Jühlke-Straße 7
99095 Erfurt, Deutschland
produktsicherheit@kolibri360.de